Sustainability of Scholarly Information

Sustainability of Scholarly Information

G. G. Chowdhury

facet publishing

© G. G. Chowdhury 2014

Published by Facet Publishing
7 Ridgmount Street, London WC1E 7AE
www.facetpublishing.co.uk

Facet Publishing is wholly owned by CILIP: the Chartered Institute
of Library and Information Professionals.

British Library Cataloguing in Publication Data
A catalogue record for this book is available from the British Library.

ISBN 978-1-85604-956-6

First published 2014

Text printed on FSC accredited material.

Typeset from author's files in 10/13 pt Bergamo and Zurich by
Flagholme Publishing Services.
Printed and made in Great Britain by CPI Group (UK) Ltd,
Croydon, CR0 4YY.

Contents

Figures and tables ix

Preface xi

1 The sustainability of information: an outline 1
    Introduction 1
    The concept of sustainability 3
    Sustainable development 4
    Information about sustainability vs sustainable information 5
    About this book 7
    Summary 12
    References 12

2 The three dimensions of sustainability 15
    Introduction 15
    Economic sustainability 16
    Social sustainability 18
    Environmental sustainability 21
    The three pillars of sustainable development 24
    An integrated approach to sustainable development 26
    The sustainability of information 28
    Summary 28
    References 29

3 The economic sustainability of information 33
    Introduction 33
    The publishing industry 34
    The generic business model for scholarly information 35
    Open access 37
    Access to digital information 41
    Access to journals and databases 44
    The economics of digital information 46
    Value-added information 50
    Summary 51
    References 52

4 The environmental sustainability of information...**57**
Introduction 57
The IPCC report and GHG emissions 58
The carbon footprint of IT 60
Green IT 63
Measuring the environmental impact of information services...................67
Summary 72
References 73

5 The social sustainability of information.......................................**79**
Introduction 79
Related studies 80
Users, community and social sustainability.......................................81
Indicators for the social sustainability of information............................84
How to study the social sustainability of information............................86
Information systems and services for sustainable development...............88
Legal and policy frameworks...89
Technology, infrastructure and social sustainability 92
Users, culture and social sustainability 94
Summary 96
References 97

6 Printed vs digital content and sustainability issues **103**
Introduction 103
Estimating the carbon footprint of printed content 104
Factors responsible for GHG emissions from printed and digital
     content 108
Summary 113
References 114

7 Open access models and the sustainability of information **117**
Introduction 117
Open access policies of institutions and funding bodies 118
Open access content and data...128
Gold open access and the sustainability of information.........................131
Summary 136
References 137

**8 Sustainable management of open access information: a conceptual
   model** **141**
Introduction 141
Managing open access information 142
Attributes of a new open access content and data management system.143
The conceptual model...145
Opportunities and challenges 148
The sustainability of the proposed open access content and data
     management system...149

Summary 154
References 155

9   Green information services: a conceptual model 157
Introduction 157
Cloud computing...158
A framework for green information services for the higher education
    sector 163
Summary 169
References 170

10 Information access and sustainability issues..............................175
Introduction 175
Cloud computing and information retrieval research...............................177
Measuring the environmental impact of information access: the
    lifecycle analysis approach 179
Measuring the environmental impact of information retrieval: an
    alternative approach 181
Green user behaviour..184
Summary 185
References 186

11 The sustainability of information models.....................................191
Introduction 191
The three pillars of sustainable information services 191
Scholarly communication processes 192
An integrated approach to research on the sustainability of digital
    information 194
The sustainability of specific information services...................................196
Summary 199
References 200

12 Research on sustainable information...203
Introduction 203
Open access and a paradigm shift in information management,
    education and research...203
Facilitating content-specific access and use 204
Information research directions..205
Conclusion 217
References 218

Index..223

Figures and tables

Figure 2.1   The three forms of sustainability...27

Figure 3.1   A generic business model for scholarly information 36

Figure 3.2   An emerging business model for scholarly information...........40

Figure 4.1   Factors responsible for GHG emissions from an information
service..68

Figure 5.1   A framework for the study of social sustainability of digital
information...87

Table 6.1   Processes and factors for GHG emissions for printed and
digital content 109

Figure 7.1   RCUK's decision tree for authors...126

Figure 8.1   A conceptual model of an open access content and data
management system 146

Figure 9.1   The green digital information services model...........................166

Figure 11.1 Scholarly communication processes..192

Figure 11.2 Research issues and challenges in sustainable digital
information services 195

Preface

Within the last few decades, there have been many new developments and challenges in the information industry and information services sector. Consequently, information management activities, and the corresponding professional and research skills, had to change and adapt continuously to changing information and communication technologies (ICTs) and global developments. Contrary to the old practices where information professionals had to play the role of an intermediary between content users and content producers, primarily commercial content providers, modern-day information professionals need to play a whole range of new roles comprising a number of different functions and activities. Such new roles and responsibilities include facilitating access to relevant information that is available through a multitude of services and platforms, creating and managing specific content and data services in the form of institutional repositories and open access digital libraries, preserving content to ensure future access, managing user-generated content, and so on. Modern information managers who use emerging web and social networking technologies to gather more user and usage data, in order to provide the best possible services to the user community, require a variety of new skills to link commercial, open access and user-generated content and data within specific contexts.

The rapidly changing scenario in the information industry and marketplace – the increasing volume of scholarly information resources vis-à-vis increasing user demands, increasing competition from a variety of new web-based information systems and services, fast changing technologies and new government regulations – raise several questions:

- How sustainable are today's information systems and services?
- How can we ensure the sustainability of information throughout its lifetime – from its generation to management and use?
- Can today's information systems and services face the new economic

challenges and yet maintain the quality of their services in order to provide easy and equitable access to information to everyone?

- Can the level and quality of information services be sustained over a long period of time?
- Can all these activities be performed in an environment-friendly manner so that an ecological balance can be maintained?

This book aims to find answers to some of these sustainability questions especially in the context of scholarly information systems and services. It argues that in order to build sustainable digital information systems and services, it is necessary to identify the challenges associated with the design, delivery, access, use and preservation of digital information. The issues of sustainability can be considered in the context of the major factors influencing the lifecycle of information – from creation to management, use or re-use, and disposal (when required, for example, disposal of analogue information resources or of computing infrastructure and equipment). These issues have been discussed by researchers in the context of various technological, economic and social issues associated with the scholarly communication processes in general, and information systems and services in particular.

Some past research papers have indirectly touched on different forms of sustainability of digital information systems and services. For example, some economic aspects and alternative business models of information have been studied in the context of e-books and e-journal subscription models in libraries (Chapter 3), and in the context of open access models (Chapter 7). Similarly many evaluation studies have focused on the traditional library and information services, and more recently there have been some studies on the impact of digital library services, but very few of these studies tried to address all the three forms of sustainability of digital information systems and services: economic, social and environmental. Similarly, a significant amount of research has taken place in the broad area of user studies and human information behaviour, resulting in several thousand research papers. Of late many studies have examined users and Web 2.0 and social networking technologies that shed new light on users' new and emerging behaviour in the digital age. Many researchers have pointed out the challenges posed by the emerging ICTs and web technologies on those in today's society who cannot or do not use ICTs. This group of studies has been classed under the topic digital divide. A large volume of research literature has also been produced in related areas like information and digital literacy and social inclusion, but very few researchers have focused on the social sustainability of digital information systems and services per se.

Many previous research studies have generated valuable findings and models on users, community and society that can shed light on the social sustainability of digital information systems and services. Many researchers have focused on designing technologies and tools for building digital libraries and information services that are particularly suitable for users and communities in the less technologically advanced countries and societies. However, the environmental sustainability of digital information systems and services has remained a relatively unexplored area of research until very recently.

This book discusses different aspects of sustainability in the context of scholarly information systems and services. It also shows how the various issues of sustainability are related to, and often influence, each other. It proposes some new models for the study of the economic, social and environmental sustainability of information systems and services, especially in the context of scholarly communications. It also provides an integrated model for study of the sustainability of digital information systems and services, and argues in favour of concerted research efforts in all three areas of sustainability of digital information systems and services.

This book takes the approach of a research monograph based on literature review and meta-analysis – environmental scanning and critical analysis of relevant literature, reports and reviews, and so on – of different issues and challenges associated with the various forms of sustainability of digital information systems and services. Based on research and critical analysis of developments in related areas, some new models are proposed for study and research in different forms of sustainability of digital information systems and services.

The book will be useful for those in the information research community – postgraduate research students and other researchers in information science and related disciplines – who wish to understand this new and hugely significant area of research: the sustainability of information. It will also open up several new directions and avenues of research in digital information systems and services leading to sustainability. For example, for researchers in user studies it will open up new discussions and debates as to how best user behaviour and interactions can be modelled and introduced in the design of different components of information systems in order to achieve economic and social sustainability of the resulting information services. Similarly, it will open up new debate in different aspects of the design of digital information systems and services – ranging from system architecture to user interfaces, retrieval and access – that are socially and environmentally sustainable.

It is expected that the book will also open up new areas of discussion and research in relation to various management and policy issues in the context of the economic, social and environmental sustainability of information systems and services. This will in turn facilitate the design of information systems and services that can achieve a social and ecological balance in their operations, and can support information and knowledge access, creation and sharing for sustainable development in specific areas such as education and research, health, business, and so on, as envisaged in various United Nations and other international and national policy documents, some of which are addressed.

Overall, it is expected that this book will not only open up new teaching and research areas with regard to the sustainability of digital information, but also promote integrated research in different areas of sustainability of information. It will be useful for decision-makers and senior management in different sectors of the information industry and services. It will promote discussion on the future directions of the information services sector from the perspectives of creation, management, access and the long-term preservation of digital information in economically, socially and environmentally sustainable ways.

Gobinda Chowdhury

The sustainability of information: an outline

Introduction

Information professionals have traditionally focused on managing formally published information resources in hard copies, often called analogue sources. A variety of information services appeared over the years that aim to make the analogue collection of documents available to users effectively and efficiently. The nature of library and information activities changed towards the middle of the 20th century when the emphasis, especially in some research organizations, was laid on providing access to the latest scientific and research information through specialized information services called current awareness services, and selective dissemination of information services. These information services improved significantly in the second half of the 20th century with the introduction of computers in preparing catalogues and indexes of scholarly information resources.

Since the 1960s the nature and scope of library and information services changed significantly with the appearance of online databases, which made it possible for users to access bibliographic databases remotely. Information services and management activities in those days centred around building and using various tools, technologies and standards for handling analogue information resources and computerized bibliographic databases. Soon online library catalogue databases provided online access to library's holdings and these were soon followed by a new set of software, broadly called library management systems, which automated various library and information management activities such as collection management, circulation, and so on. The main objective of all these activities was to provide better and easier access to information – documents and text, mostly abstracting, databases. So information management activities, especially in the western world, changed significantly from the 1970s onwards. Increasingly information professionals needed to acquire a broad range of professional skills in order to be able to operate with the traditional tools, techniques and standards that were primarily designed for managing analogue resources and the corresponding services, and also to acquire a new set of skills to work with various remote online databases and the local library management systems. At the same time, interest in research and development activities grew significantly in different areas of user studies, focusing on the understanding and analysis of user information behaviour and their information seeking and retrieval strategies; development and testing of various information search and retrieval techniques; and development of tools and techniques for use and evaluation of various online databases and library management systems.

In the 1980s, especially with the arrival of personal computers, content such as abstracts and the full text of some journal and conference papers, and some reference works like dictionaries, encyclopedias and yearbooks began to appear – published or distributed – on portable media like CD-ROMs. During this time various local text databases were created. This required information management professionals to acquire new sets of skills for working in the personal computer environment and with various local and portable CD-ROM databases. Some information management professionals, especially those who had a technical background or an interest in computing technologies, became engaged in building algorithms and software for various information management activities ranging from information retrieval to the management of various library management operations.

In the 1990s the world of information management changed significantly with the advent and proliferation of the internet and web technologies. These technologies opened up new opportunities for digital publishing, and facilitated remote access to digital content, which was expensive and limited to a select few through specific library and information services. Internet and web technologies soon gave rise to scores of digital libraries and internet-based information services such as database search services, e-journals and reference services.

With the rapid advances in ICTs, especially web and mobile technologies, over the past decade, the role of information professionals and the nature of information management activities have changed dramatically. Information management professionals now need to acquire a whole set of new skills in internet, web and social networking technologies on top of their more traditional skills of managing information resources and services based on analogue and digital information resources. With the development of internet technologies, digital information resources began to grow very rapidly in volume, variety and complexity, and various search engine services were introduced, providing free access to online information resources. These developments were not within the boundaries of the conventional information profession or the information industry, but nevertheless had a profound influence on society at large, and on the research and professional practices in the information profession.

The concept of sustainability

Sustainability has now become a key issue of discussion in every sphere of business, institution and industry. Consequently today's information personnel, and academics and researchers in information, need to understand and address many sustainability related questions and challenges. While some aspects of sustainability have been studied in recent literature, so far no integrated research has taken place that studies the sustainability of information systems and services. This book aims to bridge this gap by addressing some questions related to the sustainability of information systems and services. Although some general issues and broad questions of sustainability have been considered elsewhere, this book focuses on scholarly communications. Various issues of sustainability of information systems and services are discussed in the context of higher education and research, and some new models and research issues related to the sustainability of information, especially in the context of scholarly communications, are provided.

The adjective sustainable means 'able to be maintained at a certain rate or level' (OUP, 2013), or '[something] that can continue or be continued for a long time' (OUP, 2011). However, if a service or product, or the rate of a development process, is to be sustainable, it is important not only to maintain its level of quality but also to do so in a way that does not deplete natural resources or the environment to an extent that might affect future generations. Thus sustainability or the capacity to endure should not deprive or disadvantage current or future generations of our society.

There is another definition of the word sustainable: 'conserving an ecological balance by avoiding depletion of natural resources' (OUP, 2013). The two meanings of sustainability – maintaining a continuing level of progress or quality of a product, service or development, while at the same time maintaining an ecological balance – bring a number of challenges to those who wish to ensure the sustainability of information systems and services. However, as it involves multiple factors and their intricate relationships, the definition of sustainability can be controversial (Wu and Wu, 2012).

Sustainability, and sustainable development in particular, has become a major topic of discussion in every major international and national policy document, with implications for almost every modern-day business, institution and activity. A report published by the World Commission on Environment and Development in 1987, called *Our Common Future* (also known as the Brundtland report), provided the 'classic' definition of sustainable development: 'development which meets the needs of the present without compromising the ability of future generations to meet their own needs' (United Nations, 1987).

It is generally accepted that sustainable development calls for a convergence between the three pillars of economic development, social equity and environmental protection (Drexhage and Murphy, 2010). According to the US Environmental Protection Agency (EPA), sustainability creates and maintains the conditions under which humans and nature can exist in productive harmony, which permit the social, economic and ecological requirements of present and future generations to be fulfilled (EPA, 2010).

Thus there are three dimensions, often called three pillars, of sustainability: economic sustainability, social sustainability and environmental sustainability. They are inter-related and inter-dependent. In order to achieve sustainable development, there is a need for an integrated approach to the three dimensions of sustainable development – economic development, environmental protection and social development (BIS, 2009, 8).

In order to achieve sustainable development in any sector – government, business, education, health, and so on – we need to build systems and services that are economically, environmentally and socially sustainable. Increasingly in most countries legislation requires businesses to comply with minimum social and environmental rules, and it is recognized that a sustainable business works towards minimizing environmental and social impacts while ensuring financial stability (Dimireva, 2012). Many countries and international bodies have introduced specific measures and oblige businesses to comply with the sustainability requirements. Consequently businesses in every sector are taking the necessary measures to comply with sustainability regulations and requirements, which cause a number of changes in business workflow, products and services. However, sustainability has not been studied and practised within the information science or information services sector as much as it has in other sectors (Chowdhury, 2010, 2012a, 2013; Nathan, 2012; Nolin, 2010).

Sustainable development

Sustainable development, which can be achieved by appropriate integration of various economic, environmental and social development activities, has remained important for the United Nations. The United Nations Division for Sustainable Development (UNDSD) identified a number of topics and issues related to sustainable development, some of which are social and economic while others are related to environment or natural resource management (United Nations, 2009).

Sustainable development in every sector is necessary to achieve the millennium development goals: to eradicate extreme poverty and hunger; ensure there is universal primary education; promote gender equality and empower women; reduce child mortality; improve maternal health; combat HIV/Aids, malaria and other diseases; ensure environmental sustainability; form a global partnership for development; and form part of a blueprint of sustainable development by 2015 (United Nations, 2013a).

The United Nations Conference on Sustainable Development (UNCSD) or Rio+20 took place in Rio de Janeiro, Brazil, in June 2012 (United Nations, 2013b). The objective of this conference was to take stock of the 20 years of actions at all levels to promote sustainable development, and to discuss the future. For this the UNCSD created a document, *Sustainable Development in the 21st Century*, with an objective 'to construct a coherent vision of sustainable development in the 21st century, which will contribute to the success of the Rio+20 conference' (United Nations, 2013c). One of the main outcomes of the Rio+20 conference was the agreement by member states to launch a process in order to 'develop a set of sustainable development goals (SDGs), which will build upon the Millennium Development Goals' (United Nations, 2013a).

Information about sustainability vs sustainable information

The importance of information and knowledge for sustainable development has been recognized and mentioned by several international bodies. Terms like information society and knowledge economy have become common over the past decade, and they are now used in conjunction with sustainability in many high-level discussions and policy documents produced by international agencies like the United Nations and UNESCO to the European Union, and specific national governments and agencies. In the canonical text on sustainable development, *Our Common Future* (United Nations, 1987), the importance of information for sustainable development has been directly and indirectly mentioned in various contexts and thus 'information technology, information gathering, information databases, information sharing and information analyses have been seen as crucial' (Nolin, 2010).

The importance of information and knowledge sharing has been recognized over and over again in many UN policy documents. For example, participants in the Expert Consultation on Knowledge and Capacity Needs for Sustainable Development in Post Rio+20 Era, organized by the United Nations Office for Sustainable Development (UNOSD) and partners, held in Incheon, Republic of Korea, in March 2013, observed: 'We are of the view that transition towards sustainability requires efforts on several fronts, but knowledge sharing and capacity building should be the fundamental platform for these efforts' (United Nations, 2013d, 1).

They recommended that 'UNOSD should collaborate with other knowledge providers, and both promote and facilitate the linking and sharing of data and knowledge through open networks, avoiding the duplication of existing initiatives' (United Nations, 2013d, 3).

The UN General Assembly Resolution called *The Future We Want* made a series of recommendations for achieving sustainable development in different areas (United Nations General Assembly, 2012). The document clearly recognizes the importance of information for sustainable development. For example, it states:

- We underscore that broad public participation and access to information and judicial and administrative proceedings are essential to the promotion of sustainable development (p.8).
- We further acknowledge efforts and progress made at the local and subnational levels, and recognize the important role that such authorities and communities can play in implementing sustainable development, including by engaging citizens and stakeholders and providing them with relevant information, as appropriate, on the three dimensions of sustainable development (p.8).
- We recognize that improved participation of civil society depends upon, inter alia, strengthening access to information and building civil society capacity and an enabling environment. We recognize that information and communications technology is facilitating the flow of information between governments and the public. In this regard, it is essential to work towards improved access to information and communications technology, especially broadband networks and services, and bridge the digital divide, recognizing the contribution of international co-operation in this regard (pp.8–9).
- We recognize that integrated social, economic and environmental data and information, as well as effective analysis and assessment of implementation, are important in decision-making processes (p.20).
- We recognize that there is a need for global, integrated and scientifically based information on sustainable development (p.48).

United Nations General Assembly (2012)

The importance of the need for access to, and sharing of, information was mentioned in several places in *The Future We Want* (United Nations General Assembly, 2012). The need for access to, and sharing of, information has been mentioned more specifically in the context of various sectors of development, for example, in the context of sustainable development in agriculture (p.23), food markets (p.23), the sexual and reproductive health of women (p.28), the employment market and job creation (p.29), conserving coral reef and mangrove ecosystems and marine life protection (p.34), hazard and risk assessment (p.39), biodiversity and ecosystems (p.40), climate and weather management (p.41), hazardous chemicals (pp.42–3), education and training (p.44), technology transfer (p.51), space technology and geospatial development policies (p.51), and so on. The fact that information plays a key role in today's information society and digital economy has also been recognized in many other national and international policy documents created by the European Commission (2010), the Organization for Economic Co-operation and Development (OECD) (2010, 2011), and studies commissioned by the British government (for example, Hargreaves, 2011). Thus the global community clearly recognizes the importance of management and sharing of appropriate data, information and knowledge for sustainable development in every sphere of our activity and society. It is therefore extremely important to build sustainable information systems and services that can support sustainable development as envisaged in *The Future We Want*, and various other policy documents, discussed above.

Since access to, and use and sharing of, appropriate information is an essential requirement for any sustainable development, creation of sustainable information systems and services for every sector is an absolute necessity. A number of stakeholders are involved in, and a number of challenges are associated with, today's digital world of information systems and services. Nathan (2012) comments that information science, human–computer interactions, and participatory research approaches can help citizens develop practices that reduce negative ecological, economic and social impacts of our information practices.

Sustainable information is a term for the resources that facilitate integration of the three parts of sustainable development – social, economic and environmental – and it contributes to strengthening the processes in which society is transformed, according to the ideals of sustainable development. So far there have not been many systematic studies to address the economic, environmental and social sustainability of information with special reference to digital information systems and services that form the backbone of a knowledge society and digital economy (Chowdhury, 2012a, 2012b, 2012c; 2013). This book aims to fill that gap.

About this book

The sustainability of information systems, especially the environmental impact of information systems, has been studied well in the recent past. While reviewing the literature on green IT and green information systems, Jenkin, Webster and McShane (2011) note that almost half of the research papers on this subject addressed the environmental impact of IT equipment and infrastructure, focusing primarily on the design, development and implementation of hardware and/or software. Clearly green information systems has been an area of research for some time. This book focuses on information services, especially scholarly information services.

The definition and scope of information and information science as a discipline or area of study has been discussed and debated for a long time (see, for example, Astrom, 2010; Bates, 2007; Bawden and Robinson, 2012, Chapter 1; Buckland, 2012; Robinson, 2009; Zins, 2007). However, just like Bawden and Robinson (2012), the author prefers to define information science as an interdisciplinary field of study, which is concerned with the different principles, practices, systems, technologies and tools required to produce, manage, access and use recorded information. Hence in this book the various sustainability issues are considered in the context of the lifecycle of recorded information – from creation to management, access and use. Although sustainability issues associated with the creation of recorded information and the information industry and marketplace are discussed, special emphasis has been given to the sustainability of digital information services.

Digital information services have always been based on one or more information systems and they make extensive use of ICT. This book focuses on the sustainability of information services where a sustainable information service may be defined as a sustainable information system that is designed to manage data and information, and produces information as an output in order to support specific research, scholarly and/or decision-making activities. Thus, it is different from the information systems as reviewed in Jenkin, Webster and McShane (2011), which are systems designed to perform a variety of transactions such as online operations, monitoring, control and management of specific equipment and machineries; online sales and purchase transactions; online supply chain management; and so on. The focus of sustainable information services is on the content, user and technologies that generate information as the output to meet the specific information needs of a user or community in a specific context. Several examples are drawn from the scholarly information and data management services in the higher education and research sector; these discussions and models can be extended and used in any other sector where information is required to achieve sustainable development.

There are 12 chapters. The first two set the background. The basic concepts of sustainability and sustainable development are considered in this chapter, and the three dimensions of sustainability – economic, social and environmental sustainability – are discussed in Chapter 2, as are the relationships between the three dimensions of sustainability and their inter-dependence. Thus the first two chapters are essential for beginners in the area of sustainability, and they set the background for further discussions of the sustainability of information systems and services that appear in the subsequent chapters. As the sustainability of information has so far been a poorly studied area in information science, these two chapters will be useful for everyone – students, academics, researchers and practitioners in every field of information.

Chapter 3 discusses various issues that are responsible for the economic sustainability of information, including aspects of various subjects taught in information science and information management programmes especially in relation to the business and management aspects of information services. It begins by presenting a generic business model of scholarly information, which has been developed and practised for several years and is based on the print information world. It then looks at how the internet, web and associated technologies have changed the traditional business model, and a new business model of scholarly information is discussed. The chapter then considers the various prevailing business models in the context of e-books, e-journals and open access journals, and factors responsible for the economic sustainability of digital libraries and digital preservation. Thus, this chapter examines various factors that need to be considered in order to achieve the economic sustainability of printed and digital information services. Examples from different library and information services, especially from the academic sector, are drawn to illustrate and support the discussions. Relationships of these factors with those associated with the social and environmental sustainability of information are examined in subsequent chapters of the book. Thus this chapter will be essential reading for those interested in several subjects, such as the management of information systems and services, collection management, digital libraries and digital preservation.

Chapter 4 looks at various issues related to the environmental sustainability of information. This is a new area in information studies, and as addressing environmental and climate change issues forms a major part of the strategies and management of every business, so it should also form part of the management of the information business – information industry and information services sector. The chapter begins by examining the origin and basic concept of environmental sustainability, the carbon footprint and greenhouse gas (GHG) emissions, how they are measured, and so on. It discusses the concepts of green IT and green information systems and explains what green information services are. It discusses the attributes of green information services, and how they can be measured. Thus this chapter helps readers to build a basic understanding of the environment and climate change in the context of information technology and information services, which are essential for every information academic, professional and researcher.

Chapter 5 examines the social sustainability aspects of information. Various factors that are responsible for, or associated with, the social sustainability of information have been addressed in the information science literature, although they have not been considered in the context of social sustainability of information per se. Some indicators of the social sustainability of information have been identified and a generic framework for study of these factors has been provided. This chapter shows that many factors are responsible for the social sustainability of information – user and context, user information behaviour, information seeking and retrieval, information access and user interface and retrieval. Thus the discussions in this chapter form part of several subjects in information science and information management programmes. This chapter provides a new perspective on all these topics, and can therefore form part of the basic reading in several subjects in information science and information management courses that are related to users and society.

For centuries library and information services have dealt with printed information resources, and consequently various business models and management practices have been built primarily around the printed information world. The situation has changed somewhat since the 1960s with the introduction of electronic databases and various computerized library management systems, and of late it changed again significantly with the introduction of the web and various related technologies. Library and information services in today's world provide a combination of print-based and digital information sources and services. The sustainability of such information services is influenced by the environmental sustainability of the printed information sources, and social and economic sustainability is influenced by the prevailing regulatory frameworks that control the information industry and information services. Chapter 6 discusses various issues related to the environmental sustainability of print-based information services, and some copyright and digital rights management issues related to the print and digital information world. This chapter will be useful not only for sustainability researchers but also for managers and policy-makers in library and information services when they assess the environmental impact of printed information resources, and the impact of current copyright and digital rights management on the sustainability of information services.

The open access movement, which began in the early 1990s, brought a major change in the information industry and services. Of late many government agencies and research funding bodies have introduced open access policy guidelines as a condition for research funding. These new policies and consequent developments will have significant implications for the economic, social and environmental sustainability of information. Chapter 7 discusses the recently introduced open access policies of some agencies like the Australian Research

Council, Research Councils UK (RCUK), the US National Institutes of Health (NIH) and the Wellcome Trust, and the US government directives to various federal funding agencies in relation to open access. It also considers the implications of these open access policies for the sustainability of information, and some associated information access and management challenges. Chapter 7 shows that as a result of the implementation of various open access policies, more and more scholarly information and data will be available in the public domain in coming years. This will have significant implications for the management of scholarly publications and research data. The chapter examines how recently introduced open access policies of various government and funding agencies will influence scholarly communications processes, and the information industry and information services sector. This chapter will be useful for researchers and students in different areas of information ranging from collection management, information systems and services, information retrieval systems and usability studies to legal and policy issues.

In Chapter 8 a conceptual model for management of open access scholarly communications is proposed. This chapter will be useful for those interested in a number of subject areas in information science, including the management of information systems and services, specific areas of information users and information retrieval.

Research in green IT and green information systems shows that cloud computing technologies can make significant contributions in achieving the economic and environmental sustainability of information. Chapter 9 discusses the basics of green IT and cloud computing technologies and addresses the concept of green information services. Basic design requirements of green information services in the context of higher education are also examined in this chapter. The chapter will be useful for practitioners in a number of subject areas in information science ranging from design of information systems and services, and their usability and evaluation, to the general management of information systems and services.

One of the major requirements of sustainable information systems and services is green information access. Essential features of green information retrieval systems and services, the assessment of the carbon footprint of information retrieval systems and specific measures and research requirements for green information access are discussed in Chapter 10. It will be useful for people working in a number of subject areas in information science, especially information retrieval and access.

A generic model for study and research in different areas related to the sustainability of information is proposed in Chapter 11, based on the discussions earlier in the book. Ways in which the model can be used to identify factors responsible for the economic, environmental and social sustainability of information are considered. This chapter looks at how the various factors in the proposed sustainability model can influence each other and how these interactions can influence the overall sustainability of scholarly communication processes in general, and the underlying information systems and services in particular. The model can be used to study the sustainability of any digital library or information service. This chapter will be useful for researchers in a variety of subjects in information science, ranging from the general management of information systems and services to user studies and information system design.

A variety of research and management issues are associated with the design and management of sustainable information. Chapter 12 discusses a number of research issues associated with the economic, social and environmental sustainability of scholarly communications in general, and information systems and services in particular. This chapter identifies a number of emerging research areas that will be useful for every information researcher in the near future.

Summary

Sustainable development has become a major area of concern for various international, regional and local governments, and consequently every business sector is taking specific measures in order to achieve the economic, environmental and social sustainability of their business processes. However, environmental sustainability in information science has not been researched well to date. This book looks at different aspects of the economic, social and environmental sustainability of information – ranging from the creation of information in print or digital form to its management, access and use. Some new models for the study of sustainability and for the management of sustainable information systems and services have been proposed. Various emerging research challenges associated with the sustainability of scholarly communications in general, and sustainable information systems and services in particular, have been discussed.

References

Astrom, F. (2010) The Visibility of Information Science and Library Science Research in Bibliometric Mapping of the LIS Field, *Library Quarterly*, **80** (2), 143–59.

Bates, M. (2007) Defining the Information Disciplines in Encyclopedia Development, *Information Research*, **12** (4), http://informationr.net/ir/12-4/colis/colis29.html.

Bawden, D. and Robinson, L. (2012) *Introduction to Information Science*, Facet Publishing.

BIS (2009) *Sustainable Development Action Plan: 1 August – 31 March*, Department for Business, Innovation & Skills, UK, www.bis.gov.uk/assets/biscore/business-sectors/docs/09-p59-bis-sustainable-development-action-plan-2009-11.pdf.

Buckland, M. (2012) What Kind of Science Can Information Science Be?, *Journal of the American Society for Information Science and Technology*, **63** (1), 1–7.

Chowdhury, G. G. (2010) Carbon Footprint of the Knowledge Sector: what's the future?, *Journal of Documentation*, **66** (6), 934–46.

Chowdhury, G. G. (2012a) Building Sustainable Information Services: a green IS research agenda, *Journal of the American Society for Information Science and Technology*, **63** (4), 633–47.

Chowdhury, G. G. (2012b) An Agenda for Green Information Retrieval Research, *Information Processing and Management*, **48** (6), 1067–77.

Chowdhury, G. G. (2012c) How Digital Information Services Can Reduce Greenhouse Gas Emissions, *Online Information Review*, **36** (4), 489–506.

Chowdhury, G. G. (2013) Sustainability of Digital Information Services, *Journal of Documentation*, **69** (5), 602–22.

Dimireva, I. (2012) Doing Business in the UK: sustainability, *Eubusiness*, 20 February, www.eubusiness.com/europe/uk/sustainable-business/.

Drexhage, J. and Murphy, D. (2010) Sustainable Development: from Brundtland to Rio 2012, background paper prepared for consideration by the High Level Panel on Global Sustainability at its first meeting, 19 September, International Institute for Sustainable Development, www.un.org/wcm/webdav/site/climatechange/shared/gsp/docs/GSP1-6_ Background%20on%20Sustainable%20Devt.pdf.

EPA (2010) *Inventory of US Greenhouse Gas Emissions and Sinks: 1990–2008*, executive summary, US Environment Protection Agency, http://epa.gov/climatechange/emissions/downloads10/US-GHG-Inventory-2010_ExecutiveSummary.pdf.

European Commission (2010) A Digital Agenda for Europe, communication from the Commission to the European Parliament, the Council, the European Economic and Social Committee and the Committee of the Regions, COM(2010), 245, http://ec.europa.eu/information_society/digital-agenda/documents/digital-agenda-communication-en.pdf.

Hargreaves, I. (2011) *Digital Opportunity: a review of intellectual property and growth*, www.ipo.gov.uk/ipreview-finalreport.pdf.

Jenkin, T. A., Webster, J. and McShane, L. (2011) An Agenda for 'Green' Information Technology and Systems Research, *Information and Organization*, **21** (1), 1–24.

Nathan, L. P. (2012) Sustainable Information Practice: an ethnographic investigation, *Journal of the American Society for Information Science and Technology*, **63** (11), 2254–68.

Nolin, J. (2010) Sustainable Information and Information Science, *Information Research*, **15** (2), http://informationr.net/ir/15-2/paper431.html.

OECD (2010) Committee on Information, Communications and Computer Policy, www.oecd.org/dataoecd/18/39/37328586.pdf.

OECD (2011) OECD Resources on Policy Issues Related to Internet Governance, OECD and the World Summit on the Information Society (WSIS), www.oecd.org/ document/21/0,2340,en_21571361_34590630_35282901_1_1_1_1,00.html.

OUP (2011) *Oxford Advanced Learner's Dictionary*, Oxford University Press.

OUP (2013) Oxford Dictionaries, Oxford University Press, http://www.oxforddictionaries.com/.

Robinson, L. (2009) Information Science: communication chain and domain analysis, *Journal of Documentation*, **65** (4), 578–91.

United Nations (1987) *Our Common Future: report of the World Commission on Environment and Development*, Brundtland Report, www.un-documents.net/wced-ocf.htm.

United Nations (2009) *Sustainable Development Topics*, UN Department of Economic and Social Affairs, Division for Sustainable Development.

United Nations (2013a) *We Can End Poverty 2015: millennium development goals*, www.un.org/millenniumgoals/.

United Nations (2013b) *Sustainable Development Knowledge Platform*, UN Conference on Sustainable Development, Rio+20, http://sustainabledevelopment.un.org/rio20.html.

United Nations (2013c) *Sustainable Development Knowledge Platform: sustainable development in the 21st century*, http://sustainabledevelopment.un.org/sd21.html.

United Nations (2013d) Bridging Knowledge and Capacity Gaps for Sustainability Transition: a framework for action, UN Office for Sustainable Development, 8 March, http://sustainabledevelopment.un.org/content/documents/ 1681Framework%20for%20Action.pdf.

United Nations General Assembly (2012) *The Future We Want*, resolution adopted by the General Assembly, A/RES/66/288, 11 September, http://daccess-dds-ny.un.org/doc/UNDOC/GEN/N11/476/10/PDF/N1147610.pdf?OpenElement.

Wu, J. and Wu, T. (2012) Sustainability Indicators and Indices: an overview. In Mandu, C. N. and Kuei, C.-H. (eds), *Handbook of Sustainability Management*, World Scientific Pub Co, 65–86.

Zins, C. (2007) Conceptions of Information Science, *Journal of the American Society for Information Science and Technology*, **58** (3), 335–50.

The three dimensions of sustainability

Introduction

History shows us that human civilization has progressed over several centuries through different stages of development, and in doing so it has used natural resources in a number of different ways. The use and exploitation of natural resources has significantly increased since the beginning of the industrial revolution in the 18th century. Hundreds of thousands of miles of roads, railways, canals and bridges were built; scores of factories and mills were set up; many cities and towns appeared; and this transformation created a whole new world in which we live today. Exploitation and use of natural resources increased significantly over the last century, and is continuing in this century, because of the increased population, rapid industrialization, increasing demands, improved lifestyles and higher standard of living, massive increases in the use of fossil fuels in industries and transportation, and of late increasing use of ICT in every sphere of life. These developments make extensive use of natural resources, and produce directly and indirectly a number of substances that are harmful for natural resources and the environment.

In fact everything that we do – relating to our health and well-being, our economy, our education, our business, science and technology, our progress and our civilization – in some way or the other depends on, and makes use of, natural resources and environment. The natural world has a cycle to sustain, and understanding and managing this cycle (the normal cycle of change) in a positive way is one of the core concepts of sustainability research (University of Idaho, 2013). It is therefore extremely important that we try to understand and protect nature and the environment while at the same time make progress in every sphere of our life and civilization.

Systematic studies and research on sustainable development and various sustainability issues resulted from a number of factors, such as the recognition:

- of the need to conserve natural resources, which resulted in conservation laws emerging in the late 19th century
- of the harmful effects of various chemical and physical agents on natural resources, which resulted in the formation of bodies like the EPA in the USA, the Environment Agency in the UK, and so on
- that the rapid growth of population and civilization seriously damages our ecosystem, which resulted in the formation of various national and international bodies like the United Nations Division for Sustainable Development to organize international summits to develop policies to promote the idea of sustainable development and formulate measures and practices for the protection of nature and the environment.

National Research Council (2011)

This chapter discusses the basic concepts and objectives of the three dimensions of sustainability – economic sustainability, social sustainability and environmental sustainability. It then considers what each of these three dimensions of sustainability means in the context of digital information systems and services. Details of each dimension of sustainability for digital information, especially in the context of scholarly information, are examined in subsequent chapters.

Economic sustainability

Broadly speaking economic sustainability means sustainable economic growth. Spangenberg comments that 'in the economic debate, sustainable development is most often described as the need to maintain a permanent income for humankind, generated from non-declining capital stocks' (2005). Within a business context, economic sustainability may be defined as 'using the assorted assets of the company efficiently to allow it to continue functioning profitably over time' (BusinessDictionary.com, 2013).

In the context of a society, economic sustainability is associated with the sustained economic growth that can be measured in gross domestic product (GDP), and in the context of a business, economic sustainability may mean sustained monetary profits – a steady growth in revenues and profit margins (Soderbaum, 2008). Few other economic sustainability criteria such as innovativeness, competitiveness and public debt, or even inflation and trade imbalance are also used in the macro-economic debate (Spangenberg, 2005). Economic growth of a society generally correlates with overall improvements in quality of life, higher levels of education and life expectancy at country level (OECD, 2008).

While economic growth is essential for business or society, we need to consider various questions such as how this growth is achieved, whether or not it is lasting, who benefits and who is left behind, and to understand whether this growth is going to affect anyone adversely in the near or long-term future. Thus focusing only on the economic sustainability measured as profit or financial growth is not enough for the future of a business or society. Blackburn (2007) provides an interesting simile: like air to a human, money to a company is the most urgently needed requirement for survival; but like lack of water and food in a person's life, lack of adequate social and environmental performance in a company's future can be fatal.

A variety of indicators for sustainability have been proposed in the literature. Traditional macro-economic measures, such as gross national product (GNP) and GDP, are used to measure economic growth, but in the context of sustainable development other factors such as human capital and natural capital are also used. Therefore alongside GDP, the new indicators of economic sustainability include human and natural capital, water consumption, waste management, emission of harmful gases, quality of life, life expectancy, educational attainment, health and well-being (WorldBank Group, 2000a).

The OECD proposes the 'capital approach' for measuring sustainability. It is a framework to measure sustainable development, which operates on the principle that sustaining well-being over time requires ensuring that we replace or conserve wealth in its different components. It further stresses that a society's total capital base encompasses the following five individual types, and all of these should be taken into consideration as capital inputs in the production of well-being:

- financial capital, like stocks, bonds and currency deposits
- produced capital, like machinery, buildings, telecommunications and other types of infrastructure
- natural capital in the form of natural resources, land and ecosystems providing services like waste absorption
- human capital in the form of an educated and healthy workforce
- social capital in the form of social networks and institutions.   OECD (2008)

Measuring the economic sustainability of a service sector is a major challenge, because the outcome of a service sector is rather difficult to measure in dollars or increase in direct profits or tangible assets. The service sector produces 'intangible' goods, some of which are well known, such as government, health, education, and so on, and some are relatively new, such as modern communications, information and business services (WorldBank Group, 2000b). One of the indirect measures of economic sustainability of service sectors is the growth in human capital that is capable of engaging in sustainable development using fewer natural resources, and alternative and innovative technologies and resources.

According to the WorldBank Group:

> Most high-income countries today are postindustrializing – becoming less reliant on industry – while most low-income countries are industrializing – becoming more reliant on industry. But even in countries that are still industrializing, the service sector is growing relative to the rest of the economy. By the mid-1990s services accounted for almost two-thirds of world GDP up from about half in the 1980s.
>
> WorldBank Group (2000b, 52)

In the UK the Department for Business, Innovation & Skills (BIS) noted that there has been a 'long-term shift towards services, with manufacturing as a share of overall GDP in the UK declining from 32% in 1970 to its current level of around 12%. This broad shift in gross value added and employment from manufacturing to services is a long-term trend and common to all G7 economies' (BIS, 2010, 9). Gross value added is a measure of contribution to the economy of an industry or sector.

Social sustainability

Many researchers note that the issues of social sustainability have been explored less than those of economic and environmental sustainability (Hawke Research Institute, 2010; Omann and Spangenberg, 2002; Partridge, 2005). An EU study specifically observed that: 'there is a tendency in the FP funded research (and the SDS [sustainable development strategy] itself) to reduce sustainable development to its economic and environmental dimensions while disregarding social aspects' (Adelle and Pallemaerts, 2009). By analysing a set of definitions of social sustainability provided by different researchers, Colantonio (n.d.) comments that the concept of social sustainability 'has been under-theorised or often oversimplified in existing theoretical constructs and there have been very few attempts to define social sustainability as an independent dimension of sustainable development'.

One of the main challenges comes from the definition of the concept of social sustainability. Broadly speaking social sustainability may be defined as the maintenance and improvement of well-being of current and future generations (Mak, Peacock and Clinton, 2011). However, the concept of well-being can be defined differently in different contexts such as the equity of access to essential services, healthy life and well-being, democratic and informed citizenship, promotion and sharing of positive relations and culture, and so on. McKenzie (2004) defined social sustainability as a 'life-enhancing condition within communities, and a process within communities that can achieve that condition' (14).

Often modern studies and policy documents peg social sustainability with environmental sustainability, though some researchers argue that 'social sustainability must first be defined as distinct from environmental or economic sustainability for it to develop its own models of best practice. Once this process of definition has been achieved, parameters can be established to measure the effect of equitable social policies and institutions on environmental outcomes. This will result in a truly interdisciplinary model of eco-sustainability' (Hawke Research Institute, 2010).

Many indicators of sustainable development have been proposed in various studies and initiatives. As many as 96 indicators of sustainable development have been identified by the United Nations, and many EU-funded research projects have developed indicators for different aspects of sustainable development (Adelle and Pallemaerts, 2009). Reviews of different initiatives that attempted to define indicators of sustainability show that there have been as many as 255 indicators for sustainable development (Hutchins and Sutherland, 2008; Hutchins, Gierke and Sutherland, 2009). However, Colantonio (n.d.) comments that our understanding of social sustainability is still fuzzy and limited by theoretical and methodological constraints stemming from its context and disciplinary-dependent definitions and measurements.

Colantonio (n.d.) discusses various indicators of social sustainability that have been identified by researchers and categorizes them as follows:

- basic needs (Baines and Morgan, 2004; Hans-Böckler-Stiftung, 2001; Sinner et al., 2004)
- capability to withstand external pressures (Chambers and Conway, 1992)
- community participation (Bramley et al., 2006)
- community stability (Bramley et al., 2006)
- consumption (Omann and Spangenberg, 2002)
- cultural and community diversity (Baines and Morgan, 2004; Sinner et al., 2004)
- democracy (Sachs, 1999)
- education (Omann and Spangenberg, 2002)
- employment (Omann and Spangenberg, 2002; Sachs, 1999)
- empowerment and participation (Baines and Morgan, 2004; Sinner et al., 2004)

- enabling social innovation (Hans-Böckler-Stiftung, 2001)
- equal opportunities to participate in a democratic society (Hans-Böckler-Stiftung, 2001)
- equitable access to resources and social services (Sachs, 1999)
- equitable income distribution (Sachs, 1999)
- equity (Baines and Morgan, 2004; Chambers and Conway, 1992; DfID, 1999; Sachs, 1999; Sinner et al. 2004)
- experience (Omann and Spangenberg, 2002)
- human rights (Sachs, 1999)
- inclusion (DfID, 1999)
- income (Omann and Spangenberg, 2002)
- interactions in the community or social networks (Bramley et al., 2006)
- livelihood (Chambers and Conway, 1992; DfID, 1999)
- needs of future generations (Baines and Morgan, 2004; Sinner et al., 2004)
- paid and voluntary work (Hans-Böckler-Stiftung, 2001)
- participation (Omann and Spangenberg, 2002; Thin, Lockhart and Yaron, 2002)
- personal disability (Baines and Morgan, 2004; Sinner et al., 2004)
- poverty (DfID, 1999)
- pride and sense of place (Bramley et al., 2006)
- safety nets (Chambers and Conway, 1992)
- security (Thin, Lockhart and Yaron, 2002)
- security (crime) (Bramley et al., 2006)
- skills (Omann and Spangenberg, 2002)
- social capital (Baines and Morgan, 2004; Sinner et al., 2004)
- social homogeneity (Sachs, 1999)
- social justice (DfID, 1999; Thin, Lockhart and Yaron, 2002)
- social security (Hans-Böckler-Stiftung, 2001)
- solidarity (Thin, Lockhart and Yaron, 2002).

The above list of indicators of social sustainability is not exhaustive, and it may be noted that some of the identified indicators are very broad, for example, basic needs, consumption and skills. Similarly, some indicators are relatively difficult to assess, e.g. needs of future generations. Again, some indicators overlap, e.g. equity, equitable access to resources and social services, and equitable income. Nevertheless, the list gives an idea of the different indicators, and more importantly the difficulties that may be associated with measuring such a diverse list of indicators of social sustainability. Over the years there has been a broad shift within the sustainability discourse from 'hard' themes such as equity, poverty reduction and livelihood towards 'softer' concepts such as identity and sense of place (Colantonio, n.d.).

Environmental sustainability

The Financial Times Lexicon (2013) defines environmental sustainability as 'a state in which the demands placed on the environment can be met without reducing its capacity to allow all people to live well, now and in the future'. A more formal definition has been provided by Goodland, according to whom environmental sustainability is a 'set of constraints on the four major activities regulating the scale of the human economic subsystem: the use of renewable and nonrenewable resources on the sources side, and pollution and waste assimilation on the sink side' (Goodland, 1995, 10).

Although the concept of environmental sustainability has received a significant amount of attention only in the past two decades, its origin can be traced back over five decades. In the USA, the first establishment of a national policy for environmental sustainability came in 1969 with the passage of the National Environmental Policy Act (NEPA), and the EPA began to operate on 2 December 1970, as a national agency to protect and preserve the quality of the environment (EPA, 2013). This followed the UN Conference on Human Environment held in Stockholm in 1972, also known as the Stockholm conference, at which representatives from several countries expressed concerns about the impact of increasing global developments on the environment. This gave rise to the United Nations Environment Programme (UNEP), which was established in 1972 with the mission to provide leadership and encourage partnership in caring for the environment by inspiring, informing and enabling nations and peoples to improve their quality of life without compromising that of future generations (UNEP, n.d.). In 1983, the UN Secretary General formed a special independent commission, called the World Commission on Environment and Development, under the chairmanship of the then Prime Minister of Norway, Gro Harlem Brundtland, to re-examine the environmental and developmental problems around the world, and to formulate specific proposals to address them. The Brundtland Commission concluded its work in 1987 and published its report as *Our Common Future* (also known as the Brundtland report) (United Nations, 1987). As mentioned in Chapter 1, this canonical document defined the concept of sustainable development and emphasized the need for an ecological balance. An important outcome of the Brundtland report was the Earth Summit in Rio de Janeiro in June 1992.

The Rio Declaration on Environment and Development (United Nations

General Assembly, 1992), also known as Agenda 21, was adopted at the United Nations Conference on Environment and Development held in Rio de Janeiro, Brazil, in June 1992. This has subsequently given rise to several major international summits and conferences and has resulted in a major policy document, the Kyoto Protocol (United Nations, 1998), which was adopted in Kyoto, Japan, on 11 December 1997 and entered into force on 16 February 2005, setting binding targets for 37 industrialized countries and the European Community for reducing GHG emissions (discussed in the next section) to an average of 5% against the 1990 levels over the five-year period of 2008 to 2012 (United Nations, 2011).

Consequently various governments and international bodies have geared up their activities for combating climate change, and several new measures have been proposed. As in other fields, tough measures are being proposed by governments to ensure that higher education sectors comply with government policies in reducing their carbon footprint or GHG emissions. In March 2009, the US EPA proposed the mandatory GHG reporting rule, which would require any US entity emitting more than 25,000 metric tonnes of carbon dioxide (CO_2)-equivalent to report to a centralized federal agency, and any educational institution in the USA that produces more than 25,000 tonnes of CO_2-equivalent will come under this regulation (St Arnaud et al., 2009). In the UK the Government planned to link cutting emissions to funding agreements for higher education and a target has been set to reduce CO_2-equivalent emissions by 26% by 2020 (over 1990 figures), and as much as 80% by 2050 (Denham, 2009). According to a law introduced in the Canadian province of British Columbia, if any public-sector institutions, such as hospitals, colleges and universities, schools, museums, and municipal government, fail to become carbon-neutral, they must purchase carbon offsets from the Pacific Carbon Trust at the price of $25 (Canadian dollars)/tonne, fixed and regulated by the Trust (St Arnaud et al., 2009).

The 2012 UN Conference on Sustainable Development took the following resolution, which reinforces the UN's overall commitment to environmental sustainability:

> We, the Heads of State and Government and high-level representatives, having met at Rio de Janeiro, Brazil, from 20 to 22 June 2012, with the full participation of civil society, renew our commitment to sustainable development and to ensuring the promotion of an economically, socially and environmentally sustainable future for our planet and for present and future generations.
>
> United Nations General Assembly (2012)

The climate change debate

Environmental sustainability research covers a range of broad areas and issues, such as:

- climate change issues
- human settlements and habitats
- energy systems
- terrestrial systems
- carbon and nitrogen cycles
- aquatic systems.   Molden, Janouskova and Hak (2012)

Consequently a variety of indicators and targets have been set by various international agencies like the UN, OECD and EU, and national governments (Molden, Janouskova and Hak, 2012). Environmental sustainability is often assessed by using environmental performance indicators, which focus on assessing current environmental conditions (Wu and Wu, 2012).

It is now widely recognized that the global climate is changing for the worse, largely because of human-produced GHGs that cause increases in air and ocean temperature, melting of snow and ice, rising sea levels affecting atmospheric and ocean circulation, changing patterns of rainfall and wind causing adverse effects on human life, flora and fauna, and so on. Different terms are used to denote the factors responsible for climate change, the most common ones being the carbon footprint and GHG emissions. There are many definitions of GHG, some of which only talk about the emission of CO_2; a broader definition covers emission of not only CO_2 but other harmful gases like nitrous oxide, ozone, hydrocarbons and chlorofluorocarbons, plus black carbon (Wiedmann and Minx, 2008). However, often GHG emission is measured and expressed in metric tonnes (1000 kg) of CO_2 equivalent ($mTCO_2e$) (IPCC, 2007).

The Intergovernmental Panel on Climate Change (IPCC) was established jointly by the World Meteorological Organization (WMO) and the UNEP in 1988 as the leading advisory body for the assessment of climate change, and it now has 194 countries as members (IPCC, 2011). The IPCC 2007 report on climate change warns that the 'continued GHG emissions at or above current rates would cause further warming and induce many changes in the global climate system during the 21st century that would very likely be larger than those observed during the 20th century' (IPCC, 2007, 23).

The UN, IPCC and various other international bodies have urged governments and world leaders to step up their efforts to develop appropriate climate change policies to curb GHG emissions. The US EPA noted that human activities are changing the composition of the atmosphere, and that increasing the concentration of GHG will change the planet's climate (EPA, 2010). The UK Government promised to halve carbon emissions by 2025, from 1990 levels (BBC News, 2012). In Europe, the Directorate-General for Climate Action was established in February 2010 in order to develop and implement 'cost effective international and domestic climate change policies and strategies in order for the EU to meet its targets for 2020 and beyond, especially with regard to reducing its greenhouse gas emissions' (European Commission, 2011).

This sort of concern and examples of some of the many national and international efforts to combat climate change demonstrate the gravity of the situation and clearly point to the urgent need for action. Various national governments, international bodies and other organizations have provided figures showing the major contributors to GHG emissions in today's world. For example, in the USA, Bianco et al. (2010) suggested these come from:

- power plants: 34%
- residential and commercial heating: 7%
- transportation: 29%
- industry: 15%
- agriculture, forestry: 7%
- others (landfills, natural gas, coal mines, etc.): 8%.

Further breakdowns of GHG emissions produced by different types of industries and businesses in different sectors are also available. However, despite many initiatives at global, regional and national levels, environmental sustainability is still a contentious issue in many countries, and there are differences of opinion among those in developed and developing countries, and especially rapidly emerging economies like China, India and Brazil.

The three pillars of sustainable development

The recent global economic crisis reinforced the fact that sustainable development cannot only be based on economic progress (Molden, Janouskova and Hak, 2012). It is now globally recognized that sustainable development cannot be achieved by only one or a handful of nations, rather a concerted effort is needed by every country in the world. Consequently efforts are now being made to reach a global consensus and a policy framework for sustainable development. The UN Rio+20 conference resulted in a document entitled *The Future We Want*, which made a series of recommendations to bring about sustainable development in different areas (United Nations General Assembly, 2012).

As discussed in Chapter 1 and earlier in this chapter, there are three dimensions of sustainability – economic sustainability, social sustainability and environmental sustainability – but often national and international bodies focus on only one dimension of sustainability, for example:

- The UNEP, the environmental protection agencies of many countries and many non-governmental organizations focus on environmental issues.
- The World Trade Organization (WTO) and the OECD focus mostly on economic growth.
- The OECD and some UN bodies give some attention to social sustainability, like war reduction, peace and justice.

However, some progress has been made over the past few decades, and several government agencies, local authorities and their associations, professional and academic institutions and grassroots organizations have come up with some successful plans for sustainable development. A database of best practice cases and tools for sustainable development has been created as part of the Best Practices and Local Leadership Programme (UN Habitat, n.d.). The objective of the programme is 'to raise awareness of decision-makers on critical social, economic and environmental issues and to better inform them of the practical means and policy options to improve the living environment' (UN Habitat, n.d.).

Several issues and challenges are associated with each dimension of sustainable development. It may not always be easy to achieve all three forms of sustainability at the same time, and sometimes measures taken to bring about one form of sustainability may affect or compromise the other form(s) of sustainability. For example, in order to attain economic sustainability, one may try to do business using cheap sources of energy, inefficient industries and technologies, or a cheap and unregulated labour market. Such an effort to realize economic sustainability (by reducing costs) may compromise environmental sustainability, and also in some way social sustainability, by creating inequality in the labour market, standard of living, standard of health and well-being of the population, and so on. On the other hand, if one wants to use only clean energy and the most advanced industries and technologies, then the resulting businesses and products may be environmentally sustainable, but they are also likely to be expensive, at least to begin with, and therefore they may not be economically sustainable. This may also create social inequality by compromising the cost of living, well-being and quality of life of the population.

Although the three dimensions of sustainability are equally important and are the three pillars of sustainable development, they may be affected by a number of factors. When countries face severe austerity measures, the importance of economic and social sustainability takes priority over environmental sustainability. Even social sustainability may be affected in a number of ways because of the lack of funding for NGOs and charities that do a significant amount of work in achieving social sustainability. Similarly when a war breaks out or a natural disaster takes place social sustainability of development take priority. For many years the main priority of developing countries has been to attain economic and social development rather than environmental sustainability.

An integrated approach to sustainable development

Our Common Future, the report of the World Commission on Environment and Development, also known as the Brundtland report (United Nations, 1987), pointed out that there was a need to develop indicators for sustainable development. Subsequently the 1992 Rio Declaration on Environment and Development (United Nations General Assembly, 1992) urged countries to develop indicators of sustainable development in order to 'illustrate to policy makers and the public the linkages and trade-offs between economic, environmental and social values; to evaluate the longer term implications of current decisions and behaviours; and to monitor progress towards sustainable development goals by establishing baseline conditions and trends' (Stevens, 2005).

A report by the OECD observes that economic growth will not in itself solve problems of a country or society unless it is inclusive, equitable and sustainable and that 'natural capital accounts for an estimated 26% of total wealth in low-income countries, compared with 2% of wealth in advanced economies' (OECD, 2013). Thus, rapid depletion of natural resources for achieving a sustained growth, especially in the low-income countries, can lead to a disaster in the near future. Therefore OECD recommends that economic, environmental and social sustainability need to be fostered at all levels nationally and internationally (OECD, 2013).

Stevens (2005) notes that 'measuring sustainable development requires both simple measures that inform decision-makers about major trends and issues as well as more detailed measures to support in-depth analysis. Attention should be given to the "supply side" – how statistics and related indicators can best be constructed – as well as to the "demand side" – how these indicators can be interpreted and used most appropriately.' He further emphasizes that the frameworks developed for the purpose should assess sustainability at all levels – local, national, regional and global.

An OECD diagram (Stevens, 2005), produced in Figure 2.1, shows the impact of one form of sustainability on another:

- Economic growth and development leading to economic sustainability have an impact on environmental sustainability through use of resources, pollutants and waste discharge, and so on (arrow 1).
- Environmental services leading to environmental sustainability have an impact on the economy through natural resources, sink functions (where excess CO_2 is absorbed) and contributions to economic efficiency and employment (arrow 2).
- Environmental sustainability parameters have an impact on different aspects of society, e.g., access to resources and amenities, contributions to health, and living and working conditions (arrow 3).
- Social sustainability variables have an impact on the environment, e.g., demographic changes, consumption patterns, environmental education and information, and institutional and legal frameworks (arrow 4).
- Social sustainability variables have an impact on the economy, e.g., labour force, population and household structure, education and training, consumption levels, and institutional and legal frameworks (arrow 5).
- Economic sustainability variables have an impact on different aspects of society, e.g. income levels, equity and employment (arrow 6).

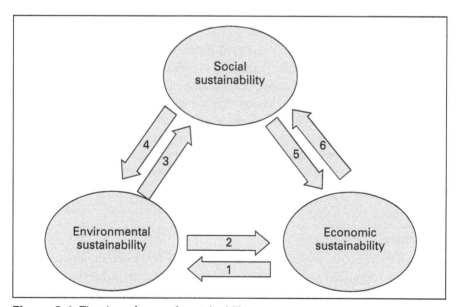

Figure 2.1 The three forms of sustainability

Thus for any business, system or service one should ask the following questions:

- From the perspective of economic sustainability: does our business, system or service promote sustainable growth that can be measured in direct or indirect economic terms such as better performance, better education, better research, better living, and so on?
- From the perspective of social sustainability: does our business, system or service contribute to the social well-being of people and communities who are our clients, and to society in general?
- From the perspective of environmental sustainability: do we carry out businesses, activities, systems and services in a way that causes minimum damage to the environment so that present and future generations are not affected by them?

Given the interdependencies and other complexities of sustainability, it is not possible for any one organization or institution to achieve all the three forms of sustainability on their own; the quest for sustainability must therefore be a joint effort (Blackburn, 2007).

The sustainability of information

According to Nolin (2010), sustainable information can consist of information for sustainable development, which includes the contribution of information studies to the communicative aspects of sustainable development, and development of sustainable information, which includes development of clean ICTs that contribute to more efficient usage of energy than other technologies.

Chapter 1 described how the importance of information for sustainable development has been recognized by several international bodies. Yet, no systematic study nor research agenda has addressed the economic, environmental and social sustainability of information systems and services with special reference to digital information services, which form the backbone of a knowledge society and digital economy (Chowdhury, 2012; Nolin, 2010).

Summary

Although the concepts of sustainability and sustainable development originated over four decades ago (EPA, 2013), only in the past two decades have they attracted significant attention at international level. Sustainable development has now become a major matter of concern for the United Nations and various other international and national bodies. Several high-level international meetings and conferences have taken place over the past few years in order to formulate guidelines and develop action plans to achieve sustainable development. It is now well recognized that sustainable development relies on the three pillars of sustainability – economic sustainability, social sustainability and environmental sustainability. Although these dimensions of sustainability have been discussed globally, regionally and nationally in the context of a number of business and development activities, and the importance of information for sustainable development has also been well recognized, to date very little research and systematic study has taken place on the sustainability of information systems and services. The rest of this book examines various issues and challenges related to the economic, social and environmental sustainability of information systems and services in the context of scholarly communications.

References

Adelle, C. and Pallemaerts, M. (2009) *Sustainable Development Indicators: an overview of relevant framework programme funded research and identification of further needs in view of EU and international activities*, European Commission, European Research Area, Seventh Framework Programme, www.ieep.eu/assets/443/sdi_review.pdf.

Baines, J. and Morgan, B. (2004) Sustainability Appraisal: a social perspective. In Dalal-Clayton, B. and Sadler, B. (eds), *Sustainability Appraisal: a review of international experience and practice*, International Institute for Environment and Development, 95–111.

BBC News (2012) Millions in UK 'lack basic online skills', 8 November, www.bbc.co.uk/news/technology-20236708.

Bianco, N. M., Litz, F. T., Gottlieb, M. and Damassa, T. (2010) *Reducing Greenhouse Gas Emissions in the United Sates Using Existing Federal Authorities and State Action*, World Resources Institute, http://pdf.wri.org/reducing_ghgs_using_existing_federal_authorities_and_state_action.pdf.

BIS (2010) *A Strategy for Sustainable Growth*, Economic Annex, Department for Business, Innovation & Skills (UK), July, https://www.gov.uk/government/uploads/system/uploads/attachment_data/file/31998/10-1059-sustainable-growth-economic-annex.pdf.

Blackburn, W. R. (2007) *The Sustainability Handbook: the complete management guide to achieving social, economic and environmental responsibility*, Environmental Law Institute.

Bramley, G., Dempsey, N., Power, S. and Brown, C. (2006) What is 'Social Sustainability' and How do our Existing Urban Forms Perform in Nurturing it?, paper presented at the conference *Sustainable Communities and Green Futures,* Bartlett School of Planning, University College London, 5–7 April.

BusinessDictionary.com (2013) Economic Sustainability,
    www.businessdictionary.com/definition/economic-sustainability.html#
    ixzz2OdJ61yXN.

Chambers, R. and Conway, G. (1992) *Sustainable Rural Livelihoods: practical concepts for the*
    21st century, IDS Discussion Paper 296, Institute of Development Studies.

Chowdhury, G. G. (2012) Building Sustainable Information Services: a green IS research
    agenda, *Journal of the American Society for Information Science and Technology*, **63** (4), 633–47.

Colantonio, A. (n.d.) *Social Sustainability: linking research to policy and practice*, Oxford
    Institute for Sustainable Development, Oxford Brookes University,
    http://ec.europa.eu/research/sd/conference/2009/papers/7/andrea_colantonio_-
    _social_sustainability.pdf.

Denham, J. (2009) letter dated 21 January 2009,
    www.hefce.ac.uk/news/hefce/2009/grant/letter.htm.

DfID (1999) Sustainable livelihoods guidance sheets, Department for International
    Development (UK).

EPA (2010) *Inventory of US Greenhouse Gas Emissions and Sinks: 1990–2008*, executive
    summary, US Environmental Protection Agency, http://epa.gov/climatechange/
    emissions/downloads10/US-GHG-Inventory-2010_ExecutiveSummary.pdf.

EPA (2013) *History of Sustainability: creation of EPA and NEPA*, US Environmental
    Protection Agency,
    http://yosemite.epa.gov/r10/oi.nsf/8bb15fe43a5fb81788256b58005ff079/
    398761d6c3c7184988256fc40078499b!OpenDocument.

European Commission (2011) Climate Action,
    http://ec.europa.eu/dgs/clima/mission/index_en.htm.

Financial Times Lexicon (2013) Definition of Environmental Sustainability,
    http://lexicon.ft.com/Term?term=environmental-sustainability.

Goodland, R. (1995) The Concept of Environmental Sustainability, *Annual Review of*
    Ecological Systems, **26**, 1–24,
    http://are.berkeley.edu/courses/ARE298/Readings/goodland.pdf.

Hans-Böckler-Stiftung (ed.) (2001) *Pathways Towards a Sustainable Future*, Setzkasten.

Hawke Research Institute (2010) Eco-social Sustainability of the Murray-Darling Basin,
    University of South Australia,
    http://w3.unisa.edu.au/hawkeinstitute/research/ecosocial/eco-background.asp.

Hutchins, M. and Sutherland, J. W. (2008) An Exploration of Measures of Social
    Sustainability and Their Application to Supply Chain Decisions, *Journal of Cleaner*
    Production, **16** (15), 1688–98.

Hutchins, M. J., Gierke, J. S. and Sutherland, J. W. (2009) Decision Making for Social
    Sustainability: a lifecycle assessment approach, *IEEE International Symposium on*
    Technology and Society, ISTAS '09, 18–20 May, 1–5.

IPCC (2007) *Climate Change 2007: synthesis report*, Intergovernmental Panel on Climate Change, www.ipcc.ch/pdf/assessment-report/ar4/syr/ar4_syr.pdf.

IPCC (2011) Intergovernmental Panel on Climate Change, www.ipcc.ch/.

Mak, M., Peacock, Y. and Clinton, J. (2011) Social Sustainability: a comparison of case studies in UK, USA and Australia, *17th Pacific Rim Real Estate Society Conference*, Gold Coast, 16–19 January, www.prres.net/papers/Mak_Peacock_Social_Sustainability.pdf.

McKenzie, S. (2004) Social Sustainability: towards some definitions, Hawke Research Institute, http://w3.unisa.edu.au/hawkeinstitute/publications/downloads/wp27.pdf.

Molden, B., Janouskova, S. and Hak, T. (2012) How to Understand and Measure Environmental Sustainability: indicators and targets, *Ecological Indicators*, **17**, 4–13.

National Research Council (2011) *Sustainability and the US EPA*, Committee on Incorporating Sustainability in the US Environmental Protection Agency, NRC, www.nap.edu/openbook.php?record_id=13152&page=16.

Nolin, J. (2010) Sustainable Information and Information Science, *Information Research*, **15** (2), http://informationr.net/ir/15-2/paper431.html.

OECD (2008) *Sustainable Development: linking economy, society, environment*, Organisation for Economic Co-operation and Development, www.oecd.org/insights/41773991.pdf.

OECD (2013) *Better Policies for Better Lives*, Organisation for Economic Co-operation and Development, www.oecd.org/.

Omann, I. and Spangenberg, J. H. (2002) Assessing Social Sustainability: the social dimension of sustainability in a socio-economic scenario, paper presented at the *7th Biennial Conference of the International Society for Ecological Economics* in Sousse, Tunisia, 6–9 March.

Partridge, E. (2005) 'Social Sustainability': a useful theoretical framework?, paper presented at the *Australasian Political Science Association Annual Conference*, Dunedin, New Zealand, 28–30 September, http://auspsa.anu.edu.au/proceedings/publications/Partridgepaper.pdf.

Sachs, I. (1999) Social Sustainability and Whole Development: exploring the dimensions of sustainable development. In Egon, B. and Thomas, J. (eds), *Sustainability and the Social Sciences: a cross-disciplinary approach to integrating environmental considerations into theoretical reorientation*, Zed Books, 25–36.

Sinner, J., Baines, J., Crengle, H., Salmon, G., Fenemor, A. and Tipa, G. (2004) *Sustainable Development: a summary of key concepts*, Ecologic Research Report 2, www.ecologic.org.nz.

Soderbaum, P. (2008) *Understanding Sustainability Economics: towards pluralism in economics*, Earthscan.

Spangenberg, J. H. (2005) Economic Sustainability of the Economy: concepts and indicators, *International Journal of Sustainable Development*, **8** (1/2), www.environmental-expert.com/Files/6471/articles/6328/f211108463951127.pdf.

St Arnaud, B., Smarr, L., Sheehan, J. and Defanti, T. (2009) *Climate Change and Higher Education*, **44** (6), www.educause.edu/EDUCAUSE+Review/EDUCAUSEReviewMagazineVolume44/ ClimateChangeandHigherEducatio/185218.

Stevens, C. (2005) *Measuring Sustainable Development*, Statistics in Brief, Organisation for Economic Co-operation and Development, www.oecd.org/std/35407580.pdf.

Thin, N., Lockhart, C. and Yaron, G. (2002) *Conceptualising Socially Sustainable Development*, Department for International Development and World Bank.

UN Habitat (n.d.) Best Practices and Local Leadership Programme, www.unhabitat.org/categories.asp?catid=34.

UNEP (n.d.) United Nations Environment Programme, www.unep.org/.

United Nations (1987) *Our Common Future: report of the World Commission on Environment and Development*, Brundtland Report, www.un-documents.net/wced-ocf.htm.

United Nations (1998) Kyoto Protocol to the United Nations Framework Convention on Climate Change, http://unfccc.int/resource/docs/convkp/kpeng.pdf.

United Nations (2011) Kyoto Protocol, UN Framework Convention on Climate Change, http://unfccc.int/kyoto_protocol/items/2830.php.

United Nations General Assembly (1992) *Report of the United Nations Conference on Environment and Development*, Rio de Janeiro, 3–14 June, www.un.org/documents/ga/conf151/aconf15126-1annex1.htm.

United Nations General Assembly (2012) *The Future We Want*, resolution adopted by the General Assembly, A/RES/66/288, 11 September, http://daccess-dds-ny.un.org/doc/UNDOC/GEN/N11/476/10/PDF/N1147610.pdf?OpenElement.

University of Idaho (2013) Principles of Sustainability: an exploration of sustainability, www.webpages.uidaho.edu/sustainability/chapters/ch01/index.asp.

Wiedmann, T. and Minx, J. (2008) A Definition of 'Carbon Footprint'. In Pertsova, C. C. (ed.), *Ecological Economics Research Trends* (1–11), Nova Science Publishers, Inc.

WorldBank Group (2000a) *Beyond Economic Growth: meeting the challenges of global development*, Chapter XVI, 'Indicators of development sustainability', www.worldbank.org/depweb/beyond/global/chapter16.html.

WorldBank Group (2000b) *Beyond Economic Growth: meeting the challenges of global development*, Chapter IX, 'Growth of the services sector', www.worldbank.org/depweb/beyond/beyondco/beg_09.pdf.

Wu, J. and Wu, T. (2012) Sustainability Indicators and Indices: an overview. In Mandu, C. N. and Kuei, C.-H. (eds), *Handbook of Sustainability Management*, World Scientific Pub Co, 65–86.

The economic sustainability of information

Introduction

The previous chapter explained that measuring the economic sustainability of a service sector is rather difficult, and often some indirect measures and different parameters need to be considered. Information systems and services are designed to support the activities of specific institutions such as the research and scholarly activities in universities, patient treatment and research activities in hospitals, and day-to-day business in government and business organizations. The economic sustainability of information systems and services depends on a number of indirect measures.

The importance of information in sustainable development has been recognized in many international and national policy documents and reports. According to Robert B. Zoellick, World Bank Group President, knowledge is power: 'Making our knowledge widely and readily available will empower others to come up with solutions to the world's toughest problems. Our new Open Access policy is the natural evolution for a World Bank that is opening up more and more' (World Bank, 2012).

In the UK, BIS observes that 'imperfect information makes it difficult for both investors and businesses to make optimal investment decisions. The high cost of obtaining information on the viability of small and medium-sized enterprises relative to the size of funding they are seeking leads to potentially viable businesses not being able to raise finance' (2010, 18) ... 'Information failures, both among learners and firms, may lead to suboptimal levels of investment in training' (2010, 21).

The economic success or value for money of information systems and services is difficult to measure. The impact of information systems and services may be noted indirectly through developments in different areas, such human resources, education and research, innovative and efficient systems for business processes, and long-term social developments such as healthy living and informed citizenship.

This chapter examines the economic sustainability issues of information systems and services, especially in the context of higher education. There are two aspects to the economic sustainability of information:

- sustainability of the information industry, which, as discussed below, makes a significant contribution to a country's economy and the higher education and research sector
- sustainability of information services, which is influenced by a variety of new policies introduced recently by various government and other agencies.

A number of new services have appeared in the digital information landscape in the recent past that have made a significant impact on the information industry and information services sector. Examples, especially in the context of scholarly information, include general search engine services and some specific services like Google Books, Google Scholar, Mendeley and Microsoft Academic Search. A number of e-book service providers like Amazon and Barnes & Noble, specific e-book readers like the Kindle and Sony e-book reader, and multipurpose e-book reading devices like the iPad and tablets have also been introduced, bringing in a number of changes in the information services sector. Similarly a large number of open access journals, digital libraries and repositories have had a significant impact on the information industry and information services sector. A number of new initiatives and regulations have been introduced that have significant implications for the entire information landscape in general, and the information industry and information services for the higher education and research sector in particular. This chapter discusses some of these issues, while details of specific initiatives and related developments, such as open access, are considered in Chapters 7 and 8.

The publishing industry

Traditionally library and information services in higher education and research institutions have dealt primarily with commercial content that is available through publishers, although part of their content includes special and institutional (home grown) collections. Conventionally the publishing industry relied on sales of information products – books, journals, and so on – directly to readers through book stores and various other intermediaries, and indirectly through library and information services. New business models have appeared over the past four decades with the introduction of online databases, e-journals, e-books, and so on. The economy of the information industry has changed drastically over the past two decades with the appearance of internet and web technologies.

Overall the publishing industry makes a significant contribution to the economy of many countries. The following figures provide an indication of the size and contributions of the publishing industry:

- It is estimated that the publishing industry in the UK alone employs 194,650 people and generates over £10 billion gross value added (Prospects, 2011).
- According to the Publishers Association in 2012 the total physical and digital book sales have grown by 4%, reaching £3.3 billion, showing a very healthy growth in the British publishing industry (Publishers Association, 2013).
- The book publishing industry in the USA employs 77,977 people and has a revenue of US$26 billion (IBISWorld, 2013a), and the magazine and periodical publishing industry has a revenue of US$36 billion and employs 135,148 people in the USA (IBIS World, 2013b).
- It is estimated that nearly 2 million scholarly journal papers are produced every year around the world, and higher education institutions in the UK spend around £150 million every year on the purchase of journals (Finch, 2012).

These figures demonstrate the size and importance of the publishing industry to the economy. Consequently, any major changes introduced in knowledge creation, distribution and access processes in order to achieve sustainability in the information industry and services sector should be such that the overall economy of a country is not affected. Many changes are now taking place in the publishing industry in order to respond to the emerging technologies that are rapidly changing the information marketplace and user expectations.

The generic business model for scholarly information

The traditional business model for scholarly information – from creation to management and use of information – is shown in Figure 3.1 on the next page. It is based on the scenario of scholarly communications, and library-based access to information. Simply speaking the main objective of a library and information service in a higher education institution is to enable users to discover and access relevant information with minimum effort. For a long time, the information industry and the information services sector have followed a model that was developed for the printed information world. Although the model has been modified to accommodate electronic databases of abstracts and full texts of journals and conferences, and more recently to include electronic books, the fundamental model has not changed too much.

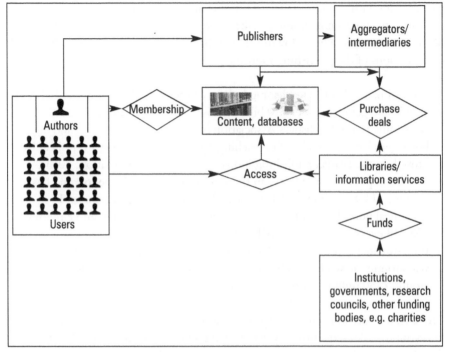

Figure 3.1 A generic business model for scholarly information

This traditional model shows that people access and use information through a library or an information service that is funded by their parent institution, government, research council or other funding body. Libraries and information services use the funds to purchase content – in analogue and/or digital format – directly from publishers or aggregators, and sometimes they purchase content through a co-operative or consortium. A small percentage of users may obtain access to content directly, for example through subscription or membership of professional bodies or learned societies.

In the context of scholarly communications, content creators – authors – publish the outcome of their scholarly activities – books, journal articles and conference papers – through the publishers. When books are published a formal contract is usually drawn up between the author and publisher, and the author may receive a royalty from book sales as a return for their intellectual contributions. The publisher in such cases not only prints, distributes and sells the books, but adds value through the review and editorial process and thus provides some form of quality assurance. For journal and conference papers, the authors usually do not receive any royalty, and the peer review process is conducted largely voluntarily by the academic and scholarly community.

To provide their users with access to books, journal articles and conference papers, library and information services have to purchase or license content directly through publishers or indirectly through aggregators or intermediaries. For analogue content, library and information services purchase information resources, and store and process them in a manner that facilitates easy discovery and access by users. For digital content, library and information services purchase a right to access, which allows users to discover and access the content, usually through a specific search system provided by the publisher, aggregator or intermediary. In this model, publishers and aggregators are usually commercial organizations, although there are some not-for-profit publishers, such as professional bodies and learned societies. The publishers and aggregators make profits by selling content either directly to users, usually for books, or indirectly through library subscriptions, for books, journals and databases.

This generic business model continued for a long time with some modifications introduced as electronic journals and databases became available over the past four decades. In this model the publishing industry remained a key player because without it the authors could not publish their research and scholarly output, and without it library and information services, and by extension users themselves some of whom are content creators, could not discover and access the information required for their scholarly activities. Over the past few decades, the cost of books and (especially) journals and databases increased very rapidly, and consequently library and information services began to be unable to afford to acquire and maintain their collections at the required level and quality. As a result, increasingly library and information users began to find it difficult to get the information they required – for research and scholarship, decision making, and other purposes such as living a healthy lifestyle, or better and informed citizenship. This situation, coupled with the new opportunities introduced by internet and web technologies, gave rise to the open access movement.

Open access

The previous section observed that libraries in higher education institutions have struggled to keep up with the ever-increasing price of scholarly publications, especially journals, over the past few decades making it increasingly difficult for users to access the scholarly information they need when libraries could no longer afford to stock these publications. Meanwhile, publishers have continued to maintain, if not increase, their profit margins. Even in the recent global financial crisis the major science, technology, engineering and medicine (STEM) publishers continued to keep their profit margins at over 35%. A report in *The Economist* on 26 May 2011 noted that in Great Britain 65% of the money spent on content in academic libraries went on journals, and that Elsevier, the biggest publisher of journals, made a profit of £724 million on revenues of £2 billion, an operating profit margin of 36% (The Economist, 2011).

Researchers, academics and information professionals have for some time been looking for alternative ways to make research and scholarly information freely available to more people, if not everyone. This gave rise to the open access movement, which emerged in the early 1990s with the establishment of the open archive known as arXiv.org (formerly xxx.lanl.gov) intended to provide free access to literature on high-energy physics. It subsequently extended its scope to cover other related disciplines such as physics, mathematics, computer science, nonlinear sciences, quantitative biology and statistics. The Santa Fe Convention in 1999, in which the Open Archives Initiative was launched, and subsequently the Budapest Open Access Initiative (BOAI) in 2002, brought a new era in scholarly communications promising free access to scholarly information, especially journal papers. The BOAI declaration recognized that open access to journal literature is the goal, and self-archiving and introducing a new generation of open access journals are the ways to attain this goal (Budapest Open Access Initiative, 2002). The following statement shows the wide scope of the open access initiative:

> By 'open access' to [peer-reviewed research literature], we mean its free availability on the public internet, permitting any users to read, download, copy, distribute, print, search, or link to the full texts of these articles, crawl them for indexing, pass them as data to software, or use them for any other lawful purpose, without financial, legal, or technical barriers other than those inseparable from gaining access to the internet itself.
>
> Budapest Open Access Initiative (2012)

A large number of open access journals have emerged over the past few years providing free access to articles published in those journals. For commercial journals, there are two models of open access:

- the green open access model, where the author self-archives published articles, usually after a certain period of embargo imposed by the journal publisher, to a repository that can be accessed by anyone for free
- the gold open access model or 'author-pays model', where the publication cost of a journal article is recovered from the authors and in return it is made available for free to everyone.

The Open Access Open Data Conference (www.oaod2010.de/index.php?id =home) held in Cologne, Germany, in December 2010 discussed several issues and changes to open access and noted that open access has been changing the scholarly communication system (Giglia, 2011). Many researchers have compared the benefits of the green and gold open access models and reviewed the progress of open access publishing over the past few years (for example, Bird, 2010; Bjork, 2012; Lewis, 2012; Oppenheim, 2008). In general all these studies observe there has been an increase in interest in open access but the uptake has been slow for a variety of reasons: the most common for the gold route is the lack of a general policy and institutional framework to support article-processing charges; the most common for the green route is confusion among academics and scholars about self-archiving publications, and lack of interest in doing so. These two routes to open access and their implications for the sustainability of the information industry and information services are discussed in more detail in Chapter 7.

A modified business model for scholarly information services

The internet made it possible for authors to create content through open access journals, and of late some authors have begun to self-publish on the internet, using various tools and technologies, without having to go formally through a publisher. Internet technologies boosted the open access movement as users and library and information services can build alternative routes for access to scholarly information. Thus the traditional business model for information, as shown in Figure 3.1, changed and a new business model appeared. Figure 3.2 on the next page shows the new business model for information, which appeared over the past few years with the advent of the internet.

Figure 3.2 illustrates two major developments that took place over the past few years:

- Many open access publishing options arose, which gave content creators an alternative route to publishing scholarly information. Such content could be accessed by users without them having to use a library or information service.
- A number of open access repositories and digital libraries began to appear where users can freely search and access content. Such repositories, especially institutional repositories, are funded by institutions, governments, research councils and often charities. Details of the funding models for open access and institutional repositories are given in Chapter 7.

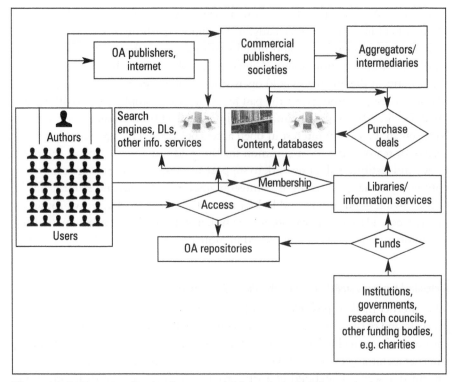

Figure 3.2 An emerging business model for scholarly information

Search engines and internet services have greatly facilitated the discovery of information. Scholarly information that earlier could be found only by searching through library or proprietary commercial databases can now be easily searched using freely available web-based search tools. In some cases such content can also be accessed for free where an open access copy is available on the web, or through a local library. In some cases, such content can be purchased directly from the publisher or online stores. Thus increasingly scholarly information is being made available through open access, and search engines are being used as an alternative tool to discover scholarly information; often they add a lot of value to the retrieved information (discussed later in this chapter).

Internet and web technologies have brought many other changes to the prevailing business models of the information industry and information services sector. A variety of business and subscription models have appeared for different types of digital content. Similarly a variety of new services appeared, e.g. search engine services like Google Books, Google Scholar and Microsoft Academic

Search; digital libraries like Europeana, PubMed and National Science Digital Library (NSDL); and specific information services like the Internet Public Library. All these services are free at the point of use, with alternative business models to sustain them, and together have begun to challenge the classical business model that has been followed by the information industry and information services sector for a long time. These are discussed briefly in later sections of this chapter, or in detail later in the book, for example, in the context of a sustainability of information model in Chapter 11, and research issues and challenges in Chapter 12.

Access to digital information

Nowadays a variety of alternative models is available to individual users for purchase of e-books through online e-book stores and e-book service providers. Similarly, a variety of business models and service providers is available for libraries for subscription to e-books and electronic databases of journal and conference papers. While library users have had access to journal and conference papers in electronic databases for some time, use of e-books in libraries is just beginning. Many studies show that students and researchers prefer e-books; the main reason why they prefer online material over print is ease of access (Bunkell and Dyas-Correia, 2009; Higher Education Consultancy Group (n.d.); Nicholas, Rowlands and Jamali, 2010). Various models of acquiring e-books, e-journals and databases are discussed in the following sections.

Business models for e-books

Details of prevailing e-book business models appear in a number of research reports and scholarly papers (Ashcroft, 2011; Bunkell and Dyas-Correia, 2009; CILIP, 2012; Content Complete Ltd and OnlyConnect Consultancy, 2009; Grigson, 2011; Jisc, 2009; Pool, 2010; Vasileiou, Hartley and Rowley, 2012). Some publishers, including Elsevier, Springer Science+Business Media, Wiley and Cambridge University Press, supply e-books directly to libraries (CILIP, 2012). In some cases e-books can be bought and downloaded to users' computing devices via specific services like eBooks.com or CourseSmart. A number of aggregator services provide access to e-books from different publishers; typical examples include EBSCOhost, the top vendor employed by US academic libraries for e-books, followed by Gale Virtual Reference Library and Ebrary (Library Journal, 2012). Examples of other e-book aggregator services include 123Library, Dawsonera, EBL (E-Book Library) and MyiLibrary. Some publishers offer lecturers the opportunity to create custom textbooks and students can purchase the customized titles. In some cases publishers provide supplementary e-resources that support adopted textbooks, and institutions can upload them into their virtual learning environment and access them online. Some libraries form consortia to acquire e-books and other print and electronic products. Examples of such consortia for academic and research libraries in the UK include the English Academic Library Consortia and the Scottish Digital Library Consortium, and for public libraries, LibrariesWest and the London Libraries Consortium (CILIP, 2012).

Amazon is now selling more Kindle books than paperback books. In 2011, for every 100 paperback books Amazon sold, the company sold 115 Kindle books (Estelle, 2011). A more recent study shows about 82% of power buyers (those who acquire e-books weekly) prefer e-books over print and nearly 70% of non-power buyers now prefer e-books over print (Bowker, 2013). Recent studies also show that e-book consumers are decidedly shifting to multi-function tablets and away from dedicated e-readers. A 2012 survey by the Book Industry Study Group shows that tablets have risen by about 25% over the past year as the first choice for respondents' e-reading devices, while dedicated e-readers have fallen by the same amount (Bowker, 2012). A more recent survey shows that multi-function tablets have become consumers' preferred e-reading devices, overtaking dedicated e-readers for the first time (Bowker, 2013). Often e-books are cheaper than their printed counterparts, for example, in 2011 *Abnormal and Clinical Psychology: an introductory textbook* was available in e-book format for £17.37 as opposed to £35 in print format (Estelle, 2011).

Libraries can buy individual titles of e-books, or can buy them as a package comprising many titles. A variety of business models are used by publishers and aggregators of e-books including outright purchase, annual subscription, rental, selected chapters and pay-per-view, the last two being driven by user demands (Grigson, 2011). However, the e-book marketplace and corresponding business models are still emerging, and library and information services are working hard to get the best deals to justify the value for money. Harris (2013) comments that libraries often have to buy collections of e-books, just like the bundles of journals in the 'big deal', where many e-books are seldom, or never, used. A project by the Joint Information Systems Committee (Jisc) aims to develop a digital infrastructure and guidance for institutions on meeting the challenges of e-books: 'Self-publication is making it much easier for academics to bypass traditional publishing business models. Consequently, we may see that the current business models of publishers may change to reflect actual usage by institutions and learners. These changing models will replace those based on historical printed-book models' (Jisc, 2012).

A survey on e-books in US academic libraries conducted by the Library Journal in 2012 noted that the average amount spent on e-books by respondents (in selected US universities) during the 2011–12 academic year was US$67,400, and an average of 9.6% of academic libraries' total acquisition budgets was spent on e-books. The researchers predicted that e-books would represent 19.5% or even more of acquisition budgets by 2017. The report noted that 'perpetual access' was the most popular (83%) form of access in libraries followed by the 'subscription model' (71%), although 'user-driven acquisition' is a growing option for many libraries, up from 16% in 2010 to 31% in 2012 (Library Journal, 2012).

A CILIP study in 2012 found that by 2013 e-textbooks were expected to encompass 18.3% of the global textbook business, a significant rise from 3.4% in 2011. This study provides the following figures, showing the e-book market for university libraries in the UK (based on 2010–11 figures):

- 17,612,276 e-books were purchased.
- 1089 e-book databases were purchased.
- Expenditure on e-books was £12,751,342.
- The mean average of e-books/100 full-time equivalent students is 1168.

CILIP (2012)

The growing cost of academic books and uncertainty among publishers in the changing marketplace is a cause for concern for the economic sustainability of information services. A recent CILIP study notes that:

> The academic monograph is under threat due to increased costs and lower print runs. This is impacting on the principle means by which researchers share their knowledge and disseminate their findings. To address this, academics and academic libraries are pursuing alternate approaches to collection development, such as 'open access'.
>
> CILIP (2012, 2)

In addition to the purchase or subscription costs of e-books, there is a concern for preservation and long-term access. E-books from different suppliers use different software and tools for access that may change over time. Therefore, long-term access to e-books is also a concern, and libraries should address this in their licence terms in order to achieve long-term sustainability of their services.

While the introduction of e-books has brought a major change in the way we access and use books in today's world, the Google Books service has brought another revolution in the information world. In fact, Google Books has introduced a step change in the process of searching and accessing books online. The project has been backed and supported from the beginning by many leading libraries, but legal controversies persisted over the issue of out-of-print but in-copyright books and orphan works (Paula, 2009; Reuters, 2009; Venkatraman, 2009). The Google Books initiative is described as an effort to privatize knowledge or called the Google monopoly (Joint, 2009; Pike, 2009; Wood, 2009).

The most significant contribution of Google Books is the provision of full-text search facilities for millions of books, which was hitherto not available, nor planned by any person or organization on such a grand scale. Within a very short span of time Google Books has become a very useful tool for full-text search of books. Chen (2012) observed that Google Books can retrieve almost all the books catalogued in WorldCat. Google Books can link to a local library catalogue 75% of the time, and some retrieved books in Google Books have free full views. Services like Google Books and Google Scholar often provide better citation counts than scholarly databases. A study by Kousha, Thelwall and Rezaie (2011) comparing the citation counts to 1000 books submitted to the UK research assessment exercise in 2008 from Google Books and Google Scholar with Scopus database citations across seven disciplines – archaeology; law; politics and international studies; philosophy; sociology; history; and communication, cultural and media studies – notes that Google Books and Google Scholar citations to books were 1.4 and 3.2 times more common than were Scopus citations, and their medians were more than twice and three times as high as were Scopus median citations, respectively.

While the e-book industry is increasing fast, the market is still evolving and therefore the economic sustainability of information services based on e-books is still not certain. Free full-text search facilities, and sometimes free access to the full text of e-books, through services like Google Books has a significant positive implication for the social sustainability of information through the provision of easier and equitable access to information (discussed in Chapter 5).

Access to journals and databases

Access to journals in a variety of formats – hard copies, soft copies or born e-journals, and databases of abstracts or full-text articles of journals – has remained a major area of concern for libraries. Research shows that large commercial publishers strongly advocate the status quo – the reader-pays business model (McCabe and Snyder, 2013). In this model publishers have always remained in an advantageous position because libraries have no choice but to pay high prices as journals are monopolists over the articles they carry, and if a scholar served by a given library needs an article in a journal for their research, there is no convenient substitute for it. It is estimated that the science-publishing industry generated

US$9.4 billion in revenue in 2011 and published around 1.8 million English-language articles – an average revenue per article of roughly US$5000 (Van Noorden, 2013). This has been the case until very recently, before the beginning of the open access movement, which began in 1992. However, researchers are now beginning to realize that scholarly publications can be produced at a much lower cost and they can create a win–win situation for scholarly content creators and users (van Noorden, 2013).

Journal publishers, especially the big ones, have preferred to lock library and information service customers into a long-term deal when they subscribe to journals and databases. The journal industry is led by some major publishers like Elsevier, Wiley-Blackwell and Springer. Elsevier publishes around 2000 journals, including *The Lancet* and *Cell*. Wiley-Blackwell publishes around 1500 journals (Jump, 2011). As a result, major publishers continue to make a huge profit through library subscriptions, while library and information services struggle to maintain their preferred journal collections. Consequently, Research Libraries UK (RLUK) told Elsevier and Wiley-Blackwell that they would not renew their existing deals when they expire unless the concession is made; the deal was subsequently signed, and RLUK claimed that the group saved more than £20 million per year following a revised deal (Jump, 2011).

The so called 'big deal' – whereby publishers force library and information services to bulk purchase journals – made the job of library and information services managers very difficult, especially with regard to the complexities of the various deals and licensing agreements with the publishers. Therefore library and information services have formed different kinds of consortia in order to get the best out of a licensing deal from the publishers. In the UK Jisc has developed what is known as Jisc model licences, which are 'a collection of licences specially drafted by Jisc and Jisc Collections to include all of the terms and conditions that an educational institution and its users need in order to make sure that they can get the most out of the online resources they subscribe to' (Jisc Collections, n.d.).

Business models for open access journals

A large number of open access journals have appeared over the past two decades, following a number of business models, sometimes in combination:

- *Community publishing*: This model is common for journals in small, niche areas of research, and especially (but not exclusively) in the arts and humanities. Journals can be accessed for free, and the costs are kept low through voluntary peer review and editing and production. Often such journals use dedicated journal production systems like Open Journal Systems, a journal management and publishing system developed by the Public Knowledge Project through its federally funded efforts to expand and improve access to research.

- *Advertising revenues*: Some journals, like *British Medical Journal*, recover some of their costs by generating advertising revenues.
- *Institutional subsidy*: Some journals are supported by institutions. They receive support through a university press or a publishing operation by the library. Although the sustainability of this model may seem unclear, it is likely to grow and funding bodies may channel some of their resources to support such open access publishing and open scholarship (discussed more in Chapter 7).
- *Institutional membership schemes*: Some open access journals generate revenues through institutional membership. For example, BioMed Central has introduced a scheme with various tiers of payment for institutions where institutions pay an annual fee in advance for articles that their authors would publish in BioMed Central, and Hindwai Publishing Corporation has introduced a flat-rate annual payment for institutions.
- *Collaborative purchasing models*: the Sponsoring Consortium for Open Access Publishing in Particle Physics is a group of institutions, research laboratories and scholarly societies, which together with national research funders pays fees to the publishers of journals in high-energy physics in return for making the entire contents of those journals open access. These and other methods of article-processing charges are discussed in Chapter 7 in the context of the gold open access model.

OASIS (2012)

The economics of digital information

The current state of the digital textbook market can be summarized as follows:

- There is an increasing demand for digital books among students and academics.
- Increasingly publishers are making their published content available online.
- The current e-book marketplace is too complex, with many different players, complex licences and terms of access.
- Librarians often find the prevailing business models to be expensive and complicated.
- A number of new players and services have appeared in the information marketplace that provide alternative routes for accessing digital information.
- The open access policies of various funding bodies and governments will

bring in a major change in the information industry and the information services sector (for details see Chapter 7).

All of these factors make those in the information industry and information services sector uncertain about the future of scholarly communications in general, and information systems and services in particular.

Several studies have taken place exploring alternative business models for digital information services, especially in the context of various open access models. The most notable among these are the various Jisc-funded research projects in the UK that studied open access business models for books and journals (for example, Content Complete Ltd and OnlyConnect Consultancy, 2009; Estelle, 2011; Houghton et al., 2009; Swan, 2010). These studies provide enough justification to support the fact that in order to achieve economic sustainability, it would be necessary to go for e-only publications and preferably in open access mode. They also prove that in addition to direct cost savings from production and distribution, e-only publications would also help libraries save a significant amount of money from reduced storage and handling costs, and other expenses.

The results of these studies can be used to argue that economic sustainability of information services in the higher education sector, indeed in any sector, can be achieved by moving all kinds of content into digital format and adopting the open access model. However, this is just one part of the problem and such a move may have consequences for the social and environmental sustainability of information services. Before making an irreversible move in this direction, it is necessary to study how such a move might affect:

- the publishing industry and knowledge sector as a whole, e.g. library and information services
- users and the overall knowledge or information culture in specific sectors, e.g. the higher education sector
- GHG emissions (see Chapter 4).

The economic sustainability of digital libraries

Several major digital libraries have been established around the world over the past two decades. Some are based on commercial models of publishers or learned societies, for example the ACM Digital Library. They require payment or subscriptions. However, many others are free at the point of use, funded in different ways, for example by:

- *government agencies*, e.g. the US National Science Foundation providing support for the NSDL, or the National Library of Medicine as part of the US NIH providing PubMed
- *specific countries, institutions or consortia*, e.g. various EU countries providing support for Europeana
- *funding bodies*, e.g. the US NIH providing support for the PubMed Central services
- *charities*, e.g. the Wellcome Library supported by the Wellcome Trust.

Sustainable funding is still a major problem for many large digital libraries. Europeana produced a factsheet showing that in 2011 funding from the EU for the entire Europeana service platform totalled some €30–35 million, out of which Europeana required €5 million (2011 level) to run the services, a figure expected gradually to rise to €7 million by 2020 (Europeana, 2012). However, another report on the funding of Europeana noted that Europeana had a funding gap for 2011, 2012 and 2013 of €1.2 million (Europeana Foundation, 2011).

Very few digital library evaluation studies have focused primarily on the economic sustainability of digital libraries (Chowdhury, McMenemy and Poulter, 2008), but the Europeana case for funding document (Europeana, 2013) draws on some data that indirectly justify the economic sustainability of the Europeana service, pointing out that 'over the past five years, initial EU investment of 150 million euros has resulted in 70 million euros of co-funding from Ministries in 21 countries'. These investments have facilitated massive digitization in different EU member countries and as a result 27 million digital objects are available through Europeana, and as of 2013 '770 businesses, entrepreneurs, educational and cultural organizations are exploring ways of including Europeana information in their offerings (websites, apps, games and so on) through our API'. The document notes that Europeana has helped create new jobs: 'In Hungary, for example, over 1,000 graduates are now involved in digitizing heritage that will feed in to Europeana. Historypin in the UK predicts it will double in size with the availability of more open digital cultural heritage.'

The economic sustainability of digital preservation

Economic sustainability has also remained a major challenge within digital preservation research. Dobreva and Ruusalepp (2012) comment that over the past decade digital preservation research has mainly focused on design, architecture and software solutions for management of digital collections and creation of various preservation tools. Several attempts have been made to create a research agenda for digital preservation over the past five years:

- In 2007, the DigitalPreservationEurope project identified ten fields of research in digital preservation (DigitalPreservationEurope, 2006).
- A research seminar organized within the Dagstuhl series in 2010 identified seven major topics of research (Chanod et al., 2010).
- In May 2011 an expert seminar organized by the European Commission (Billenness, 2011) identified ten topics for future research.

None of these projects identified the economic and social sustainability of digital preservation as a major area of research. The EU DPimpact study demonstrated that 'investing efforts and resources in securing future access to digital content makes a lot of sense in economic terms, as impacts – direct and indirect – will be clearly positive and growing as the DP [digital preservation] market starts to "Cross the Chasm" [contemporary or topical] by penetrating and developing the mainstream markets of the Information Society' (DPimpact, 2009, 103–4). However, the study also noted that memory institutions had 'very limited' funding for preservation, compared with 'limited' funding in scientific and research institutions; and funding for preservation in businesses, companies and enterprises is awarded by project and charged to overheads (DPimpact, 2009, Table 2A, 34).

According to the Blue Ribbon Task Force on Sustainable Digital Preservation and Access (2008), economically sustainable digital preservation requires:

- recognition of the benefits of preservation on the part of key decision-makers
- incentives for decision-makers to act in the public interest
- a process to select digital materials for long-term retention
- mechanisms to secure an ongoing, efficient allocation of resources to digital preservation activities
- appropriate organization and governance of digital preservation activities.

The Blue Ribbon Task Force final report recommends that 'sustainable digital preservation requires a compelling value proposition, incentives to act, and well defined roles and responsibilities. Digital preservation is a challenge for all of society because we all benefit from reliable, authentic information now and into the future' (Blue Ribbon Task Force on Sustainable Digital Preservation and Access, 2010, 5). It concludes that sustainable preservation is a societal concern and transcends the boundaries of any content domain, and therefore all parts of society – national and international agencies, funders and sponsors of data creation, stakeholder organizations and individuals – have roles in achieving sustainability. Recognizing the lack of a continuous source of funding for digital preservation, a recently completed EUFP7 research project called SHAMAN proposed an enterprise architecture-based approach, which enables the accommodation of digital preservation concerns in the overall architecture of an organization with the justification that although the preservation of contents is not a main business requirement, it is required to enable delivery of value in the primary business (SHAMAN Reference Architecture, 2012). Although this may resolve some problems of preservation of digital records within an institution, this does not specially resolve the issues that digital libraries and information services, for example institutional repositories, face for preservation of digital data and content to ensure future access.

Increasingly library and information services are moving towards a shared or consortia-based approach for digital preservation. The HathiTrust Digital Library brings together huge collections of partner institutions in digital form, preserving them securely for current and future access. In a recent move, seven European countries have launched the 4C Project (Collaboration to Clarify the Costs of Curation) to help public and private European organizations invest more effectively in digital curation and preservation, sustaining the long-term value of all types of digital information (Jisc, 2013). The 4C partners involved are Danish National Archives (Denmark), Data Archiving and Network Service (DANS) (Netherlands), Deutsche Nationalbibliothek (Germany), Digital Curation Centre (UK), Digital Preservation Coalition (UK), Humanities Advanced Technology and Information Institute (UK), Institute for Information Systems and Computing Research (Portugal), Jisc (UK), Keep Solutions (Portugal), National Library of (Estonia), Royal Library of Denmark (Denmark), Secure Business (Austria) and UK Data Archive (UK). It is widely recognized that the costs of curation are currently hard to predict and that the short term benefits are hard to define because curation implicitly addresses long-term challenges. It is reported that 4C will address both concerns and provide practical guidance that will help practitioners persuade executives to invest in new services (Jisc, 2013).

Value-added information

As discussed earlier in this chapter, and shown in Figure 3.2, a number of changes in the business model of the information industry and information services have been introduced since the arrival of the internet. In many cases people can now discover scholarly information through search engines, which was not possible before when users could search for information only through a database or information service subscribed to by a library. As stated earlier in this chapter Google Books now enables people to search for the full text of books which was not possible earlier.

Over the years online databases added a number of very useful features to their search interfaces in order to enable users not only to discover and access information, but also to manipulate their search results in a number of useful ways. These value-added services from online databases may be considered as specific features of their business models, whereby they not only provide content, but also provide user-centred services. Similar services are also available from some search engine services like Google Scholar and Microsoft Academic Search. This is an important development with implications for the business model and therefore the sustainability of digital information services. For example, search engine services not only allow people to discover scholarly information, but also add a lot of value that has traditionally been part of online database services, for which they charge library and information services.

There may also be other kinds of value-added service. For example, the Europeana repository has 20 million metadata records with a CC0 licence (a Creative Commons licence with no rights reserved), which will enable creative users to make appropriate use and re-use of digital content and thereby facilitate the creative culture and economy (Europeana, 2013). As more and more scholarly information becomes available through open access repositories, more free value-added services will be provided by information services facilitating easy discovery, access and use of scholarly information. This is discussed in more detail later in this book.

Summary

Economic sustainability of information systems and services depends significantly on a number of factors ranging from the business models of the information industry to various emerging systems and services such as search engine services, digital libraries, open access repositories and information services, various new initiatives such as the open access initiatives and regulations introduced by government agencies and funding bodies. Several parallel funding models are now being introduced and tested, including traditional user-pays or institution-pays models, author-pays models, institutional repository models introduced by open access initiatives, and alternative revenue models such as the advertisement revenues that run search engines and similar services, co-operative models and consortia-pay models.

The variety of business models and practices, new free search engines and digital library services bring a number of benefits to users, but also uncertainty in relation to the economic sustainability of scholarly communications in general, and information systems and services in particular. Some of the emerging business models and practices and their consequences with regard to various sustainability issues are discussed later in this book, for example in the context of open access models in Chapter 7, and cloud computing and green information services models in Chapter 9.

References

Ashcroft, L. (2011) Ebooks in Libraries: an overview of the current situation, *Library Management*, **32** (6/7), 398–407.

Billenness, C. (2011) *The Future of the Past – Shaping New Visions for EU-research in Digital Preservation, Report on the Proceedings of the Workshop Organised by the Unit Cultural Heritage and Technology Enhanced Learning, European Commission, Information Society and Media Directorate-General, Luxembourg, 4–5 May*,
http://cordis.europa.eu/fp7/ict/telearn-digicult/future-of-the-past_en.pdf.

Bird, C. (2010) *Continued Adventures in Open Access: 2009 perspective*, Learned Publishing, **23** (2), 107–16.

BIS (2010) *A Strategy for Sustainable Growth*, Economic Annex, Department for Business, Innovation & Skills (UK), July,
https://www.gov.uk/government/uploads/system/uploads/attachment_data/file/31998/10-1059-sustainable-growth-economic-annex.pdf.

Bjork, B.C. (2012) The Hybrid Model for Open Access Publication of Scholarly Articles: a failed experiment? *Journal of the American Society for Information Science and Technology*, **63** (8), 1496–504.

Blue Ribbon Task Force on Sustainable Digital Preservation and Access (2008) *Economic Sustainability in a Digital Preservation Context*,
http://brtf.sdsc.edu/econ_sustainability.html.

Blue Ribbon Task Force on Sustainable Digital Preservation and Access (2010) *Sustainable Economics for a Digital Planet: ensuring long-term access to digital information*,
www.jisc.ac.uk/media/documents/publications/reports/2010/brtffinalreport.pdf.

Bowker (2012) Tablets Gain Dedicated E-readers, Says New BISG Study,
www.bowker.com/en-US/aboutus/press_room/2012/pr_11142012.shtml.

Bowker (2013) As E-books Market Evolves, Correlation Between Genre Preference and Device Selection Is Revealed, Says New BISG Study, 5 April, www.bowker.com/en-US/aboutus/press_room/2013/pr_04052013.shtml.

Budapest Open Access Initiative (2002) *Read the Budapest Open Access Initiative*,
www.budapestopenaccessinitiative.org/read.

Budapest Open Access Initiative (2012) *Ten Years on from the Budapest Open Access Initiative: setting the default to open*, www.budapestopenaccessinitiative.org/boai-10-recommendations.

Bunkell, J. and Dyas-Correia, S. (2009) E-Books vs. Print: which is the better value?, *Serials Librarian*, **56** (1–4), 215–19.

Chanod, J. P., Dobreva, M., Rauber, A., Ross, S. and Casarosa, V. (2010) *10291 Dagstuhl Seminar Report – Automation in Digital Preservation*, Automation in Digital Preservation, Dagstuhl Seminar Proceedings 10291, Dagstuhl, Germany, 2010. Schloss Dagstuhl – Leibniz-Zentrum für Informatik, Germany, http://drops.dagstuhl.de/opus/volltexte/2010/2899/pdf/10291.Report.2899.pdf.

Chen, X. T. (2012) Google Books and WorldCat: a comparison of their content, *Online Information Review*, **36** (4), 507–16.

Chowdhury, G., McMenemy, D. and Poulter, A. (2008) MEDLIS: Model for Evaluation of Digital Libraries and Information Services, *World Digital Libraries,* **1** (1), 35–46.

CILIP (2012) Ebook Acquisition and Lending Briefing: public, academic and research libraries, www.cilip.org.uk/get-involved/policy/statements%20and%20briefings/Documents/E-book%20acquisition%20and%20lending%20by%20libraries%20-%20longer%20briefingv2.pdf.

Content Complete Ltd and OnlyConnect Consultancy (2009) *Study on the Management and Economic Impact of e-Textbook Business Models on Publishers, E-book Aggregators and Higher Education Institutions: Phase One Report.*

DigitalPreservationEurope (DPE) (2007) *Access to and Preservation of Cultural and Scientific Resources: research roadmap*, www.digitalpreservationeurope.eu/publications/reports/dpe_research_roadmap_D72.pdf.

Dobreva, M. and Ruusalepp, R. (2012) Digital Preservation: interoperability *ad modum*. In: Chowdhury, G. G. and Foo, S. (2012) *Digital Libraries and Information Access: research perspectives*, Facet Publishing, 193–215.

DPimpact (2009) *Socio-economic Drivers and Impact of Longer Term Digital Preservation*. Final Report, http://cordis.europa.eu/fp7/ict/telearn-digicult/dpimpact-final-report.pdf.

The Economist (2011) *Academic Publishing: of goats and headaches: one of the best media businesses is also one of the most resented*, 26 May, www.economist.com/node/18744177.

Estelle, L. (2011) E-books Models and Joint Purchasing, RLUK Members' Meeting, 24–25 November, www.rluk.ac.uk/.../Estelle_ebook%20models%20RLUK%20members%2025.11.11.ppt.

Europeana (2012) Support for Europeana and its Ecosystem in the Connecting Europe Facility (CEF), factsheet, June, http://pro.europeana.eu/documents/900548/c878ddbd-204e-4f70-b375-d80416f13f5b.

Europeana (2013) Europeana – the case for funding, http://ciber-research.eu/Europeana/Europeana-The_Case_for_Funding.pdf.

Europeana Foundation (2011) Europeana Funding Gap, 2012 and 2013,
    http://pro.europeana.eu/documents/844813/851970/Funding+Gap+Paper.pdf.
Finch, J. (ed.) (2012) *Accessibility, Sustainability, Excellence: how to expand access to research
    publications*, report of the Working Group on Expanding Access to Published Research
    www.researchinfonet.org/wp-content/uploads/2012/06/Finch-Group-report-FINAL-
    VERSION.pdf.
Giglia, E. (2011) Open Access, Open Data: paradigm shifts in the changing scholarly
    communication scenario. Conference report, *D-Lib Magazine*, **17** (3/4),
    www.dlib.org/dlib/march11/giglia/03giglia.html.
Grigson, A. (2011) An Introduction to E-book Business Models and Suppliers. In Price,
    K. and Haavergal, V. (eds), *E-books in Libraries: a practical guide*, Chapter 2, Facet
    Publishing, http://digirep.rhul.ac.uk/file/bf558385-a28c-b465-582e-0e9da35be076/
    1/1-2-AG-Providers.pdf.
Harris, S. (2013) Libraries Learn to Love E-books, *Research Information*, **65**, April/May,
    12–14.
Higher Education Consultancy Group (n.d.) *A Feasibility Study on the Acquisition of E-books
    by HE Libraries and the Role of JISC*, www.jisc.ac.uk/.../jisc.../e-
    books%20final%20report%205%20oct.doc.
Houghton, J., Rasmussen, B., Sheehan, P., Oppenheim, C., Morris, A., Creaser, C.,
    Greenwood, H., Summers, M. and Gourlay, A. (2009) *Economic Implications of
    Alternative Scholarly Publishing Models: exploring the costs and benefits*, Jisc,
    www.jisc.ac.uk/publications/reports/2009/economicpublishingmodelsfinalreport.aspx
    #downloads.
IBISWorld (2013a) *Book Publishing in the US: market research report*, February,
    www.ibisworld.com/industry/default.aspx?indid=1233.
IBISWorld (2013b) *Magazine & Periodical Publishing in the US: market research report*,
    February, www.ibisworld.com/industry/default.aspx?indid=1232.
Jisc (2009) *National E-books Observatory Project: key findings and recommendations*, Joint
    Information Systems Committee, www.jisce-booksproject.org/.
Jisc (2012) *The Challenge of Ebooks: a JISC project*, wiki, Joint Information Systems
    Committee, http://ebookchallenge.org.uk/.
Jisc (2013) *13 Partners from across Europe Join Together to Improve Digital Curation*, Joint
    Information Systems Committee, www.jisc.ac.uk/news/stories/2013/03/4C.aspx.
Jisc Collections (n.d.) JISC Model Licence, www.jisc-collections.ac.uk/Help-and-
    information/How-Model-Licences-work/Guide-to-Model-Licence/.
Joint, N. (2009) The Google Book Settlement and Academic Libraries, *Library Review*,
    58 (5), 333–40.
Jump, P. (2011) Libraries Reject 'Raw Deal' on E-journals, *Times Higher Education*, 18
    August, www.timeshighereducation.co.uk/417157.article.

Kousha, K., Thelwall, M. and Rezaie, S. (2011) Assessing the Citation Impact of Books: the role of Google Books, Google Scholar, and Scopus, *Journal of the American Society for Information Science and Technology*, **62** (11), 2147–64.

Lewis, D. W. (2012) The Inevitability of Open Access, *College & Research Libraries*, **73** (5), 493–5.

Library Journal (2012) E-book Usage in US Academic Libraries, third annual survey sponsored by ebooks on EBSCOhost, http://c0003264.cdn2.cloudfiles. rackspacecloud.com/Ebook-Usage-Report-Academic.pdf.

McCabe, M. J. and Snyder, C. M. (2013) The Best Business Model for Scholarly Journals: an economist's perspective, *Nature*, www.nature.com/nature/focus/accessdebate/28.html.

Nicholas, D., Rowlands, I. and Jamali, H. (2010) E-textbook Use, Information Seeking Behaviour and its Impact: case study business and management, *Journal of Information Science*, **36** (2), 263–80.

OASIS (2012) Open Access Journals: business models, Open Access Scholarly Information Sourcebook, www.openoasis.org/index.php?option=com_ content&view=article&id=347&Itemid=377.

Oppenheim, C. (2008) Electronic Scholarly Publishing and Open Access, *Journal of Information Science*, **34** (4), 577–90.

Paula, H. J. (2009) Settlement Opposition, New Options, and Search Developments Top the News, *Information Today*, **26** (6), 7, 11–13.

Pike, G. H. (2009) Google Books Settlement Still a Bit Unsettled, *Information Today*, **26** (6), 17 and 21.

Pool, R. (2010) Open to Debate, *Research Information*, **47**, 12–14.

Prospects (2011) Publishing Overview, www.prospects.ac.uk/industries_publishing_overview.htm.

Publishers Association (2013) Publishing Industry Continues to Grow with Sales of Consumer Ebooks Rising by 134%, www.publishers.org.uk/index.php?option=com_content&view=article&id=2480: publishing-industry-continues-to-grow-with-sales-of-consumer-ebooks-rising-by-134-&catid=503:pa-press-releases-and-comments&Itemid=1618.

Reuters (2009) Google Book Deal Violates Copyright Law, 1 September, www.reuters.com/article/idUSN0149201520090901.

SHAMAN (2012) *SHAMAN Reference Architecture*, http://shaman-ip.eu/sites/default/files/SHAMAN-REFERENCE%20ARCHITECTURE-Final%20Version_0.pdf.

Swan, A. (2010) *Modelling Scholarly Communication Options: costs and benefits for universities*, report to the JISC, February, http://repository.jisc.ac.uk/442/2/Modelling_scholarly_communication_report_final1.pdf.

Van Noorden, R. (2013) Open Access: the cost of science publishing, *Nature*, **495** (7442), www.nature.com/news/open-access-the-true-cost-of-science-publishing-1.12676.

Vasileiou, M., Hartley, R. and Rowley, K. (2012) Choosing E-books: a perspective from academic libraries, *Online Information Review*, **36** (1), 21–39.

Venkatraman, A. (2009) Clicks Versus Copyright, *Information World Review*, **259**, October, 12–14.

Wood, D. (2009) Revised Google Book Search Deal 'a Massive Disappointment', ComputerWeekly.com, www.computerweekly.com/Articles/2009/11/19/239154/Revised-Google-Book-search-deal-39a-massive-disappointment39.htm.

The World Bank (2012) World Bank Announces Open Access Policy for Research and Knowledge, Launches Open Knowledge Repository, press release 2012/379/EXTOP, 10 April.

The environmental sustainability of information

Introduction

Practitioners in library and information services have been increasingly dealing with digital documents and databases. With the invention and adoption of the internet and web technologies the volume of information has significantly increased over the past two decades. These new technologies have opened up many hitherto unforeseen opportunities that have facilitated an unprecedented growth in the creation and use of digital content and data. However, the internet, web, various information systems and services, and underlying ICT infrastructure and computing devices make extensive use of energy and consequently generate a substantial amount of GHG.

Chapters 1 and 2 described how environmental sustainability has become a major matter of concern in discussions at institutional, regional, national and international level about how to encourage businesses and departments to reduce GHG emissions. Chapter 2 gave examples of some of the definitions of GHG – generally it is measured as the equivalent of CO_2 emissions, expressed in metric tonnes of CO_2 or $mTCO_2e$.

Although environmental sustainability issues are addressed in almost every business sector, studies show that very little research has been carried out on environmental sustainability in the information services sector (Chowdhury, 2012). Since ICT forms the basis of today's information systems and services, some relevant lessons can be learnt from related areas, especially green IT research.

Chapter 2 noted that although there are many different challenges and indicators involved, climate change issues, measured in GHG emissions, are often used as one of the major indicators of environmental sustainability. This chapter explains the concept of GHG as discussed in many authoritative documents and reports, especially in an IPCC report (2007a). It then considers the concepts of green IT and green information systems research, pointing out the major difficulties of measuring GHG emissions from ICT and tools. It briefly looks at the lifecycle analysis technique used to measure GHG for IT and information services and examines whether and how such a technique can be used to measure GHG emissions from information systems and services.

The IPCC report and GHG emissions

Since its inception in 1988 the IPCC has produced four multi-volume assessment reports on different aspects of climate change. The Fourth Assessment Report (AR4) of the IPCC was published in 2007, and the Fifth Assessment Report (AR5), with contributions from more than 800 international experts, will appear in 2014 (IPCC, 2013). The IPCC 2007 synthesis report (IPCC, 2007a) is based on the assessment carried out by the three working groups of the IPCC on climate change.

The IPCC Fourth Assessment Report describes the work of three working groups. Working Group I deals with the physical science basis of climate change and discusses 'those aspects of the current understanding of the physical science of climate change that are judged to be most relevant to policymakers' (IPCC, 2007b). This report shows that climate change that has taken place in the recent past and is taking place now is mostly due to human activities.

Working Group II deals with the impacts, adaptation and vulnerability of climate change and draws on over 290,000 data series to provide 'a much broader set of evidence of observed impacts coming from the large number of case studies developed over recent years' (IPCC, 2007c). This report shows the impact of climate change on different areas and their vulnerability.

Working Group III deals with the mitigation of climate change and addresses five major questions:

- What can we do to reduce or avoid climate change?
- What are the costs of these actions and how do they relate to the costs of inaction?
- How much time is available to realise the drastic reductions needed to stabilize greenhouse gas concentrations in the atmosphere?
- What are the policy actions that can overcome the barriers to implementation?
- How can climate mitigation policy be aligned with sustainable development policies?

IPCC (2007d)

The IPCC synthesis report notes:

- Continued GHG emissions at or above current rates would cause further warming and induce many changes in the global climate system during the 21st century that would *very likely* be larger than those observed during the 20th century (p.36).
- There is *high agreement* and *much evidence* that with current climate change mitigation policies and related sustainable development practices, global GHG emissions will continue to grow over the next few decades (p.36).

IPCC (2007a)

The report also states that GHGs comprise CO_2, methane (CH_4), nitrous oxide (N_2O), hydrofluorocarbons (HFCs), perfluorocarbons (PFCs) and sulphur-hexafluoride (SF_6). Human activities result in emissions of four long-lived GHGs – CO_2, CH_4, N_2O and halocarbons (a group of gases containing fluorine, chlorine or bromine) (IPCC, 2007a). The IPCC 2007 synthesis report recommends that GHGs differ in their warming influence on the climate, and these warming influences may be expressed through a common metric of CO_2-equivalent emissions, which can be defined as:

> the amount of CO_2 emission that would cause the same time-integrated radiative forcing [a measure of the influence a factor has in altering the balance of incoming and outgoing energy in the Earth-atmosphere system and is an index of the importance of the factor as a potential climate change mechanism], over a given time horizon, as an emitted amount of a longlived GHG or a mixture of GHGs. The equivalent CO_2 emission is obtained by multiplying the emission of a GHG by its Global Warming Potential (GWP) for the given time horizon. For a mix of GHGs it is obtained by summing the equivalent CO_2 emissions of each gas. Equivalent CO_2 emission is a standard and useful metric for comparing emissions of different GHGs but does not imply the same climate change responses.

IPCC (2007a, 36)

The report notes that global GHG emissions due to human activities have grown at the rate of 70% between 1970 and 2004:

- CO_2 is the most important anthropogenic GHG, and its annual emissions have grown between 1970 and 2004 by about 80%, from 21 to 38 gigatonnes (Gt), and represented 77% of total anthropogenic GHG emissions in 2004.
- The rate of growth of CO_2e emissions was much higher during the recent 10-year period of 1995–2004 (0.92 $GtCO_2$e per year) than during the previous period of 1970–1994 (0.43 $GtCO_2$e per year) (IPCC, 2007a, 36).

The IPCC 2007 synthesis report found that in 2004 the major developed countries that held a 20% share in world population produced 57% of the world's gross domestic product based on purchasing power parity (GDPPPP), and accounted for 46% of global GHG emissions. In other words, countries that have only 20% or the world's population generate nearly half the world's total GHG emissions. However, this situation is changing because of the rapid industrial growth in some developing countries like India, China and Brazil, which now generate much more GHG than previous decades. A BBC News report in 2013 reported that the daily measurements of CO_2 at a US government agency lab on Hawaii have topped 400 parts per million (ppm) – 400 molecules of CO_2 for every one million molecules in the air. It commented that the last time CO_2 was regularly above 400 ppm was three to five million years ago – before modern humans existed. The report further notes that in 1958 the measurement used to be 315 ppm; and thus the current figures demonstrate there has been a significant rise in CO_2 over the past five decades (BBC News, 2013). UNEP's *Emissions Gap Report 2012* stated that current global emissions are around 50.1 gigatonnes per year of CO_2e (GtCO_2e) and at the current rate of growth can go up to 58 GtCO_2e in 2020 (UNEP, 2013). In order to stay on track to achieve the target of not letting the global mean temperature rise to more than 2°C in 2020, while maintaining the rate of growth, global emissions have to be reduced by 8–13 GtCO_2e, which is a larger figure than earlier estimates because of higher than expected economic growth.

The carbon footprint of IT

The IPCC reports on climate change and various reports from UN offices, especially the United Nations Framework Convention on Climate Change (UNFCCC), recognize the need to achieve environmental sustainability in every development activity, and that such environmental sustainability of systems and products can be realized by reducing GHG emissions from their design, development and operations (UNFCCC, 2013). Since modern information services make extensive use of ICT and information systems, it is necessary to understand the environmental impact of ICT and information systems, and how such impact can be reduced.

It is estimated that globally ICTs contribute to about 2% of the current GHG emissions (Climate Group, 2008), and these emissions are going to increase rapidly in coming years. This is a critical issue because on the one hand we can see the benefits of using more IT in managing administrative and scholarly information in higher education and research, but on the other hand increased use of ICT will require more energy and therefore create more GHG emissions. Fortunately research also shows that appropriate use of ICT can reduce GHG emissions. The Climate Group's report *Smart2020* suggests that 'through enabling other sectors to reduce their emissions, the IT industry could reduce global emissions by as much as 15% by 2020 – a volume of CO_2e five times its own footprint in 2020' (Climate Group, 2008). It also proposes that replacing physical information products and services with their digital equivalents can help in the reduction of environmental impacts and this can be achieved by using appropriate IT and online information service models. This is discussed further in Chapter 6. However, replacing physical information resources with their digital counterparts also leads to increasing use of ICT.

A study by the Australian Computer Society noted that in 2009 Australia's ICT users consumed 13.248 million kilowatt hours (KWh) of electricity, which generated 14.248 million tonnes equivalent to CO_2 emissions, which is nearly 2.5% of Australia's total emissions (539 million tonnes) (Australian Computer Society, 2010). It is estimated that desktops and laptops comprise roughly half of the internet's total power consumption (Raghavan and Ma, 2011) and that over 500,000 tonnes of CO_2 is emitted from the electricity used to run the overall ICT infrastructure in British universities (James and Hopkinson, 2009). According to Carbon Monitoring for Action (CARMA) statistics, there are 1662 power stations in the UK and together they emit 174.6 million tonnes of CO_2e (CARMA, 2013). Therefore the annual GHG emissions from energy required to run the ICT infrastructure in British universities would be equivalent to the annual emissions from about five typical power stations! This is only for running the ICT infrastructure, and if the environmental costs of the full lifecycle of all the computing and networking equipment are considered (Chowdhury, 2012) then there will be a manifold increase in the emission figures. This clearly indicates that current practices are not environmentally sustainable and appropriate green ICT measures have to be taken.

According to the EU IT work programme (2011–12) report, 'the ICT sector has been identified as a potential major player in the fight against climate change – in particular its role in improving energy efficiency' (European Commission, 2011, 4). Similar observations have been made by other researchers. For example, Forge et al. (2009) note that 'IT occupies a leading role in the fight against climate change, contributing to a sustainable low-carbon economy'. However, improved and appropriate use of ICT infrastructure and computing equipment can reduce 'annual man-made global emissions by 15% by 2020 and deliver energy efficiency savings to global businesses of over EUR 500 billion' (Climate Group, 2008).

The carbon footprint of information infrastructure and services

Information infrastructure and services use a variety of computing tools and technologies, each of which has its own carbon footprint. Hence measuring the environmental impact of information infrastructure and services is a complex task involving a number of assumptions and generalizations. As a result, estimates vary over the environmental impact of the information infrastructure and services such as the internet and search engine services.

According to some estimates, the internet releases 'around 300 million tonnes of CO_2 a year – as much as all the coal, oil and gas burned in Turkey or Poland, or more than half of the fossil fuels burned in the UK' (Clark and Berners-Lee, 2010). One study estimates that the internet consumes between 170 and 307 gigawatt (GW) of electricity, which is equivalent to 1.1–1.9% of the total energy usage of humanity (estimated to be 16 terrawatt (TW)) (Raghavan and Ma, 2011). More recently researchers from the Centre for Energy-Efficient Telecommunications and Bell Laboratories explain that the ICT industry, which delivers internet, video, voice and other cloud services, produces more than 830 million tonnes of CO_2e (ACS News Service, 2013). However, all such estimates are based on several assumptions about the number and types of computing devices used, the amount of time used by people to perform the millions of jobs on the internet, the amount of energy consumed throughout the lifecycle of all these computing devices and the overall ICT infrastructure used to run the internet, energy consumptions and cooling requirements of the numerous large data centres that hold and process internet data.

According to one report, in 2010 Google's overall consumption of electricity was 2.26 million MWh (Albanesius, 2011). To put this into perspective, taking the CARMA (2013) statistics, it can be estimated that Google's annual GHG emission is 1.1 million tonnes of CO_2e, or GHG emissions from Google's total energy consumption is equivalent to that from about 11 typical power stations in the UK. This is a conservative estimate for several reasons, not least that Google operates in many different countries and uses power that comes from various different types of power stations with different GHG emission ratings. According to another report, Google emits 1.5 million tonnes of CO_2e, which is slightly higher than the annual consumption of the country of Laos in south-east Asia and equivalent to the UN's operational footprint (Clark, 2011). Another report calculates that Google emitted 1.67 million tonnes of CO_2e in 2011 compared with 1.46 million tonnes in 2010; and the company's 'carbon footprint per million dollars of revenue – a measure of carbon intensity commonly used to track corporate sustainability – has decreased by an average of 10% each year since 2009' (Forbes, 2012). In any case, it may be noted that according to Google's own estimate, in 2011 Google's GHG emissions were equivalent to the annual emissions from nearly 14 typical power stations in the UK.

According to some other Google figures, 'the typical Google user creates 1.46kg of CO_2e by consuming its various services – the equivalent of filling a deep bath or buying an imported bottle of wine. It also claims that producing and shipping a single DVD uses as much energy as watching YouTube non-stop for three days' (Clark, 2011). Clark estimated that each 10 minutes of viewing on YouTube generates 1g of CO_2e and a typical Gmail user generates 1.2kg of CO_2e per year (2011). However, these emission figures do not include the client-side ICT and energy usage figures. For example, the total carbon footprint of a Dell Latitude E6400 is approximately 320–370kg CO_2e, depending on the energy source used (Dell, 2010). Laptops are typically replaced every four years. Assuming that a laptop is used for around 10 hours a day, or 3650 hours a year, for a typical 10-minute daily use of a laptop to watch video on YouTube, the client-side carbon footprint would be about 4g.

As an example of GHG emissions in a specific sector, higher education institutions in the USA produce approximately 121 million tonnes of CO_2e in a year, equivalent to nearly 2% of total annual GHG emissions in the USA, or about a quarter of the entire State of California's annual emissions (Sinha et al., 2010).

Green IT

Until very recently little research was conducted to explore how information systems, as one of the technologies embedded in almost every function and activity in today's society, can help organizations develop ecological sustainability (Chen, Boudreau and Watson, 2008). Researchers now suggest that more efficient usage of facilities, more efficient use of energy-efficient equipment, and renewable energy sources are three keys to reducing the carbon footprint of ICT (Chan et al., 2013). Broadly all these fall within the research area of green IT, which includes the initiatives and programmes that directly or indirectly address environmental sustainability (Jenkin, Webster and McShane, 2011). Green IT initiatives and measures are based on the basic premise that increasing use of ICT has a detrimental effect on the environment, and this can be reduced by adopting specific measures. For example, as stated earlier, ICTs contribute to 2% of global emissions, which is equal to that of the aviation industry, and this will double by 2020 (Climate Group, 2008). The environmental impact of ICT is increasing mainly because:

• ICT equipment and networks have short product life spans

- the manufacture and disposal of ICT equipment cause toxic waste
- ICTs consume a large amount of electricity (Jenkin, Webster and McShane, 2011; Siegler and Gaughan, 2008).

The objective of green IT is to reduce the overall environmental impact of ICT by adopting a number of measures ranging from taking environment-friendly approaches to the production and use of ICT equipment and facilities to optimizing the use of ICT equipment and network infrastructure in order to reduce energy consumption at every stage. Green IT initiatives and practices make efficient use of computing and network resources that can reduce energy consumption, and this in turn can reduce the carbon footprint of the ICT and the specific business or services concerned. Several tools have been developed to estimate the energy costs of ICT equipment; for example, the energy calculator for PC equipment by EU Energy Star (n.d.). The SusteIT toolkit has been developed to estimate the energy consumption of specific ICT and computing devices in higher education institutions (SusteIT, n.d.); and the Jisc-funded U-CARE project sought to benchmark energy costs in university labs and server rooms (Graham et al., 2012). It is estimated that active implementation of IT efficiency measures in computer centres in Germany could have saved €3.6 billion from electricity from 2009 to 2013 (Metz and Seadle, 2012).

Green information systems research aims to develop and use improved business practices by using improved and more efficient ICT tools and techniques, for example, by developing better ICT-based production and supply chain management, reducing travel for business meetings through the use of teleconferencing and videoconferencing facilities, using more energy-efficient equipment and processes, and turning off ICT equipment when it is not in use. The EU ICT work programme (2011–12) report notes that 'the ICT sector has been identified as a potential major player in the fight against climate change – in particular its role in improving energy efficiency' (European Commission, 2011).

Some research in green IT and green information service focuses specifically on the environmental impact of IT on:

- businesses (Baliga et al., 2011; Carballo–Penela and Domenech, 2010; Harmon et al., 2010; Harmon, Daim and Raffo, 2010)
- countries (Hertwich and Peters, 2009)
- cities (Sovacool and Brown, 2010)
- households (Jones and Kammen, 2011).

Green IT can reduce the environmental impact directly by using improved materials and technology in the manufacturing of IT components, and making IT equipment and infrastructure more energy-efficient; or indirectly by developing more efficient information systems and technology solutions to support business initiatives in reducing their negative environmental impacts.

One of the early works on the energy consumption of IT and internet was that of Gupta and Singh (2003) which noted that a significant amount of energy savings can be achieved by putting network interfaces and other router and switch components to sleep at idle times.

Research shows that the printed content industry generates a significant amount of GHG emissions and the modern information services sector based on this industry is not environmentally sustainable (Chowdhury, 2012; Moberg, Borggren and Finnveden, 2011). Dematerialization – replacement of printed content with digital information resources and services – may be one way to reduce some of the environmental impacts of information services (Chowdhury, 2010), but other measures need to be taken into consideration in order to build sustainable information services, which are discussed further in Chapter 6.

While reviewing the literature on green IT and green information systems, Jenkin, Webster and McShane (2011) note that almost half of the research papers they examined studied the environmental impact of IT equipment and infrastructure, focusing primarily on the design, development and implementation of hardware and/or software. They categorized research on green information systems as studies:

- examining how the software development lifecycle can be modified to reduce the potential negative environmental impacts of systems (Haigh and Griffiths, 2008)
- focusing on various environmental reporting, measurement and accounting systems (Brown, Dillard and Marshall, 2005; Goodman, 2000; Isenmann, Bey and Welter, 2007; Moller and Schaltegger, 2005; Rikhardsson, 1998; Shaft, Sharfman and Swahn, 2001)
- focusing on knowledge management systems for environmental sustainability initiatives (Jain, George and Webster, 2008)
- focusing on the concept of designing for the environment – taking the environment into consideration when designing products and services (Lenox, King and Ehrenfeld, 2000; Yang et al., 2007)
- concerned with describing green technologies, such as green supercomputers (Schaffhauser, 2008) and green data centres (West, 2008).

Green information services

A green information service or system may be defined as a sustainable information system designed to manage data and information, producing information as an output in order to support specific research, scholarly and/or decision-making activities. Thus, it is different from green information systems reviewed above, which are systems designed to perform a variety of transactions such as the online operation, monitoring, control and management of specific equipment and machinery; online sales and purchase transactions; online supply chain management; and so on. The focus of green information services, as defined here, is on the user and user- or context-specific information services that generate information as the output to meet specific information needs of a user or community. In the context of scholarly communications and research such a green information service will aim to provide information services to students, scholars, and university managers and other interested parties like the government, businesses, and so on, in an economically and environmentally sustainable way. More specific examples of the features and benefits of a green information service are discussed in the following sections, while the design issues are considered in Chapter 9.

Carbon neutrality: the foundation of a green information service

By definition a green information service should be designed to minimize GHG emissions throughout its lifecycle from content creation to distribution, access, use and disposal. GHG emissions of a product or service can be calculated by using what is known as the lifecycle analysis or the 'cradle-to-grave' approach (ISO 14040:2006; Finnveden et al., 2009). This method takes into account the energy inputs and emission outputs throughout the production chain from exploration and extraction of raw materials to different stages of processing, manufacturing, storage, transportation, use and disposal. Lifecycle analysis is accredited by the ISO 14000 series standards, which reflect 'international consensus on good environmental and business practices that can be applied by organizations all over the world in their specific context' (ISO, 2009).

The UK's Department of Energy and Climate Change (DECC) guidelines suggest that carbon neutrality can be achieved by one or more of the following methods:

- reducing emissions by changing the processes of production, distribution, storage, processing, use and disposal
- adopting and encouraging 'green user behaviour'

- using alternative (environment-friendly) energy sources
- carbon sequestration, the process of removing CO_2 from the atmosphere
- offsetting residual emissions by buying carbon credits.

DECC (2009)

Ideally a green information service should try to achieve carbon neutrality by adopting a combination of approaches mentioned in the first three points above, and after taking all the necessary measures, if there are still some residual emissions then the fourth and fifth may be followed to reach the target of carbon neutrality. In order to develop a green information service, it is necessary to understand the general lifecycle of information systems and services, which will enable us to determine where and how GHG emissions can be reduced.

Measuring the environmental impact of information services

Estimating the energy consumption of a large digital library or information service, and assessing the corresponding carbon footprint or GHG emissions, is a complex process because of the global dimension of a large digital library or information service, and the arrays of equipment and tools used to build, manage and access the internet and various information services. Assumptions are always involved in deciding:

- the different types and number of devices involved in the network at the server and client sides
- the number of users involved and time spent on the specific information service
- the proportion of the life of a typical computing device that is used specifically for the information service rather than various other activities at the users' end
- the life of a typical computing device before it is replaced, and the mode of destruction
- energy sources used for the computing industry and the information services that may be spread in different part of the world, for example for a distributed digital library.

Some figures on the carbon footprint of various computing devices are available (for example, the Energy Star or the SusteIT toolkit mentioned earlier), which can calculate the carbon footprint of specific computing devices used in a digital library or information service. However, one has to estimate:

- the time used to build and manage content held and managed in a digital library or information service
- the amount of time spent by users, perhaps from transaction logs, on a given digital library or information service
- the volume of information downloaded on a client's device and the amount of time spent to use such information in order to estimate the total environmental costs of a digital information service.

One has to consider two forms of energy usage:

1 Embodied energy – the energy used to manufacture the myriads of computing and network devices that are used to run the information services
2 Socket energy – used by the devices during a typical information search or use session.

It is important to remember that some devices are always turned on, and they consume energy, irrespective of whether the information service is being used or not at a particular time. There are other factors as well; for example, the environmental costs of preservation of digital content and data. Figure 4.1 shows the various factors that need to be considered for such calculations. It may be noted that there are two major components in the calculation of energy consumption –

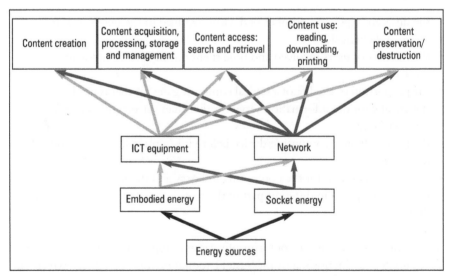

Figure 4.1 Factors responsible for GHG emissions from an information service

embodied energy and socket energy, and we need to consider both for estimating the energy costs of all the information-related activities from content creation to use and preservation, and also destruction of the ICT equipment used.

Measuring the carbon footprint of digital libraries

Figure 4.1 shows how energy consumption by computing and network devices at different stages of creating, processing, preserving, accessing and using information plays an important role in estimating overall GHG emissions of a digital library. However, it is difficult to separate out the energy consumptions of the internet for every stage of a digital library like content creation, content management, content access and use. An alternative approach may be to estimate the energy costs and corresponding GHG emissions of every stage separately and then add the internet cost component for the period that users spend on the internet for content creation and using a digital library.

Digital libraries vary in their content, architecture and target users. For example, the Europeana Digital Library focuses primarily on the cultural heritage information in Europe; the NSDL is designed to provide information on education and research in science, technology, engineering and mathematics for school students and teachers in the USA; the Networked Digital Library of Theses and Dissertations (NDLTD), as the name suggests, provides access to digital theses and dissertations produced at the universities in the USA and some other countries that are members of the organization. Many digital libraries have a distributed architecture, and even if they provide access to a central portal the content can be accessed and downloaded from specific institutional servers distributed over the internet.

There are other issues as well. For example while NDLTD and NSDL primarily deal with born digital content; some digital libraries like Europeana deal with content that is digitized for inclusion in the digital library. So, the environmental costs of digitization may be an important factor in such cases. A digital library may fall into one or more of the following categories:

- *Type 1*: born digital content
- *Type 2*: centralized vs distributed architecture – institutional repositories and distributed digital libraries like NSDL, NDLTD, Europeana
- *Type 3*: digitized content and born digital content
- *Type 4*: digital libraries with preservation role
- *Type 5*: digital libraries of content and data – data storage and processing requirements; large volumes of data processing.

The above categories are not mutually exclusive and a particular digital library may fall into more than one category; for example, the Europeana digital library falls into types 2, 3 and 4 and may be type 5 as well. Again, in order to be accurate in the estimation, the environmental costs of the software – for its creation and to manage and upgrade – used to run and manage the digital library should also be considered. However, the energy and environmental costs of a specific digital library software may be much less than the overall management and access costs, and therefore one may decide to ignore the energy costs for the software development from the overall energy and environmental costs of a large digital library.

A generic methodology

In order to estimate the carbon footprint or GHG emissions of a digital library it is necessary to estimate the embodied energy costs, and the socket energy costs for the computing devices required or used for:

- content and data creation for born digital content and digitization
- content and data storage, processing and maintenance
- software development for specific activities, for example the information retrieval software, interface and various tools for log maintenance, report generation, and so on
- content access – connect time or searches; data transfer
- content use – online use, downloading and offline use, printing, sharing, re-use
- content preservation and long-term storage
- internet access time for all the above activities.

For each of the above, we need to consider three other factors, say 'n', 'a' and 'b', where:

- 'n' denotes the type of computing device such as a server, desktop, laptop, mobile phone, and so on, used for a given activity
- 'a' denotes the proportion of the lifetime of a specific computing device that is used for an operation or activity
- 'b' is the unit power consumption figure for the given computing device, which is different for each device.

It is also necessary to consider the estimated lifespan of every type of computing device.

Thus the embodied energy for each device can be calculated as follows (some figures are taken from a study (Raghavan and Ma, 2011) conducted to estimate the energy consumption of the internet; other guides such as the Energy Star Network guides mentioned earlier, can be used):

- *Servers*: n5GJ (where 'n' is the number of servers; it is assumed that each server is used with maximum weight – full time (i.e. a=1) and a server energy consumption of 5 giga joules (GJ))
- *Desktops*: n × a × (0.01 to 1.0) × 7.5 GJ (where 'n' is the number of desktops used; the energy consumption of a desktop is 7.5 GJ; the weight 'a' can be between 0.01 to 1.0 – a desktop can be used @ 1–100% of its lifetime for using a digital library)
- *Laptops*: n × a × (0.01 to 1.0) × 5 GJ (where 'n' is the number of laptops used; the energy consumption of a laptop is 5 GJ; the weight 'a' can be between 0.01 and 1.0 – a laptop can be used @ 1–100% of its lifetime for using a digital library)
- *Smartphones*: n × a × (0.01 to 1.0) × 1 GJ (where 'n' is the number of smartphones used, assuming that the energy consumption of a smartphone is 1 GJ; the weights can be between 0.01 and 1.0 – a smartphone can be used @1–100% of its lifetime for using a digital library).

Similarly, the socket energy costs can be calculated by estimating (based on the suggested energy consumption of the devices or using a standard guideline like the Energy Star or the SusteIT guidelines):

- the socket energy consumption by each computing device used to host and maintain the digital library (for a server that hosts the digital library this will be 24 × 7) and multiplying it by per unit energy consumption figure (for example, 375 watts for servers)
- the energy consumption by each user device, based on the connect time according to transaction log analyses, and average usage for a typical device to access, use and (if necessary) print digital library content (for example, 150 watts for desktops, 40 watts for laptops and 1 watt for smartphones)
- the internet energy consumption for the duration of use and/or data transfer in a typical digital library search and retrieval session (based on the transaction log analysis).

The total energy consumption for a digital library over a period such as a year can thus be estimated by adding the embodied energy and socket energy consumptions. In order to get more accurate figures, it is also necessary to account for the internet energy costs for creation and maintenance of the digital library content and energy cost for software development for digital libraries (for example a proportion of the energy costs of a digital library software like DSpace, Fedora, Greenstone, and so on), but these figures are very difficult to estimate because they depend on the energy costs for the software lifecycle, copies of the software downloaded and used for various digital library development, and so on. These are difficult to estimate because one has to apportion these costs for a specific digital library based on the number of digital libraries that use a given software, updating and upgrading of a software, and various preservation activities. As stated earlier, these energy costs may be considered or ignored depending on the level of detail required.

Summary

Modern information systems and services make extensive use of ICT infrastructure and services in different forms, and people nowadays make extensive use of ICT for access to and use of a variety of information in their day-to-day activities and living. However, the increasing use of ICT infrastructure and equipment increases energy consumption, which in turn increases the carbon footprint or GHG emissions. This chapter described how the internet, search engine services, and even the ICT infrastructure of the higher education sector in a country generate a substantial amount of GHG, and this will keep on increasing unless appropriate measures are taken to reduce such emissions.

The library and information services sector also uses a substantial amount of energy and thus generates a substantial amount of GHG. With the increasing volume and variety of digital content, the environmental costs of long-term access to digital information will increase rapidly. IBM estimates that we create 2.5 quintillion (2.5 × 10^{18}) bytes of data every day, and it comes from everywhere: sensors used to gather climate information, posts to social media sites, digital pictures and videos, purchase transaction records, and cell phone GPS signals to name a few (IBM, 2013). Estimates show that the British Library's digital collection will grow to 300 terabytes (300 × 10^{12} bytes) in 2013 and 2 Petabytes (2 × 10^{15} bytes) in 2018; and it is estimated that for every £1 spent on running servers, £1.20 is spent on cooling (Knight, 2010). Green IT and cloud computing research hold some promise, and green information services may help us reduce the carbon footprint of information systems and services. These issues are discussed in more detail in Chapter 9.

However, climate change, especially that brought about by human activities, is caused by socio-economic developments. Hence, the new IPCC report will put greater emphasis on assessing the socio-economic aspects of climate change and implications for sustainable development, risk management and the framing of a response through adaptation and mitigation (IPCC, 2013). Issues related to the social sustainability of information are examined in Chapter 5.

References

ACS News Service (2013) Toward Reducing the Greenhouse Gas Emissions of the Internet and Telecommunications, Weekly PressPac, 2 January, www.acs.org/content/acs/en/pressroom/presspacs/2013/acs-presspac-january-23-2013/toward-reducing-the-greenhouse-gas-emissions-of-the-internet-and-telecommunications.html.

Albanesius, C. (2011) How Much Electricity Does Google Consume Each Year?, *PCMag.com*, www.pcmag.com/article2/0,2817,2392654,00.asp.

Australian Computer Society (2010) *Carbon and Computers in Australia: the energy consumption and carbon footprint of IICT usage in Australia in 2010*, Australian Computer Society, www.acs.org.au/attachments/505 ICFACSV4100412.pdf.

Baliga, J., Ayre, R. W. A., Hinton, K. and Tucker, R. S. (2011) Green Cloud Computing: balancing energy in processing, storage, and transport, *Proceedings of the IEEE*, **99** (1), January, http://ieeexplore.ieee.org/stamp/stamp.jsp?arnumber=05559320.

BBC News (2013) Carbon Dioxide Passes Symbolic Mark, 10 May, www.bbc.co.uk/news/science-environment-22486153.

Brown, D. L., Dillard, J. F. and Marshall, R. S. (2005) Strategically Informed, Environmentally Conscious Information Requirements for Accounting Information Systems, *Journal of Information Systems*, **19**, 79–103.

Carballo-Penela, A. and Domenech, J. L. (2010) Managing the Carbon Footprint of Products: the contribution of the method composed of financial statements (MC3), *International Journal of Lifecycle Assessment*, **15** (9), 96–9.

CARMA (2013) Carbon Monitoring for Action, United Kingdom, http://carma.org/region/detail/2635167.

Chan, C. A., Gygax, A. F., Wong, E., Leckie, C. A., Nirmalathas, A. and Kilper, D. C. (2013) Methodologies for Assessing the Use-Phase Power Consumption and Greenhouse Gas Emissions of Telecommunications Network Services, *Environmental Science & Technology*, **47** (1), 485–92, http://pubs.acs.org/doi/ipdf/10.1021/es303384y.

Chen, A. J. W., Boudreau, M.-C. and Watson, R. T. (2008) Information systems and Ecological Sustainability, *Journal of Systems and Information Technology*, **10** (3), 186–201.

Chowdhury, G. G. (2010) Carbon Footprint of the Knowledge Sector: what's the future?, *Journal of Documentation*, **66** (6), 934–46.

Chowdhury, G. G. (2012) Building Sustainable Information Services: a green IS research agenda, *Journal of the American Society for Information Science and Technology*, **63** (4), 633–47.

Clark, D. (2011) Google Discloses Carbon Footprint for the First Time, *Guardian*, 8 September, www.guardian.co.uk/environment/2011/sep/08/google-carbon-footprint.

Clark, D. and Berners-Lee, M. (2010) What's the Carbon Footprint of the Internet?, *Guardian*, 12 August, www.guardian.co.uk/environment/2010/aug/12/carbon-footprint-internet.

Climate Group (2008) *SMART2020: enabling the low carbon economy in the information age*, www.theclimategroup.org/publications/2008/6/19/smart2020-enabling-the-low-carbon-economy-in-the-information-age/.

DECC (2009) Guidance on Carbon Neutrality, Department of Energy and Climate Change (UK), www.decc.gov.uk/assets/decc/What%20we%20do/A%20low%20carbon%20UK/carbonneutrality/1_20090930090921_e_@@_carbonneutralityguidance.pdf.

Dell (2010) Carbon Footprint of a Typical Business Laptop From Dell, http://i.dell.com/sites/content/corporate/corp-comm/en/Documents/dell-laptop-carbon-footprint-whitepaper.pdf.

EU Energy Star (n.d.) Energy Calculator for PC Equipment, www.eu-energystar.org/en/en_008.shtml.

European Commission (2011) ICT: information and communication technologies: a theme for research and development under the specific programme 'cooperation' implementing the Seventh Framework Programme (2007–2013) of the European Community for research, technological development and demonstration activities, work programme 2011–12, ftp://ftp.cordis.europa.eu/pub/fp7/ict/docs/ict-wp-2011-12_en.pdf.

Finnveden, G., Hauschild, M., Ekvall, T., Guinée, J., Heijungs, R., Hellweg, S., Koehler, A., Pennington, D. and Suh, S. (2009) Recent Developments in Life Cycle Assessment, *Journal of Environmental Management*, **91** (1), 1–21.

Forbes (2012) Google's Business Is Booming, Its Carbon Emissions Are Not, 9 December, www.forbes.com/sites/toddwoody/2012/09/12/googles-business-is-booming-its-carbon-emissions-are-not/.

Forge, S., Blackman, C., Bohlin, E. and Cave, M. (2009) *A Green Knowledge Society: an ICT policy agenda to 2015 for Europe's future knowledge society*, a study for the Ministry of Enterprise, Energy and Communications, Government Offices of Sweden, by SCF Associates Ltd, Final Report, September, http://ec.europa.eu/information_society/eeurope/i2010/docs/i2010_high_level_group/green_knowledge_society.pdf.

Goodman, A. (2000) Implementing Sustainability in Service Operations at Scandic Hotels, *Interfaces*, **30**, 202–14.

Graham, E., Strachan, P., Lees, M., Parkinson, D. and Swindells, S. (2012) U-Care, Joint Information Systems Committee, http://www.jisc.ac.uk/media/documents/ programmes/greeningict/finalreports/UCare/UCAREFinalReport.pdf.

Gupta, M. and Singh, S. (2003) Greening of the internet. In Feldmann, A., Zitterbart, M., Crowcroft, J. and Wetherall, D. (eds), *Proceedings of the ACM SIGCOMM 2003 Conference on Applications, Technologies, Architectures, and Protocols for Computer Communication*, 25–29 August, Karlsruhe, Germany, 19–26.

Haigh, N. and Griffiths, A. (2008) The Environmental Sustainability of Information Systems: considering the impact of operational strategies and practices, *International Journal of Technology Management*, **43**, 48–63.

Harmon, R., Daim, T. and Raffo, D. (2010) Roadmapping the Future of Sustainable IT Technology Management for Global Economic Growth (PICMET). In *Proceedings of PICMET '10*, Phuket, Thailand, 18–22 July, 1–10.

Harmon, R., Demirkan, H., Auseklis, N., Reinoso, M., Jones, C. M. and Kammen, D. M. (2010) From Green Computing to Sustainable IT: developing a sustainable service orientation, paper given at *43rd Annual Hawaii International Conference on System Sciences*, HICSS-43; Koloa, Kauai, HI, 5–8 January, 1–10.

Hertwich, E. G. and Peters, G. P. (2009) Carbon Footprint of Nations: a global, trade-linked analysis, *Environmental Science and Technology*, **43** (16), 6414–20.

IBM (2013) Big Data at the Speed of Business, www-01.ibm.com/software/data/bigdata/.

IPCC (2007a) *Climate Change 2007: synthesis report, contribution of Working Groups I, II and III to the fourth assessment report of the Intergovernmental Panel on Climate Change*, www.ipcc.ch/publications_and_data/publications_ipcc_fourth_assessment_report_ synthesis_report.htm.

IPCC (2007b) *Climate Change 2007: Working Group I: the physical science basis*, Intergovernmental Panel on Climate Change, www.ipcc.ch/publications_and_data/ar4/wg1/en/frontmatterspreface.html.

IPCC (2007c) *Climate Change 2007: Working Group II: impacts, adaptation and vulnerability*, Intergovernmental Panel on Climate Change, www.ipcc.ch/publications_and_data/ar4/wg2/en/frontmattersforeword.html.

IPCC (2007d) *Climate Change 2007: Working Group III: mitigation of climate change*, Intergovernmental Panel on Climate Change, www.ipcc.ch/publications_and_data/ar4/wg3/en/frontmatterspreface.html.

IPCC (2013) *Activities*, Intergovernmental Panel on Climate Change, www.ipcc.ch/activities/activities.shtml.

Isenmann, R., Bey, C. and Welter, M. (2007) Online Reporting for Sustainability Issues, *Business Strategy and the Environment*, **16**, 487–501.

ISO (2009) *Environmental Management: the ISO 14000 family of international standards*, International Organization for Standardization, www.iso.org/iso/theiso14000family_2009.pdf.

ISO 14040:2006 *Environmental Management – Life Cycle Assessment – Principles and Framework*, International Organization for Standardization.

Jain, R., George, R. and Webster, R. (2008) Sustainable Deconstruction and the Role of Knowledge-Based Systems, *International Journal of Environmental Technology and Management*, **8**, 261–73.

James, P. and Hopkinson, L. (2009) *Green ICT: managing sustainable ICT in education and research*, www.jisc.ac.uk/publications/programmerelated/2009/ sustainableictfinalreport.aspx.

Jenkin, T. A., Webster, J. and McShane, L. (2011) An Agenda for 'Green' Information Technology and Systems Research, *Information and Organization*, **21** (1), 1–24.

Jones, C. M. and Kammen, D. M. (2011) Quantifying Carbon Footprint Reduction Opportunities for US Households and Communities, *Environmental Science and Technology*, **45** (9), 4088–95.

Knight, B. (2010) *The Carbon Footprint of Preservation*, British Library, www.bl.uk/blpac/pdf/dareknight.pdf.

Lenox, M., King, A. and Ehrenfeld, J. (2000) An Assessment of Design-for-Environment Practices in Leading US Electronics Firms, *Interfaces*, **30**, 83–94.

Metz, K. and Seadle, M. (2012) Green Publishing With Green Technologies, *Library Hi Tech*, **30** (3), 381–3.

Moberg, Å., Borggren, C. and Finnveden, G. (2011) Books from an Environmental Perspective, Part 2: e-books as an alternative to paper books, *International Journal of Life Cycle Assessment*, **16**, 238–46.

Moller, A. and Schaltegger, S. (2005) The Sustainability Balanced Scorecard as a framework for Eco-Efficiency Analysis, *Journal of Industrial Ecology*, **9**, 73–83.

Raghavan, B. and Ma, J. (2011) The Energy and Emergy of the Internet. In *Proceedings of the ACM Workshop on Hot Topics in Networks (Hotnets)*, Cambridge, MA, November, www.cs.berkeley.edu/~jtma/papers/emergy-hotnets2011.pdf.

Rikhardsson, P. M. (1998) Information Systems for Corporate Environmental Management Accounting and Performance Measurement, *Greener Management International*, Spring, **98**, 51–70.

Schaffhauser, D. (2008) *New Green Supercomputer Powers up at Purdue*, CampusTechnology.com, www.campustechnology.com/articles/64516/.

Shaft, T. M., Sharfman, M. P. and Swahn, M. (2001) Using Interorganizational Information Systems to Support Environmental Management Efforts at ASG, *Journal of Industrial Ecology*, **5**, 95–115.

Siegler, K. and Gaughan, B. (2008) A Practical Approach to Green IT, Webinar, www.itmanagement.com/land/green-it-webinar/?tfso=2058.

Sinha, P., Schew, W. A., Sawant, A., Kolwaite, K. J. and Strode, S. A. (2010) Greenhouse Gas Emissions from US Institutions of Higher Education, *Journal of Air and Waste Management Association*, **60** (5), 568–73.

Sovacool, B. K. and Brown, M. A. (2010) Twelve Metropolitan Carbon Footprints: a preliminary comparative global assessment, *Energy Policy*, **38** (9), 4856–69.

SusteIT (n.d.) Resources: ICT energy and carbon footprinting tool, www.susteit.org.uk/files/category.php?catID=4.

UNEP (2013) *The Emissions Gap Report 2012: a UNEP synthesis report*, www.unep.org/publications/ebooks/emissionsgap2012/.

UNFCCC (2013) *Background on the UNFCCC: the international response to climate change*, https://unfccc.int/essential_background/items/6031.php

West, J. E. (2008) The *Green Grid's Datacenter Metrics: experience from the field*, HPCwire, www.hpcwire.com/features/The_Green_Grids_Datacenter_Metrics.html.

Yang, X., Moore, P. R., Wong, C. B., Pu, J. S. and Chong, S. K. (2007) Product Lifecycle Information Acquisition and Management for Consumer Products, *Industrial Management & Data Systems*, **107**, 936–53.

The social sustainability of information

Introduction

Chapters 1 and 2 described how the three dimensions of sustainability – economic, environmental and social sustainability – are inter-related and to some extent inter-dependent. Chapter 2 looked at a variety of social sustainability indicators for sustainable development and noted that easy access to and use of relevant information is a prerequisite for sustainable development in any sector.

By its very nature, information services play a key role in providing easy access to information as a shared resource, and hence promote the concept of equity of access to information. The advent and proliferation of the web, social networking and mobile technologies have significantly facilitated access to knowledge in a number of ways, for example through a large number of digital libraries and web resources, a variety of search engine services, and so on. All these new technologies in some way promote the social sustainability of information because in principle they provide wider access to information for every sphere of life and activity. However, it may be argued that these technologies also create some inequalities. Many researchers have discussed different socio-political implications of modern ICT, web and mobile technologies in the context of information systems and services (for a critical review of such works see Feather, 2013), but the social sustainability of information systems and services has not been researched well, so indicators for social sustainability of information systems and services have not been developed. Nevertheless, some valuable lessons may be learnt from related studies. For example, while assessing the social sustainability of a telecentre in Malaysia, Badsar et al. (2011), identified three sets of parameters:

- specific characteristics of individual users, such as computer skills and innovativeness

- specific characteristics of telecentres, such as location, infrastructure and type and quality of telecentre services
- information characteristics of telecentres, such as access to local content and relevance of content for the local community.

Some of these parameters apply to any information system or service. Similarly researchers in a variety of fields in information studies including human information behaviour, information seeking and retrieval, usability and accessibility of information have developed models, tools, techniques and indicators that can contribute to the social sustainability of information systems and services. Similarly, many related issues such as the digital divide (manifested by the economic, social and technological divide), literacy (including digital and information literacy), social inclusion, use and impact of information on various sectors and activities, can contribute to our understanding of the various issues associated with the social sustainability of information systems and services.

This chapter discusses the social sustainability of information with special reference to scholarly information systems and services. It should be noted that as in any other field of sustainable development, measuring the social sustainability of information systems and services is a challenging task. Some indicators for assessing the social sustainability of information services are identified in this chapter. This is followed by an examination of research and development activities in different areas of information that have implications on the social sustainability of information. A generic framework for study of the social sustainability of digital information systems and services has been proposed. Some research questions are listed that can help us understand the various social sustainability issues of information.

Related studies

The main beneficiaries of sustainable information systems and services are users (of specific information systems and services) and society at large. Users have remained the focus of information science research and development activities for several decades. A significant volume of research literature exists in the broad area of user studies – human information behaviour, information seeking and retrieval, and so on. A quick search in early 2013 on the topic of user studies in the ISI Web of Knowledge database retrieved over 13,000 results within the discipline of library and information science alone. The number would be much higher if the search was extended to related disciplines like computer science, engineering, psychology, and so on. Similarly, a large volume of research literature has been produced in various user-related fields like information and digital literacy, the digital divide and social inclusion, usability and user-centred design. These research studies have indirectly addressed different social sustainability issues of information systems and services.

Many research studies over the past two decades have focused specifically on different aspects of users' access to web and digital information systems and services. They have addressed different issues of usability, digital literacy and information skills, web accessibility, social inclusion, and so on, that can shed light on various social sustainability issues of digital information systems and services. Of late many studies have investigated users and Web 2.0 and social networking technologies to shed some light on the emerging behaviour of users in the digital age. Many researchers have also pointed out the challenges created by emerging ICT and web technologies on the sections of today's society that cannot or do not use ICT, web and digital information services. This group of studies has been classed under the topic of digital divide (for details of such studies in the context of information access, see Chowdhury and Chowdhury, 2011, Chapter 9; Feather, 2013). Many researchers have also focused on designing technologies and tools to build digital libraries and information systems that are particularly suitable for users and communities in less technologically advanced countries and societies (discussed later in this chapter).

So, in effect many research studies have generated valuable findings and models on users, community and society, which can shed light on the social sustainability of digital information systems and services. In some recent publications, Chowdhury provides a conceptual view of the sustainability of digital libraries and information systems and services in general (Chowdhury, 2013a, 2013b) and social sustainability of digital libraries in particular (Chowdhury, 2013c). These generic models and frameworks can provide directions for research in social sustainability of information systems and services in different contexts.

Users, community and social sustainability

Human information behaviour has remained a major area of research in information studies for nearly six decades (Wilson, 2009). Researchers have identified a number of barriers to information access (for details, see Ingwersen, 1996; Wilson, 2009). These barriers may be related to one individual user or a community or sometimes the overall environment of the user. They may be considered as barriers to achieving the social sustainability of information services. Many other researchers have proposed models to explain the process of information seeking and retrieval. Ingwersen (1996) identified five different sets of parameters or barriers that may affect users' information seeking and retrieval, related to information objects, intermediaries or the interface, information retrieval systems or models, users' cognitive space, and the environment or domain. A closer look at the barriers identified in this model will reveal that each one of these barriers is influenced by a variety of economic and technological factors. For example, information objects in today's digital world may be obtained in a variety of forms and formats through a variety of different computing devices and interfaces supported by a variety of search engines running behind the interfaces. Access to such diverse sets of digital objects – data and content – are dependent on the economic and technological affordability and accessibility of individual users and their community and context – workplaces, institutions, countries, social and political environment, and so on.

Many studies show increasing interest in the use of specific types of digital information products. A number of earlier studies have focused specifically on the use of e-books (for example, Bailey, 2006; Borchert et al., 2009; Jisc, 2009). Bunkell and Dyas-Correia (2009) suggested that the number of loans per volume for print books is very small at 0.18 to 1.3 accesses per volume per year whereas the number of accesses per volume for digital books is 12 to 45 accesses per volume per year. Some researchers have investigated how specific titles in e-book collections are accessed and used (for example, Christianson, 2005; Christianson and Aucoin, 2005; Grigson, 2009; Nicholas et al., 2008, Walters, 2013). Overall these studies show a similar pattern, with most usage concentrated in a few high-use titles while for the majority of titles there is little or no use. In the Jisc National E-books Observatory project, Nicholas et al. (2008) noted that 45% of the use for one collection was generated by three- to six-year-old books. More recent research shows a rapid increase in the e-book usage across the board (ALA, 2012; Martin and Quan-Haase, 2013; McLure and Hoseth, 2012), but there are differences among different categories of users of e-books (Lamothe, 2013).

Recent usability studies of digital libraries demonstrate the various factors that interplay in the access and use of digital information, and the rapid changes in user information behaviour and expectations. Several researchers have commented that the perceived convenience of digital books for users is compromised by poor usability and other interface features (Pei, Yan and Siew, 2009; Shelburne, 2009; Wacholder, 2008). In a usability study of Europeana digital library it was found that young users' information needs and search strategies and expectations were different from those of more mature users (Dobreva and Chowdhury, 2010) and that many younger users wanted to be able to download, annotate and share digital objects. The latter activity is relatively new and popular with the recent proliferation of Web 2.0 and social networking technologies, especially among the younger generation of users.

So, while we know that different parameters influence users' information seeking, to date there is no research showing how these parameters interplay with the social sustainability of digital information services. While many large digital libraries provide free access to information, such as Europeana, NDLTD, NSDL, PubMed, and so on, and scores of institutional repositories that have appeared over the past decade, no research has taken place so far to determine how socially sustainable they are.

Turning towards recent developments in institutional repositories (for more details see Chapter 7), it may be noted that in the UK, Jisc has played a key role in promoting the development, management and use of institutional repositories (for details see Jacobs, Amber and McGregor, 2008; Jisc, 2011). Efforts similar to those of Jisc have been made elsewhere, for example, at global level through the Digital Repository Infrastructure Vision for European Research (DRIVER) project, whose objective is to establish an appropriate infrastructure for all European and worldwide digital repositories, thereby providing scientific information in an open access model (Peters and Lossau, 2011). The OpenDOAR database at the University of Nottingham records over 2200 repositories, each repository typically holding a mix of journal articles, theses and dissertations, unpublished working papers, conference papers, books and book chapters, and multimedia and other audiovisual materials. In April 2013, out of the 1901 organizations in the OpenDOAR database, 47.1% were from Europe, 19.4% from Asia, 18.6% from North America, 7.9% from South America, 2.9% from Africa, 2.8% from Australasia, 0.9% from the Caribbean, and 0.4% from the rest of the world. Many studies point out that the progress of institutional repositories has not been as fast as was originally envisaged (Connell, 2011; Cryer and Collins, 2011; Cullen and Chawner, 2011; Davis and Connolly, 2007; MacDonald, 2011; St Jean et al., 2011). More details of institutional repositories and sustainability of information systems and services are given in Chapter 7.

Overall, the social sustainability of open access is still not known and many factors including the economic sustainability and social recognition of open access publishing need to be studied in order to generate reliable datasets. These issues are considered in chapters 7 and 8. The problems and challenges become more complex when we consider how the parameters for social sustainability influence, and are influenced by, the parameters related to the economic and environmental sustainability of digital information systems and services. This is discussed further in the following section.

Like human information behaviour, information literacy has remained a major area of research in information studies. There are other related areas of research like digital literacy, the digital divide, social inclusion, and so on. Liew comments that it would be wrong to assume that the impact of ICT has been wholly positive on every section of our society and that social exclusion is not always the result of an intentional act or intentional policy, but often 'an accumulation of isolating factors denying an individual or a group of people a means of inclusion within the society in terms of resources, rights, goods and services, and the ability to participate in the normal relationships and activities available to the majority of people in that society' (2012, 97–8). In the context of digital information services, social exclusion may be caused by a number of factors ranging from lack of adequate access to ICT infrastructure and services, to lack of digital and information literacy, which are the prerequisites for successful access to and use of digital information services. Some of these issues are discussed in the following section.

Indicators for the social sustainability of information

Chapter 2 described the indicators available to measure social sustainability in general (in the context of sustainable development). Some of them may be appropriate to measure the social sustainability of information systems and services. Two major requirements of the social sustainability of information systems and services are rights to access, and equitable access, to information in every sphere of life. Access is a rather broad term, which includes all the activities related to the discovery, access and use or re-use of information for day-to-day business, pleasure, living, well-being, knowledge and understanding.

A variety of indicators may be identified for the social sustainability of information depending on the nature of information, the information service providers, the underlying information systems and ICT frameworks, and users and their context. However, the following ten indicators may be considered appropriate for any kind of information service:

- rights to information (ideally but not necessarily free)
- ease of access to information relevant for every sphere of life
- equity of access to information
- mechanisms for community recognition and responsibility for information sharing
- mechanisms for advocacy in support of all activities related to the creation and dissemination of information
- mechanisms to protect community needs through appropriate use of information
- mechanisms to involve users in the design and usability of information systems and services

- mechanisms to transmit information awareness through generations, for example through education and training in information skills
- mechanisms to create an information society and a knowledge economy through appropriate legal and policy frameworks
- mechanisms to protect privacy and security in relation to information.

While all of these are required to achieve the social sustainability of information, some are related directly to the information systems and services concerned while others are related to wider society, such as awareness, advocacy, participation and regulations. Again, while all are related in some way, some are more inter-dependent than others. For example, the first two – the equity of, and access to, all kinds of information – are ideal goals of any information system or service, but there are a number of technological, economic and social barriers to this.

Ease of access to information has remained a major focus for information research, and a large volume of literature has appeared over the past five or so decades addressing various information access issues and challenges. Some of this research aimed at developing better information retrieval models and techniques; other research focused on how people access and use information, the major barriers, and so on. Bawden and Robinson (2012) provide a good summary of this research. Despite this huge volume of research, information systems and services still rely on how best users choose a database and how effectively they can conduct searches and filter the retrieved results. While cross database search facilities are now available for scholarly information searching, the success of information access still relies on users' search capabilities. Most digital libraries and information services still follow the print paradigm and in most cases they only provide access to the digital version of linear content. The design and delivery of these services are not aligned with the work, lifestyle and culture of users such that systems can provide the best information relevant for specific user contexts. This is discussed later in this chapter.

It should be noted that the equity of access and rights to information do not necessarily mean information should be free. While free access is ideal, it has some implications for the economic sustainability of information services. In the context of social sustainability, equity of access means given the similar circumstances, different sections of a society or a community should have similar access facilities. In some cases people may have restricted or no access to some specific information, for example, in military, business and key scientific intelligence. Nonetheless, in principle, information should be available for all kinds of activities and development, for example, for research and scholarly information to support education and research, health information to support well-being and healthy lifestyle of the population, political and government information to support informed citizenship, cultural and heritage information to ensure protection of values, support and promotion of cultural integration as and when desired by individuals and groups, and information for sustainable development and for protection of communities.

Equity of access to information should be considered for current and future generations through appropriate mechanisms of preservation of information. Rights to information should go hand in hand with the sharing of information, as far as practicable. Appropriate mechanisms need to be developed for advocacy at all levels to support all the activities related to the creation and dissemination of information among various stakeholders and the general public, as appropriate. Similarly, appropriate mechanisms need to be built so that communities can be protected through the right use of information, for example from acts of crime and terrorism, natural disasters, and so on.

Ease of access and use can be ensured only when information users are involved at every step of the design and evaluation of information systems and services. Since this is an evolutionary process, and information systems and services change fast with the advancement of technology, changing society and community needs, user involvement and user training should be a continuous process for any successful information service. Finally all these activities and steps to build a knowledge society should be governed by the appropriate legal and policy frameworks that can support all the activities related to the development of information systems and services, but at the same time protect people's rights to privacy and security. Technology and regulations should go hand in hand in order to promote free flow of, and easy access to, information, but at the same time protect people and society against the misuse and abuse of information.

How to study the social sustainability of information

Broadly speaking digital information systems and services are created in order to make digital information – data and content – available to people and machines – computers and ICT devices – when they need it. Since information is the essential fabric of today's information society and economy, we need to build information systems and services that are economically, environmentally and socially sustainable. This chapter focuses primarily on various parameters associated with the social sustainability of information systems and services. These parameters are associated with, or have some influence on, the economic and environmental sustainability of information systems and services.

Figure 5.1 presents a framework of features that need to be studied in order to understand the different factors and associated challenges of the social sustainability of digital information systems and services. Each strand of research shown in Figure 5.1 influences the overall social sustainability of information systems and services. They also influence each other, and are related to, or dependent on, the nature and characteristics of digital data and information managed by a specific digital information service (Chowdhury, 2013c). It may be noted that the research strands shown in Figure 5.1 are not mutually exclusive, and some cover generic social science and policy research issues, while others cover information issues. Each research strand has attracted a significant amount of research attention and produced a large volume of literature. Together these research findings can contribute to improving the equity and ease of access to information, rights to access to information, and so on. Thus together they can make significant contributions to achieving the social sustainability of information systems and services. They and specific research questions are discussed in more detail in the following sections.

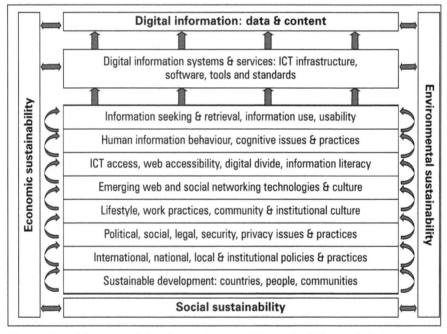

Figure 5.1 A framework for the study of social sustainability of digital information

Information systems and services for sustainable development

Chapter 1 observed that information systems and services are created to support various activities related to sustainable development in every sphere of activity, and thus play an important role in these activities. The importance of information and knowledge sharing for sustainable development has been identified and discussed in many international and national policy documents (for example, United Nations, 1987). The Expert Consultation on Knowledge and Capacity Needs for Sustainable Development in Post Rio+20 Era, organized by the UNOSD together with its partners in Incheon, Republic of Korea, in March 2013, emphasized the importance of information and knowledge sharing:

- We are of the view that transition towards sustainability requires efforts on several fronts, but knowledge sharing and capacity building should be the fundamental platform for these efforts. (United Nations, 2013, 1)
- UNOSD should collaborate with other knowledge providers, and both promote and facilitate the linking and sharing of data and knowledge through open networks, avoiding the duplication of existing initiatives. (United Nations, 2013, 3).

Chapter 1 described how UN General Assembly Resolution A/RES/66/288, called *The Future We Want*, made a series of recommendations on how to achieve sustainable development in different areas (United Nations General Assembly, 2012). Thus at the very broad level the success of digital information systems and services can be measured by their contributions to the overall sustainable development of people, society and communities. For example, in the context of institutional repositories and open access digital libraries, one measure of success of the social sustainability of digital libraries could be their contributions and impact on sustainable development in education and research. However, such measures of success depend on a number of other factors, as shown in Figure 5.1.

The social sustainability of information services

One of the major challenges for information services and information professionals with regard to social sustainability is to provide context-specific and relevant information to people, which requires minimum effort to access and use. Such services should not only be based on efficient indexing and retrieval, but also use a variety of static and dynamic data about the specific user and community of practice, context and surroundings. Such additional information about users and their specific contexts, or user intelligence, can help in providing better and more efficient information services. Most search engines use some form of user and context information, or user intelligence, in order to produce better search results.

An example of the use of specific user contexts to provide better information services can be seen in the services provided through satellite navigation systems (sat navs) used in motor vehicles. Such systems require very little input and learning skills from users. They use a variety of static and dynamic data and information (from a variety of sources or services) and process them in real time with reference to a user's spatial location and contexts such as the user's preference for the fastest or a preferred route, specific destinations, recently visited places, major attractions in cities and towns, and so on. Such information services that can contextualize and package information for ready use in a given situation, or solve a given problem, but do not require complex search skills from users, can be more easily acceptable to the user, and thus be more socially sustainable. Some digital libraries and information services now gather and use some form of user intelligence in order to filter, and sometimes contextualize, retrieved information.

However, one needs to be careful because a number of social and legal issues may crop up in the context of user modelling and contextualization, which may be required to build and provide such information services. For example, a variety of personal information held in social networks and databases through transaction logs can be used to contextualize and personalize information services available through the web. Some new systems now employ individual user information and group or collective information about similar users in order to provide more contextual and customized information services (Chen, Compton and Hsiao, 2013; Liu and Chen, 2013). Anyone gathering and storing personal information about individuals or groups of users may face many legal, security and privacy issues.

Legal and policy frameworks

When formal and informal processes, systems, structures and relationships actively support various development and activities, lifestyles and the well-being of current and future generations they are considered to be socially sustainable. Information systems and services are often governed or guided by a variety of international, regional, national and institutional regulations and policies. These indicators of social sustainability (the ninth and tenth indicators listed earlier in this chapter) influence almost all other research strands shown in Figure 5.1, and the other indicators of social sustainability discussed earlier in this chapter. Hence in the context of digital information systems and services, one may ask how far current institutional, regional, national and international level policies and practices support the objectives of digital information systems and services set up to serve specific user communities.

Two recent sets of developments in the UK and other parts of the world consider this question with reference to regulations, policies and practices and their influence on the social sustainability of information systems and services.

Intellectual property rights and digital rights management issues

Recent developments in ICT infrastructure and internet technologies have significantly increased the rate of the growth of digital information. A huge volume and variety of content is now created through conventional modes of publication and open access and user-generated mode, the last often unregulated and not peer reviewed. Side by side there have been many new players and developments, which provide better, easier and sometimes free, access to information, including Google Books, Microsoft Academic Search, Amazon Kindle and a variety of similar e-book reading devices including the Sony e-book reader, iPad, and so on. However, despite these myriads of services and devices, optimum access to and use of digital information is very much hindered because of inappropriate and often stringent intellectual property rights and complex digital rights management issues. This was identified in several studies (Chowdhury, 2009; Chowdhury and Fraser, 2011), and the Hargreaves review, commissioned by the UK prime minister in 2011 (Hargreaves, 2011). Considering the various recommendations of the Hargreaves review, the UK Government commissioned a subsequent feasibility report to establish a digital copyright exchange, which was one of the major recommendations of the Hargreaves review. The feasibility study recommended the development of a copyright hub, which will serve a number of functions including:

- information and copyright education
- registries of rights
- a marketplace for rights – licensing solutions
- help with the orphan works problem.   Hooper and Lynch (2012)

The first part of the feasibility report concluded that 'a number of issues existed with copyright licensing which meant that it was not entirely fit for purpose for the digital age', and the final report noted that 'the creative industries have responded proactively and are busy streamlining copyright licensing for the digital age' (Hooper and Lynch, 2012, 5). The main recommendation of the report is:

> the creation of a not-for-profit, industry-led Copyright Hub based in the UK that links interoperably and scalably to the growing national and international network of private

and public sector digital copyright exchanges, rights registries and other copyright-related databases, using agreed cross-sectoral and cross-border data building blocks and standards, based on voluntary, opt-in, non-exclusive and pro-competitive principles. The Copyright Hub will serve in the UK and beyond a wide range of copyright licensors (rights holders, creators and rights owners in both commercial and cultural worlds) on the supply side and a wide range of copyright licensees/users on the demand side.   Hooper and Lynch (2012, 5)

Such a copyright hub is expected to boost the social sustainability and economic sustainability of digital information services by facilitating easier discovery, access and lawful use or re-use, and distribution of digital data and content for different activities.

Open access policies of funding bodies

Increasingly research funding bodies in different countries are promoting the idea of open access (discussed in Chapter 3) by formulating specific open access policies associated with their research funding guidelines. For example, the public access policy of the US NIH requires that: 'all investigators funded by the NIH submit or have submitted for them to the National Library of Medicine's PubMed Central an electronic version of their final, peer-reviewed manuscripts on acceptance for publication, to be made publicly available no later than 12 months after the official date of publication' (NIH, n.d.). The Wellcome Trust has introduced a similar open access policy guideline, which:

requires electronic copies of any research papers that have been accepted for publication in a peer-reviewed journal, and are supported in whole or in part by Wellcome Trust funding, to be made available through PubMed Central (PMC) and Europe PubMed Central (Europe PMC) as soon as possible and in any event within six months of the journal publisher's official date of final publication.
                                                                          Wellcome Trust (2013)

The newly introduced open access policy of the European Commission (European Commission, 2014) stipulates that as of 2014 all research papers produced with funding from EU Horizon 2020 will have to be freely accessible to the public. The Australian Research Council (ARC) introduced an open access policy for ARC-funded research with effect from 1 January 2013. According to this policy the ARC requires that any publications arising from an ARC-supported research project must be deposited into an open access institutional repository within 12 months of the date of publication. Research Councils UK (RCUK) has not only introduced an open access policy since 1 April 2013, but shown a preference for providing gold open access through the provision of article-processing charges. The RCUK open access policy stipulates that research papers published through the article-processing charges should be made open access immediately, and those that are not should be made available after six or 12 months of publication (RCUK, n.d.). These open access policies will have a far reaching effect on the long-term future of the information creation (publishing process) and access (through open access systems) of scholarly communications. These are discussed in more detail in Chapters 7 and 8.

Technology, infrastructure and social sustainability

Technological infrastructure for digital information systems and services may be characterized by the ICT infrastructure running various information systems and services; design, organization, accessibility and usability of different information systems and services; and the overall technological developments such as search engines, Web 2.0 and social networking technologies, and mobile technologies. All these have a profound impact on information access and use and on user information behaviour in today's digital world.

A variety of specific issues and challenges are associated with ICT infrastructure, software and interfaces used for various digital information services, usability and impact of information services, and so on. So, while assessing the social sustainability of information systems and services, one may ask how far the ICT infrastructure, equipment and technologies – hardware, software and various tools, interfaces, and so on – are appropriate in providing easy and equitable access to information in order to support the needs of every community and citizen.

Technology infrastructure and usability of digital information systems and services are closely linked to social challenges like the digital divide and social inclusion. The digital divide can be manifested in a number of ways:

- the social divide, characterized by difference in access between diverse social groups
- the global divide, characterized by difference in access to internet technologies
- the democratic divide, characterized by the different applications and uses of digital information in order to engage and participate in social life.

Chowdhury and Chowdhury (2011)

There are different indicators for assessing these different manifestations of the digital divide which are not only prevalent in the developing world, but can also be seen among various communities within the developed nations. For example, as of April 2011 more than a third of US households did not have a broadband connection and only about two-thirds of the population in the 27 EU countries have a broadband connection at home (Chowdhury and Chowdhury, 2011). So, the vision of the Europeana digital library – to provide digital information and culture to everyone in Europe – has not been accomplished because over a third of the EU population does not have internet access (in June 2012, only 63.2% of the EU population had internet access (Internet World Stats, 2013)). In the first quarter of 2013, 43.5 million adults in the UK used the internet while 7.1 million adults (14%) had never used the internet (ONS, 2013). The situation in the third world countries is even worse; only a third of the global world population has internet access (34.3% as of June 2012 (Internet World Stats, 2013)).

Suleman (2012) notes that digital library development in the developing countries is significantly hampered by low-resource environments because of the lack of highly skilled staff to develop and manage digital library systems and services, poor ICT infrastructure, slow and unreliable network connections, and poor and unreliable energy supply. Thus, digital library systems and services that are common in developed countries cannot easily be implemented and used in such low-resource environments. Some researchers have attempted to build digital library systems and technologies for low-resource environments, typical examples being the early digital libraries produced and distributed by the Waikato digital library research team in New Zealand led by Ian Witten and colleagues in co-operation with Unesco (Bainbridge et al., 2004), and the recently built SimplyCT technology developed by Hussein Suleman and his team at the University of Cape Town in South Africa (Suleman, 2007, 2012; Suleman et al., 2010).

Evidently not everyone in any society or community has equal or optimum access to these technologies. Access to ICT and web may be affected by the digital divide, and digital and information literacy and web accessibility. All these factors influence equity of access and therefore the social sustainability of digital information services. Web accessibility is another major issue related to the ICT infrastructure and may influence the social sustainability of digital information systems and services. A variety of guidelines are now available that can improve web accessibility. Examples include Web Content Accessibility Guidelines (WCAG) 2.0, the US government guidelines for web accessibility (Usability.gov) and BS8878:2010, the British standard on web accessibility. However, to date very few digital library and information services fully comply with these standards and guidelines, so many people, especially those with special needs, cannot properly access and use digital information and levels of access to information are unequal.

Users, culture and social sustainability

One of the major goals of social sustainability is to ensure that people are informed and capable of making informed decisions about social, political and developmental processes and activities. In the context of modern digital information systems and services, one may ask how far today's digital information systems and services support this vision of building well-informed, healthy and participative communities at all levels of our society. Does everyone and every generation of our society (rich and poor, old and young, male and female, urban and rural, well educated and less educated or illiterate) have equity of access to information through digital information services?

Social sustainability also involves equity between generations. So, in the context of information systems and services, the key question is to find out how far modern digital information systems and services are compatible with, as well as support and promote, the lifestyle, work practices and culture of specific users and communities.

Many issues and challenges discussed above have been identified by researchers although not specifically in the context of social sustainability of information systems and services. For example, in an early study sponsored by the National Science Foundation in the USA on the social aspects of digital libraries, Borgman et al. (1996) proposed a number of human-centred, content-centred and systems-centred research issues in digital libraries that could be useful to achieve social sustainability of digital information systems and services.

Access to digital information services depends on users' access to ICT, web and other emerging technologies. Several research papers provide evidence that the emerging web, social networking and mobile technologies are changing user behaviour and expectations from digital information systems and services (Bates, 2010; Bennett, Maton and Kervin, 2008; Cunningham, 2010; Hargittai, 2010; Nicholas et al., 2013; Rowlands et al. 2008). These emerging technologies and their implications on users and communities have significant implications for the social sustainability of digital information services. Human information behaviour and cognitive aspects of information can be influenced by any of the factors associated with the other layers discussed in Figure 5.1. Overall, human information and cognition can significantly influence the social sustainability of digital information services.

Lifestyle, work practices, community and institutional culture have profound implications for the social sustainability of information. Every country, community and institution has some specific culture and practices with regard to lifestyle, work and professional practices. Several research studies on human information behaviour and information seeking and retrieval show that user and community culture and practices have a significant influence on users' information seeking and access behaviour. The social sustainability of digital information services thus depends on the specific community, and institutional and individual cultural, professional and work practices. Social sustainability is closely related to the community culture and practices. Information services have long been created and provided through institutions, in order to support specific communities and information-intensive activities like higher education and research, government services and specific businesses and domains like health and law, and the general public, for example through information services provided by national, state and public libraries. With the emergence of the internet and web, many new digital libraries and information services have also emerged specifically designed to provide cultural and heritage information, indigenous information, and so on.

A digital information service is influenced by one or more institutional, regional, national and international level policies, which may vary depending on the nature and characteristics of digital data and information. There may be some general policies governing any kind of data and content; for example there are specific international and national and local policies for management and handling of digital data and content – government information, public information, security and sensitive information, and so on. There are also policies associated with some specific kinds of data and information, for example, data and information related to national security, indigenous data and information, and health information. These specific policies have significant influence on the social sustainability of information services influencing people's rights to access, use and sharing of specific types of data and information for specific purposes.

All the factors discussed in the context of the other layers shown in Figure 5.1 can influence the overall information seeking and retrieval process including access to, and use or re-use of, digital information. Research on information seeking and retrieval models and techniques has significantly influenced the design and development of various software tools and techniques used in accessing and using or re-using information. However, a lot more work is needed to build information systems and services that can provide information to users and communities tailored and personalized according to the context and culture of users, and quality and relevance of information. In order to achieve this we need to be more innovative in the creation, processing, linking and managing of digital content and data. We should also reduce reliance on users' abilities and skills for searching, and instead focus more on using the power of a variety of modern ICT tools and techniques for better information retrieval, natural language processing, semantic analysis and data linking, user-centred design, and web and social networking technologies.

Digital libraries and information services should enable people to perform their jobs better, be more creative and innovative, and live a healthy life. Some innovative work is now being performed by leading researchers, which can improve some aspects of the social sustainability of information systems and digital libraries. See for example, the works of Witten and his colleagues on the creation and use of content and data in innovative ways by using open access tools and technologies like Weka (Witten, 2011) and WikiMiner (Milne and Witten, 2013); or the works of Hsinchun Chen and his team on managing health information based on the extraction of useful information from patient records using advanced text mining and data analysis techniques (Chen, Compton and Hsiao, 2013, Liu and Chen, 2013).

Summary

Social sustainability is a complex area so a large number of indicators have been proposed, and the social sustainability of information systems and services is influenced by a variety of ICT and personal or cognitive, social or community, and political and legal issues, just to name a few. This topic has not been studied, but several research studies in user studies, information seeking and retrieval, usability and evaluation, and so on, can provide significant and valuable information for the study of the social sustainability of information systems and service.

Although some progress is being made in different areas of information science in order to provide better and customized information services based on a variety of user and contextual knowledge, a lot more work needs to be done to achieve a high level of social sustainability of scholarly information systems and services. The ten indicators of social sustainability of information discussed in this chapter are inter-related and can significantly influence the overall sustainability of any digital information system or service. The framework for study of social sustainability of information systems and services shows there are various issues and challenges, which are inter-related in the context of the study of the social sustainability of information systems and services (see Figure 5.1). Some issues of social sustainability especially in the context of recent open access policies and developments are addressed in Chapters 7 and 8. Social sustainability issues are also considered in Chapter 11 in the context of an integrated model of sustainability of scholarly communications in general, and digital information systems and services in particular.

References

ALA (2012) *The 2012 State of America's Libraries: a report from the American Libraries Association*, www.ala.org/news/mediapresscenter/americaslibraries/soal2012.

Badsar, M., Samah, A. B., Hasan, A. M., Osman, N. B. and Shaffri, M. H. A. (2011) Social Sustainability of Information and Communication Technology (ICT) Telecentres in Rural Communities in Malaysia, *Australian Journal of Basic and Applied Sciences*, **5** (12), 2929–38.

Bailey, T. P. (2006) Electronic Book Usage at a Master's Level I University: a longitudinal study, *Journal of Academic Librarianship*, **32** (1), 52–9.

Bainbridge, D., Don, K. J., Buchanan, G., Witten, I. H., Jones, S., Jones, M. and Barr, M. I. (2004) Dynamic Digital Library Construction and Configuration. In Heery, R. and Lyon, L. (eds), *Research and Advanced Technology for Digital Libraries*, Springer.

Bates, M. J. (2010) Information Behavior. In Bates, M. J. and Maack, M. N. (eds), *Encyclopedia of Library and Information Sciences*, 3rd edn, CRC Press, 2381–91.

Bawden, D. and Robinson, L. (2012) *Introduction to Information Science*, Facet Publishing.

Bennett, S., Maton, K. and Kervin, L. (2008) The 'Digital Natives' Debate: a critical review of the evidence, *British Journal of Educational Technology*, **39** (5), 775–86.

Borchert, M., Hunter, A., Macdonald, D. and Tittel, C. (2009) *A Study on Student and Staff Awareness, Acceptance and Usage of E-books at Two Queensland Universities*, http://eprints.usq.edu.au/4876/.

Borgman, C. L., Bates, M., Cloonan, M. V., Efthimiadis, E. N., Gilliand-Swetland, A., Kafai, Y., Leazer, G. L. and Maddox, A. (1996) *Social Aspects of Digital Libraries*, final report to the National Science Foundation, http://is.gseis.ucla.edu/research/dig_libraries/UCLA_DL_Report.html#methods.

Bunkell, J. and Dyas-Correia, S. (2009) E-Books vs Print: which is the better value?, *Serials Librarian*, **56** (1–4), 215–19.

Chen, H., Compton, S. and Hsiao, O. (2013) DiabeticLink: a health big data system for patient empowerment and personalized healthcare. In Kou, W., Yesha, Y. and Tan, C. J. (eds), *Electronic Commerce Technologies: Second International Symposium, ISEC 2001, Hong Kong, China, April 26–28, 2001, Proceedings*, Lecture Notes in Computer Science, **2040**, 71–83.

Chowdhury, G. (2009) Towards the Conceptual Model of a Content Service Network. In *Globalizing Academic Libraries Vision 2020: proceedings of the International Conference on Academic Libraries*, Delhi, 5–8 October, Delhi Mittal Publications, 215–20.

Chowdhury, G. G. (2013a) Sustainability of Digital Information Services, *Journal of Documentation*, **69** (5), 602–22.

Chowdhury, G. G. (2013b) Social Sustainability of Digital Libraries: a research framework. In Aalberg, T., Papatheodorou, C., Dobreva, M., Tsakonas, G. and Farrugia, C. J. (eds), *Research and Advanced Technology for Digital Libraries: International*

Conference on Theory and Practice of Digital Libraries, TPDL 2013, Valletta, Malta, September 22–26, 2013, Proceedings, Lecture Notes in Computer Science, **8092**, 25–34.

Chowdhury, G. G. (2013c) Sustainability of Digital Libraries: a conceptual model. In Aalberg, T., Papatheodorou, C., Dobreva, M., Tsakonas, G. and Farrugia, C. J. (eds), *Research and Advanced Technology for Digital Libraries: International Conference on Theory and Practice of Digital Libraries, TPDL 2013, Valletta, Malta, September 22–26, 2013, Proceedings*, Lecture Notes in Computer Science, **8092**, 1–12.

Chowdhury, G. G. and Chowdhury, S. (2011) *Information Users and Usability in the Digital Age*, Facet Publishing.

Chowdhury, G. G. and Fraser, M. (2011) Carbon Footprint of the Knowledge Industry and Ways to Reduce it, *World Digital Libraries*, **4** (1), 9–18.

Christianson, M. (2005) Patterns of Use of Electronic Books, *Library Collections Acquisitions, & Technical Services*, **29** (4), 351–63.

Christianson, M. and Aucoin, M. (2005) Electronic or Print Books: which are used?, *Library Collections, Acquisitions, & Technical Services*, **29** (1), 71–81.

Connell, T. H. (2011) The Use of Institutional Repositories: the Ohio State University experience, *College & Research Libraries*, **72** (3), 253–74.

Cryer, E. and Collins, M. (2011) Incorporating Open Access Into Libraries, *Serials Review*, **37** (2), 103–7.

Cullen, R. and Chawner, B. (2011) Institutional Repositories, Open Access and Scholarly Communication: a study of conflicting paradigms, *Journal of Academic Librarianship*, **37** (6), 460–70.

Cunningham, J. (2010) New Workers, New Workplace? Getting the balance right, *Strategic Direction*, **26** (1), 5–6.

Davis, P. M. and Connolly, M. J. L. (2007) Institutional Repositories: evaluating the reasons for non-use of Cornell University's installation of DSpace, *D-Lib Magazine*, **13** (3/4), www.dlib.org/dlib/march07/davis/03davis.html.

Dobreva, M. and Chowdhury, S. (2010) A User-Centric Evaluation of the Europeana Digital Library, 12th International Conference on Asia-Pacific Digital Libraries: Gold Coast, Australia, 21–25 June. In Chowdhury, G., Koo, C., Hunter, J. (eds), *Role of Digital Libraries in a Time of Global Change*, Lecture Notes in Computer Science, **6102**, 148–57.

European Commission (2014) *Research and Innovation*, http://ec.europa.eu/research/science-society/index.cfm?fuseaction=public.topic&id =1294&lang=1.

Feather, J. (2013) *The Information Society: a study of continuity and change*, 6th edn, Facet Publishing.

Grigson, A. (2009) Evaluating Business Models for E-books Through Usage Data Analysis: a case study from the University of Westminster, *Journal of Electronic Resources Librarianship*, **21** (1), 62–74.

Hargittai, E. (2010) Digital Na(t)ives? Variation in internet skills and uses among members of the 'net generation', *Sociological Inquiry*, **80** (1), 92–113.

Hargreaves, I. (2011) *Digital Opportunity: a review of intellectual property and growth*, www.ipo.gov.uk/ipreview-finalreport.pdf.

Hooper, R. and Lynch, R. (2012) *Copyright Works: streamlining copyright licensing for the digital age*, www.ipo.gov.uk/dce-report-phase2.pdf.

Ingwersen, P. (1996) Cognitive Perspectives of Information Retrieval Interaction: elements of a cognitive IR theory, *Journal of Documentation*, **52** (1), 3–50.

Internet World Stats (2013) *Internet Usage Statistics: the internet big picture – world internet users and population stats*, www.internetworldstats.com/stats.htm.

Jacobs, N., Amber, T. and McGregor, A. (2008) Institutional Repositories in the UK: the JISC approach, *Library Trends*, **57** (2), 124–41.

Jisc (2009) *National E-books Observatory Project: key findings and recommendations*, Joint Information Systems Committee, www.jisce-booksproject.org/.

Jisc (2011) *UK's Open Access Full-Text Search Engine to Aid Research*, Joint Information Systems Committee, www.jisc.ac.uk/news/stories/2011/09/openaccess.aspx.

Lamothe, A. R. (2013) Factors Influencing the Usage of an Electronic Book Collection: size of the e-book collection, the student population, and the faculty population, *College & Research Libraries*, **74** (1), 39–59.

Liew, C. L. (2012) Towards Socially Inclusive Digital Libraries. In Chowdhury, G. G. and Foo, S. (eds), *Digital Libraries and Information Access: research perspectives*, Facet Publishing, 97–111.

Liu, X. and Chen, H. (2013) AZDrugMiner: an information extraction system for mining patient-reported adverse drug events in online patient forums. In Kou, W., Yesha, Y. and Tan, C. J. (eds), *Electronic Commerce Technologies: Second International Symposium, ISEC 2001, Hong Kong, China, April 26–28, 2001, Proceedings*, Lecture Notes in Computer Science, **2040**, 134–50.

MacDonald, R. (2011) Starting, Strengthening, and Managing Institutional Repositories, *Electronic Library*, **29** (4), 553–4.

Martin, K. and Quan-Haase, A. (2013) Are E-books Replacing Print Books? Tradition, serendipity, and opportunity in the adoption and use of e-books for historical research and teaching, *Journal of the American Society for Information Science and Technology*, **64** (5), 1016–28.

McLure, M. and Hoseth, A. (2012) Patron-driven E-book Use and Users' E-book Perceptions: a snapshot, *Collection Building*, **31** (4), 136–47.

Milne, D. and Witten, I. (2013) An Open-source Toolkit for Mining Wikipedia, *Artificial Intelligence*, **194**, 222–39.

Nicholas, D., Rowlands, I., Clark, D., Huntington, P., Jamali, H. R. and Ollé, C. (2008)

UK Scholarly E-book Usage: a landmark survey, *Aslib Proceedings: New Information Perspectives*, **60** (4), 311–34.

Nicholas, D., Clark, D., Rowlands, I. and Jamali, H. R. (2013) Information On the Go: a case study of Europeana mobile users, *Journal of the American Society for Information Science and Technology*, **64** (7), 1311–22.

NIH (n.d.) NIH Public Access Policy Details, National Institutes of Health, http://publicaccess.nih.gov/policy.htm.

ONS (2013) *Statistical bulletin: internet access quarterly update*, Office for National Statistics, Q1 2013, www.ons.gov.uk/ons/rel/rdit2/internet-access-quarterly-update/2013-q1/stb-ia-q1-2013.html.

Pei, C., Yan, L. and Siew, L. (2009) On the Design Preferences for E-books, *IETE Technical Review*, **26** (3) 213–22.

Peters, D. and Lossau, N. (2011) DRIVER: building a sustainable infrastructure for global repositories, *Electronic Library*, **29** (2), 249–60.

RCUK (n.d.) RCUK Policy on Open Access, Research Councils UK, www.rcuk.ac.uk/research/outputs/.

Rowlands, I., Nicholas, D., Williams, P., Huntington, P., Fieldhouse, M. and Gunter, B. (2008) The Google Generation: the information behaviour of the researcher of the future, *Aslib Proceedings*, **60** (4), 290–310.

Shelburne, W. A. (2009) E-book Usage in an Academic Library: user attitudes and behaviours, *Library Collections, Acquisitions, & Technical Services*, **33**, 59–72.

St Jean, B., Rieh, S. Y., Yakel, E. and Markey, K. (2011) Unheard Voices: institutional repository end-users, *College & Research Libraries*, **72** (1), 21–42.

Suleman, H. (2007) Digital Libraries without Databases: the Bleek and Lloyd Collection. In Kovacs, L., Fuhr, N. and Meghini, C. (eds), *Proceedings of Research and Advanced Technology for Digital Libraries*, 11th European Conference, 16–19 September, Budapest, Hungary, 392–403.

Suleman, H. (2012) Design and Architecture of Digital Libraries. In Chowdhury, G. G. and Foo, S. (eds), *Digital Libraries and Information Access: research perspectives*, Facet Publishing, 13–28.

Suleman, H., Bowes, M., Hirst, M. and Subrun, S. (2010) Hybrid Online-Offline Collections. In *Proceedings of the Annual Conference of the South African Institute for Computer Scientists and Information Technologists (SAICSIT 2010)*, Bela Bela, South Africa, 11–13 October, ACM Press.

United Nations (1987) *Our Common Future: report of the World Commission on Environment and Development*, Brundtland Report, www.un-documents.net/wced-ocf.htm.

United Nations (2013) *Bridging Knowledge and Capacity Gaps for Sustainability Transition: a framework for action*, UN Office for Sustainable Development, 8 March,

http://sustainabledevelopment.un.org/content/documents/1681Framework%20for%2
0Action.pdf.

United Nations General Assembly (2012) *The Future We Want*, resolution adopted by the
General Assembly, A/RES/66/288, 11 September, http://daccess-dds-ny.un.org/
doc/UNDOC/GEN/N11/476/10/PDF/N1147610.pdf?OpenElement.

Wacholder, N. (2008) How Should Users Access the Content of Digital Books?,
Proceedings of the International Conference on Information and Knowledge Management, 37–9.

Walters, W. H. (2013) E-books in Academic Libraries: challenges for discovery and
access, *Serials Review*, **39** (2), 97–104.

Wellcome Trust (2013) Open Access Policy: position statement in support of open and
unrestricted access to published research, www.wellcome.ac.uk/About-
us/Policy/Policy-and-position-statements/WTD002766.htm.

Wilson, T. (2009) On User Studies and Information Needs, *Journal of Documentation*,
62 (6), 658–70.

Witten, I. (2011) *Data Mining: practical machine learning tools and techniques*, 3rd edn,
Morgan Kaufmann.

Printed vs digital content and sustainability issues

Introduction

Libraries are social institutions; they aim to provide their members and others in society with easy and equitable access to knowledge. For many years, libraries have collected, organized and managed information resources so users can discover and access information as and when they need it. However, of late ICTs, and especially the internet, web and social networking technologies, have revolutionized the information industry, the information marketplace and consequently the information services sector. Conventional publishers are not the only channels now through which authors and institutions can create information sources, and similarly conventional library and information services are not the only gateways for people to gain access to information. There are various new players in the information services sector, ranging from a myriad of web search engine services to numerous specialized web-based information services, digital libraries and repositories. Side by side the new technologies have also brought a number of changes to typical library and information services. For example, many printed information resources have been replaced by their digital counterparts, and sometimes print and digital formats exist side by side; many analogue information resources have been converted to digital formats through massive digitization programmes; full texts of many books and journals are now searchable through a variety of search services that are outside the conventional library and information services sector; a variety of options is now available for creation and management of user-generated information in different forms; and so on. These changes are taking place very rapidly and have implications for the long-term sustainability of library and information services in general, and scholarly information systems and services in particular.

This chapter looks at the environmental costs of print-based library and information services. Other related issues, such as legal issues and open access policies and their implications for the sustainability of information systems and services are examined in Chapters 7 to 10.

Estimating the carbon footprint of printed content

Many researchers have attempted to estimate the carbon footprint of printed books (Borggren, Moberg and Finnveden, 2011; Enroth, 2009; Kozac, 2003) and journals (Lukovitz, 2009; Reed Elsevier, n.d.). Some of these studies were undertaken mainly to compare the GHG emissions from printed books and digital books or web-based content or teaching materials (Enroth, 2009; Moberg, Borggren and Finnveden, 2011; Ritch, 2009), while others compared the carbon footprint of books sold through traditional bookstores and online bookstores (Williams and Tagami, 2003). All these studies used the lifecycle assessment method (ISO 14040:2006) to determine the carbon footprint of printed books, but their results vary significantly, for example:

- The Babcock Management School report estimates that 10.2 kg of CO_2e is generated by each printed book over its lifetime (Blueskymodel.org, 2008).
- A Cleantech report estimates that an equivalent of 7.46 kg of CO_2e is generated by each printed book over its lifetime (Ritch, 2009).
- Kozac's (2003) study estimates that a book produces 6.3 kg of CO_2e over its lifetime.
- Wells et al. (2012) state that the carbon footprint of paperbacks produced in the USA and printed in Canada was 2.71 kg CO_2e per book.

Some researchers have compared the energy and environmental costs of print vs online newspapers, showing that reading newspapers online is more environmentally friendly than reading them in print (Moberg, Johansson and Finnveden, 2007; Moberg et al., 2010). Most studies comparing the energy costs of printed books with those read digitally on e-book readers have noted that e-book readers are more environmentally friendly when they are used frequently (Moberg, Borggren and Finnveden, 2011; Ritch, 2009). Surprisingly, Enroth found that the environmental impact of a web-based electronic teaching aid can be 10 to 30 times higher (depending on whether laptops or desktops are used to access materials) than printed textbooks (Enroth, 2009). There may be several reasons for this surprising result. First, the CO_2e emissions calculated for a printed book in this study was significantly lower than in the other studies: about 0.6 kg per book as opposed to 2.1 kg per book in Borggren, Moberg and Finnveden's (2011) study, 2.71 kg CO_2e per book in Wells et al.'s (2012) study, 6.3 kg in

Kozac's (2003) study, 7.46 kg in Cleantech's study (Ritch, 2009) and 10.2 kg in the Babcock Graduate School of Management study (Blueskymodel.org, 2008). Enroth (2009) cautioned that the results should be considered in the light of the types of teaching aids used, and their benefits, in comparison with a specific textbook.

None of the studies considered the environmental costs associated with the storage, handling, management and use of printed books through libraries, and especially the environmental costs of long-term storage and preservation of printed content in libraries. This is an area that needs to be researched because a typical library procures a large volume and variety of books, produced in different countries with different kinds of paper, manufacturing and transportation technologies, different water and power sources, and so on. A significant amount of energy is required to process, handle, store and manage books in libraries. Often library storage of books and other reading materials requires a considerable amount of energy because a constant temperature and humid condition has to be maintained throughout the year, and this can be for several decades over the lifetime of a typical library book.

Chowdhury (2012) estimates the carbon footprint of printed books in some Australian and New Zealand university libraries using the figures from the Cleantech report (Ritch, 2009) and the Babcock Management School report (Blueskymodel.org, 2008). These figures are higher than those proposed in other studies, but these higher figures were chosen on purpose because in countries like Australia and New Zealand most books are imported from Europe and America. Therefore a significant amount of GHG emission is caused for transportation of the books, and consequently the overall GHG emission figure becomes significantly high.

The environmental impact of printed books

The printed book market throughout the world is large but the e-book market is steadily growing. According to Bowker market research, in 2012, 28% of all book purchases in the USA and 13% of book purchases in the UK were in e-book format (Bowker, 2013). According to a report by the UK Publishers Association, 149,800 new titles were published in 2011 in the UK and digital book sales increased to £243 million, an increase of 54% on sales in 2010 (Publishers Association, 2012). The report notes that digital sales stand at 8% of overall book market sales – print and digital together.

As observed earlier, the carbon footprint of an individual book varies depending on a number of factors, such as the quality of paper, size of the book and binding, country in which the book was produced, and sources of raw materials and energy, and the overall carbon footprint from printed book publishing could be significant. For example, according to Bowker annual statistics (Bowker, 2012), 4,134,519 individual book titles (new titles, editions and reprints) were produced in the USA in 2011. Assuming there were 1000 copies of each title, over 4 billion books were produced in total. If 4 billion books were published in the USA in a year, it may be estimated that:

- even if all the books were paperbacks and produced in the USA and printed in Canada, as in the Wells et al. (2012) study, at around 2.7 kg per book for 4 billion titles the overall GHG emissions would be 10.8 million tonnes of CO_2e
- taking the higher rate of carbon footprint estimated in the Babcock Management School report (Blueskymodel.org, 2008), at around 10.2 kg of CO_2e per book, the total emission for 4 billion books would be 40.8 million tonnes of CO_2e.

In fact the actual figure is somewhere between the two extremes shown above, but whichever estimation is chosen, the overall carbon footprint of printed books just for the USA could range between 11 and 40 million tonnes of CO_2e. The IPCC Climate Change 2007 report shows that the global GHG emission figure was 49 $GtCO_2e$ (or 49 billion tonnes) (IPCC, 2007). According to the US EPA, in 2008, total US GHG emissions were 6,956 million tonnes of CO_2 (EPA, 2010). By taking these emission figures, one can estimate that the GHG emissions only from book production in the USA could be 0.16–0.6% of the annual GHG emissions for the entire country, or equivalent to 0.022–0.08% emissions of the entire world. To put this in another perspective, this would be equivalent to the annual emissions from 110 to 400 typical power stations (based on the emission figures from the power stations in the UK (CARMA, 2013). There are additional environmental costs for library storage and preservation, and so on.

It may be assumed that a significant proportion of the books published in any country are used for academic and research purposes. So, moving to a digital information service model, where books are purchased and accessed only in digital form, can help publishers and institutions reduce a significant amount of CO_2e emissions generated for production, distribution, and storage and maintenance of printed books in libraries. However, digital books and the ICT infrastructure required to use them also generate a significant amount of GHG. This is discussed later in this chapter.

The environmental impact of printed journals

Since the appearance of the first e-journal *New Horizons in Adult Education* in 1987 (Medeiros, 2009), the journal industry and journal use around the world have changed significantly. Most higher education institution libraries now have a large collection of journals that are available in digital form. Some of these journals are also collected in print form as part of a deal with the publisher or aggregator. Side by side a significant number of digital-only journals are now available, and most users in academic libraries are now used to accessing and using most of their journals in digital form. Ulrichs.com lists a total of 84,013 online serials, 38,029 online academic or scholarly journals, and 5,262 open access journals.

So, further research is needed to generate figures and benchmarks to calculate the carbon footprints of all kinds of books. This is a challenging task because the book production industry is distributed over many countries in the world, and often finished books need to be transported over a long distance before they reach libraries or users. Estimation of GHG emission figures for journals is even more challenging. Journals have a number of characteristics that are different from books, which makes estimation of their carbon footprint data more complex. Each journal has a different frequency, size, volume (number of pages), quality (text and high quality images and plates) and distribution figures (some are available only through purchase or subscription while others are given to each member of an institution as part of the membership benefits). Journals are often published in one country and distributed – often by air to avoid a time lag – to subscribing libraries around the world. Often print journals also have an online counterpart, and both are sold as a bundle to libraries. Libraries may store journals in a bound volume for a much longer period than conventional textbooks or monographs are stored, with consequent long-term storage energy and environmental costs.

Because of these and various other factors, very few studies have so far been conducted to estimate the carbon footprint of journals. A study commissioned by a leading journal publisher, Reed Elsevier, noted that the total carbon footprint used in producing the journal *Fuel* in 2007 was 'just over 40 tonnes of carbon dioxide' (Reed Elsevier, n.d.). The calculations were based on the following stages:

1 Preparation in Kidlington
2 Typesetting in India
3 Printing in and distribution from the UK (hard copy only)
4 Online hosting in the USA (electronic only)
5 End-user reading and printing.

For the production and distribution (stages 1 to 4) based on two year's data (2006 and 2007) the study noted that 'the largest impacts came from staff commuting and business travel for Kidlington (UK), where the majority of the *Fuel* staff work. Other significant impacts came from the utilities for typesetting, paper for printing, delivering hard copies and energy for hosting online content' (Reed Elsevier, n.d.). This study did not find enough reliable data to model user and use behaviour (stage 5) and how it affects the carbon footprint. This is a difficult area indeed, and if the journals are stored in higher education institution libraries, a significant carbon footprint figure needs to be added to the production figures, the emission figures from the energy costs required to maintain, bind and store print journals over a relatively long term. Later recommendations are made for further research to develop a methodology to calculate the carbon footprint of journals, especially the storage and maintenance costs in libraries. The following section looks at the GHG emission from printed journals based on the figure of 40 tonnes of CO_2 per journal.

Chowdhury (2012) estimates that at around 40 tonnes per journal, 36,800 scholarly journal titles would generate an equivalent of 1.47 million tonnes of CO_2. This is a very rough figure, and in effect the total carbon footprint figure for all the print journals acquired by libraries is much higher than this because many journals have more pages and issues or greater frequency than *Fuel*, which was used to estimate these figures.

Factors responsible for GHG emissions from printed and digital content

Table 6.1 provides a quick overview of the various stages of the lifecycle of printed and digital content and the corresponding factors that cause GHG emissions.

While comparing the environmental costs of printed and digital content, one may note that the environmental costs for production of content – typesetting, formatting, desktop publishing, and so on – is the same for printed and digital content because in today's world almost every kind of content is produced digitally irrespective of whether it is distributed in digital or analogue format. Hence, the main differences in the carbon footprint between printed and digital content appear from the production of physical content, distribution and access or use. For printed content, for example books and journals, most environmental costs come from paper, production and printing, and distribution. According to some estimates (for example, Enroth, 2009), over 90% of CO_2 emissions come from paper, production and distribution of books, while the rest comes from disposal and waste management costs.

Printed content may also have hidden or indirect environmental costs arising

Table 6.1 Processes and factors for GHG emissions for printed and digital content

Process	Printed books or journals	E-content: e-books, e-journals
Content preparation	Content preparation, digital version or desktop publishing	Content preparation, digital version or desktop publishing
Paper manufacture	Raw materials (forestry), transportation of raw materials, pulp and paper manufacture – infrastructure, energy, water and waste, transportation and storage of finished paper and boards (for binding)	Nil
Printing	Raw materials, printing and binding, storage and transportation	Nil
Distribution of final product	Transportation to warehouses, retailers and libraries; return or pulping of unsold items	Nil
Storage	Library storage – multiple copies; local or central storage; long-term storage	Content and index on multiple servers Replacement and disposal of ICT or network equipment
Access or use	Personal collection and use; library acquisition, processing, shelving, on-site use, circulation – issue and return – energy costs for travel, maintenance	Access: search and retrieval Online reading or download – data transfer Content and index updates
Reading device	No special reading devices; library reading room facilities	General multipurpose devices – desktop or laptop computers; mobile devices Special devices – e-book readers
Preservation or disposal	Donation or circulation or disposal; waste management	Digital preservation Replacement and disposal of ICT or network equipment

from the library storage and maintenance of printed materials, circulation and use of content. For example, multiple copies of books and bound volumes of back issues of journals are stored in libraries, incurring energy costs for storage and maintenance. Similarly, there are costs associated with the disposal of printed content. Such disposal costs may arise from incinerating or sending to landfill unsold books from bookstores or warehouse, and books and journals discarded by libraries and individuals at the end of the lifecycle. The amount of CO_2 produced by a single book or journal, as shown earlier in the chapter, may increase significantly when they are transported over long distances, leading to increased distribution costs between production facilities and libraries or users. For example, the environmental cost of a printed book or a journal is significantly higher for a user – individual or library – in countries like Australia and New Zealand than for a user in Europe and North America simply because a printed book or journal has to travel several thousand miles from its production or distribution facility to users in Australasia.

While moving to a digital format may reduce the carbon footprint of publications at the production stage, this does not necessarily guarantee an overall reduction in the environmental impact of information services. There are additional energy and environmental costs of accessing digital information online, and moreover digital format makes it easy, and often tempting, for the end-user to print, which has environmental consequences. These issues are discussed later in this chapter.

Green library buildings

The concept of green or sustainable library buildings has received much attention over the past few years. With various government and institutional measures and initiatives, many libraries have focused on the green library building concept by using standard green ratings to evaluate their current status or have built new green buildings by meeting different criteria for sustainable building design and obtaining a green certificate. Examples of green library building rating systems include Leadership in Energy and Environmental Design (LEED) verification of green buildings under the US Green Building Council (2005), the Green Star Education rating system of the Green Building Council Australia (2013), and Display Energy Certificates (DEC) of the UK Green Building Council (2013). These rating systems consider several factors. For example, the LEED rating is awarded on a 100 point scale, recognizing performance in five major areas: sustainable site selection and development, water efficiency, energy and atmosphere, materials and resources, and indoor environmental quality (Barnes, 2012).

Many recent research papers have discussed different aspects of sustainable library buildings. Barnes (2012) provides an overview of green building technologies and practices in order to illustrate how public libraries can use them as tools to teach their communities about sustainability and foster behaviour change. Some researchers examine the sustainable design of specific public or university libraries. For example,

- Edwards (2011) looks at sustainability issues in the context of public and university library buildings built over the past decade with some reference to the building under construction.
- Hawke (2010) discusses the design features of public libraries in several

countries: San Francisco Public Library, Eugene Public Library, Seattle Public Library, Vancouver Public Library, Surrey Public Library, Calgary Public Library, Winnipeg Public Library, Chicago Public Library, Fayetteville Public Library, Newcastle Public Library and the City of Sydney Public Library.

- Brodie (2012) describes the sustainable design of Macquarie University library in Australia.
- Cohen, Bordass and Leaman (2007) investigate the design of library buildings in two cities: Visby in Sweden and Gloucester in England.
- Linden, Reilly and Herzog (2012) report on research that aims to design a methodology for monitored and risk-managed shutdown of air handling units during unoccupied hours in selected spaces of a library building without compromising the quality of the preservation environment, which in turn would save energy while maintaining the preservation and conservation requirements of the library.

Edwards (2011) argues that an architectural approach to the 21st century library is returning to the roots of the modernist library found in Scandinavia with its emphasis on high levels of daylight, natural materials, social harmony and contact with nature. The overall goal of the green or sustainable library building initiatives is to acquire green building certifications (Hardesty, 2011) and reduce overall energy consumptions costs; for example, Brodie (2012) notes that the thermal energy storage tank used as part of the sustainable building design of Macquarie University in Australia can lead to a 17% reduction in peak energy demand and an overall 25% reduction in annual GHG emissions.

While these research studies show that green and sustainable designs are useful in reducing the energy and environmental costs of libraries, so far there has been very little research comparing the economic and environmental costs and benefits of print versus digital information, and also whether and how a shift from print to digital content can influence – positively or negatively – the social sustainability of information services.

GHG emissions from digital content creation and access

There are environmental costs relating to digital content's storage, processing and access, which need to be considered when comparing the environmental costs of printed and digital content (Chowdhury, 2010). Factors associated with the environmental costs of a digital information service were shown in Figure 4.1.

Features associated with access to digital content that need to be considered when calculating its environmental impact include the following:

- *Content creation in digital form*: Nowadays any content is almost invariably created in digital form irrespective of whether the end product is delivered and used in print or digital form. Therefore, the environmental cost for comparison purposes (between printed and digital versions) may be ignored. However, if the end product is designed for digital access and use, then standard metadata and formats need to be used, which should be embedded within the production process. This will not incur any significant additional environmental costs.
- *Storage and maintenance of digital content*: Certain environmental costs are associated with the storage and maintenance of digital content and they have to be factored in when calculating the overall environmental impact of digital materials. This calls for further research, which should take into account such factors as the size of the digital collection, where and in how many sites the digital content is stored, how often the content and hardware and software maintenance or replacement takes place, how efficient the overall ICT infrastructure (green ICT) is, and so on. Fortunately lessons can be learned from the significant amount of current research into green ICT, cloud computing, virtualization, and so on (Baliga et al., 2011; Cervone, 2010; Mell and Grance, 2011). While there are some environmental costs associated with the storage of digital content, it is expected that the overall environmental costs for data storage will be amortized with the overall environmental costs of data storage for the entire business – companies, universities, and so on. This is discussed in more detail in Chapter 9.
- *Access costs*: Accessing digital content certainly has a carbon footprint, which depends on a number of factors such as where and in how many places the content is stored, whether simultaneous searches are conducted on one or more sites, and how efficient the search and retrieval techniques are. Specific data for search and retrieval of huge volumes of digital information are not available, but the environmental costs of a Google search, or the overall energy and environmental costs of the internet, discussed in Chapter 4, provide an idea. This is examined further in Chapter 10.
- *Data transfer costs*: There is an environmental cost associated with the transfer of digital content from a storage server to users, which can be significantly reduced by optimizing the use of computing and networking capacities and automatically controlling and diversifying these resources using green ICT and cloud computing technologies (Baliga et al., 2011).
- *Use or reading costs*: No specific device is needed to read printed materials, and the only environmental costs associated with this activity come from energy costs, if any, associated with the reading space and facilities, such as lights, air

conditioning or heating. However, digital books always require a special reading device, which uses energy to run. Research is needed to compare the environmental efficiency of various reading devices such as the Amazon Kindle, Sony e-book reader, iPad, and various tablets and laptops.

- *Printing costs*: As discussed earlier, digital format often makes it easier for end-users to print content locally, and sometimes more than one copy of the same document is printed at different times. Energy and environmental costs of such printing activities should include the environmental costs of printers, ink cartridges, paper, and so on, on top of socket energy costs for the printer.
- *Digital preservation costs*: While it is the responsibility of specific users – individuals or libraries – to store and preserve printed content for future use, digital content can be stored and preserved centrally for future access by anyone. Details of the environmental costs of digital preservation are not yet available, but some issues and directions in this regard were addressed in Chapter 4.

Summary

Printed information sources generate a significant amount of GHG during their creation and throughout their lifecycle, for example, for transportation and handling, storage and disposal, and so on. Several studies have estimated the carbon footprint of printed books, but the figures vary significantly because of the different objectives and methodologies used in these studies. The carbon footprint of books also differs according to the type of paper, binding and size of books; the country in which they are produced; the sources of raw materials, water and energy used in their production; the distance and mode of transportation of the raw materials; and printing, storage and transportation of the printed books. Overall, the amount of GHG produced by printed books is significant and consequently they have some influence on the environmental sustainability of information systems and services. The cumulative environmental costs of library storage and handling of printed content can also be high. Although green library building designs can reduce the overall environmental costs of library and information services, further research is needed to estimate the environmental costs of storage and handling of different types of analogue content. Similarly research is also needed to find a way to reduce such environmental costs of printed content.

While replacing printed content with their digital counterpart may reduce GHG emissions and thus can promote environmental sustainability of information services, digital content and digital information services also have some environmental impact. It has been noted that the current copyright laws and digital rights management laws are not appropriate for dealing with digital content seamlessly on the internet. Some recent changes proposed by specific expert committees and study groups such as the Hargreaves review and the subsequent feasibility study commissioned by the UK Government (Hargreaves, 2011; Hooper and Lynch, 2012) may help us achieve an eco-sociological balance in digital information systems and services.

References

Baliga, J., Ayre, R. W. A., Hinton, K. and Tucker, R. S. (2011) Green Cloud Computing: balancing energy in processing, storage, and transport, *Proceedings of the IEEE*, **99** (1), January,
http://ieeexplore.ieee.org/stamp/stamp.jsp?arnumber=05559320.

Barnes, L. (2012) Green Buildings as Sustainability Education Tools, *Library Hi Tech*, **30** (3), 397–407.

Blueskymodel.org (2008) *Pounds of CO_2 Per Pound of Stuff, case study of the Babcock School*,
www.stewartmarion.com/carbon-footprint/html/carbon-footprint-stuff.html.

Borggren, C., Moberg, Å. and Finnveden, G. (2011) Books from an Environmental Perspective, Part 1: environmental impacts of paper books sold in traditional and internet bookshops, *International Journal of Life Cycle Assessment*, **16**, 138–47.

Bowker (2012) *New Book Titles and Editions, 2002–2011*,
www.bowker.com/assets/downloads/products/isbn_output_2002–2011.pdf.

Bowker (2013) E-reading Habits Drive Market Share Growth of e-Retailers, says New Study from Bowker, 18 March,
www.bowker.com/en-US/aboutus/press_room/2013/pr_03182013.shtml.

Brodie, M. (2012) Building the Sustainable Library at Macquarie University, *Australian Academic & Research Libraries*, March, **43** (1), 4–16.

CARMA (2013) Carbon Monitoring for Action, United Kingdom,
http://carma.org/region/detail/2635167.

Cervone, H. F. (2010) An Overview of Virtual and Cloud Computing, *OCLC Systems and Services*, **26** (3), 162–5.

Chowdhury, G. G. (2010) Carbon Footprint of the Knowledge Sector: what's the future?, *Journal of Documentation*, **66** (6), 934–46.

Chowdhury, G. G. (2012) How Digital Information Services Can Reduce Greenhouse Gas Emissions, *Online Information Review*, **36** (4), 489–506.

Cohen, R., Bordass, W. and Leaman, A. (2007) Evaluations and Comparisons of the Achieved Energy and Environmental Performance of Two Library Buildings in England and Sweden, *ASHRAE Transactions*, **113** (2), 14–26.

Edwards, B. W. (2011) Sustainability as a Driving Force in Contemporary Library

Design, *Library Trends*, **60** (1), 190–214.

Enroth, M. (2009) Environmental Impact of Printed and Electronic Teaching Aids: a screening study focusing on fossil carbon dioxide emissions, *Advances in Printing and Media Technology*, **36**, www.ipex.org/files/learning_from_text_books.pdf.

EPA (2010) *Inventory of US Greenhouse Gas Emissions and Sinks: 1990–2008*, executive summary, Environment Protection Agency (US), http://epa.gov/climatechange/ emissions/downloads10/US-GHG-Inventory-2010_ExecutiveSummary.pdf.

Green Building Council Australia (2013) Rating Tools, www.gbca.org.au/green-star/rating-tools/.

Hardesty, L. (2011) The Environmental Sustainability of Academic Libraries, *Library Issues*, **32** (1), 1–4.

Hargreaves, I. (2011) *Digital Opportunity: a review of intellectual property and growth*, www.ipo.gov.uk/ipreview-finalreport.pdf.

Hawke, B. (2010) Sustainable Libraries: report back on a study visit to public libraries in the USA, Canada & Australia (August 2009), *New Zealand Library & Information Management Journal*, **52** (1), 24–40.

Hooper, R. and Lynch, R. (2012) *Copyright Works: streamlining copyright licensing for the digital age*, www.ipo.gov.uk/dce-report-phase2.pdf.

IPCC (2007) *IPCC Climate Change 2007: synthesis report*, Intergovernmental Panel on Climate Change, www.ipcc.ch/pdf/assessment-report/ar4/syr/ar4_syr.pdf.

ISO 14040:2006 *Environmental Management – Life Cycle Assessment – Principles and Framework*, International Organization for Standardization.

Kozac, G. (2003) *Printed Scholarly Books and E-Book Reading Devices: a comparative life cycle assessment of two book options*, Centre for Sustainable Systems, University of Michigan, http://css.snre.umich.edu/css_doc/CSS03-04.pdf.

Linden, J., Reilly, J. and Herzog, P. (2012) Research on Energy Savings Opportunities in University Libraries, *Library Hi Tech*, **30** (3), 384–96.

Lukovitz, K. (2009) Common Sense Sustainability: a look at how circulation and distribution fit into the sustainability equation and efforts to maximize eco and cost savings in these areas, *Audience Development*, 10 September, www.audiencedevelopment.com/2009/common+sense+sustainability.

Medeiros, N. (2009) The Birth, Growth and Supremacy of Electronic Journals as an Information Medium. In Jones, W. (ed.), *E-journals: access and management*, Routledge, 187–200.

Mell, P. and Grance, T. (2011) *The NIST Definition of Cloud Computing: recommendations of the National Institute of Standards and Technology*, http://csrc.nist.gov/publications/drafts/ 800-145/Draft-SP-800-145_cloud-definition.pdf.

Moberg, Å., Borggren, C. and Finnveden, G. (2011) Books from an Environmental Perspective, Part 2: e-books as an alternative to paper books, *International Journal of Life*

Cycle Assessment, **16**, 238–46.

Moberg, A., Johansson, M. and Finnveden, G. (2007) Screening Environmental Life Cycle Assessment of Printed, Internet-BASED and Tablet E-Paper Newspaper. In Enlund, N. and Lovrecek, M. (eds), *34th International Research Conference of Iarigai and International Association of Research Organization for the Information Media and Graphic Arts Industries*, Grenoble, France, 9–12 September, Advances in Printing Science and Technology, **34**, 419–29.

Moberg, Å., Borggren, C., Finnveden, G. and Tyskeng, S. (2010) Environmental Impacts of Electronic Invoicing, *Progress in Industrial Ecology*, **7**, 93–113.

The Publishers Association (2012) *Annual Report 2011*, www.publishers.org.uk.

Reed Elsevier (n.d.) *Footprinting Study of the Reed Elsevier Journal 'Fuel'*, www.reedelsevier.com/corporateresponsibility08/PDFFiles/fuel-footprint-study-exec-sum.pdf.

Ritch, E. (2009) *The Environmental Impact of Amazon's Kindle: executive brief*, Cleantech Group.

UK Green Building Council (2013) Sustainable Built Environment, www.ukgbc.org/.

US Green Building Council (2005) Introducing the New LEED Online, www.usgbc.org/DisplayPage.aspx?CategoryID=19.

Wells, J.-R., Boucher, J.-F., Laurent, A.-B. and Villeneuve, C. (2012) Carbon Footprint Assessment of a Paperback Book: can planned integration of deinked market pulp be detrimental to climate?, *Journal of Industrial Ecology*, **16** (2), 212–22.

Williams, E. and Tagami, T. (2003) Energy Use in Sales and Distribution via E-commerce and Conventional Retail: a case study of the Japanese book sector, *Journal of Industrial Ecology*, **6** (2), 99–114.

Open access models and the sustainability of information

Introduction

For centuries libraries have acquired and managed journals in order to provide their users with access to scholarly information. However, the price of journals has skyrocketed over the past few decades, making it increasingly difficult for libraries to maintain their journal subscription levels, which has affected users' access to scholarly information. Research shows that while libraries and higher education institutions have continued to struggle to keep up with the rising cost of scholarly publications, especially journals, journal publishers have continued to maintain, if not increase, their profit margins.

Chapter 3 explained how the open access movement emerged in the early 1990s with the establishment of the open archive known as arXiv.org (formerly xxx.lanl.gov) in order to provide free access to research and scholarly information in high-energy physics. The Santa Fe Convention in 1999, in which the Open Archives Initiative was launched, and subsequently the BOAI in 2001, brought about a new era in scholarly communications promising free access to scholarly information. Two models for open access emerged:

- *the gold route*, where the cost of publication would be recovered from authors and in return the resulting publications would be made available to everyone free of charge
- *the green route*, where the published papers would be made available to everyone free of charge after a certain period of time (called the embargo period).

The green route is based on the principle of self-archiving where authors are required to submit a final copy of their paper to a repository that can be accessed by everyone free of charge.

The overall goal of both routes to open access is to facilitate free access to scholarly information. However, this very mission of the open access initiatives is bound to bring forth a paradigm shift in the ways people access and use information, and in some cases how scholarly information is published. This in turn will significantly influence the information industry and information services sector, and thus the overall sustainability of information systems and services.

The implications of the green and gold open access routes on the sustainability of information systems and services are discussed in this chapter: open access policies of some funding bodies and their potential implications for the sustainability of scholarly information systems and services; green open access and its implications for the development of institutional repositories and their sustainability issues; and sustainability issues related to the gold open access and the funding mechanisms.

Open access policies of institutions and funding bodies

Research and funding bodies and institutions in many countries support the idea of open access, and have come up with specific open access policies. The European Commission recommends the following two options for open access:

- *gold open access*: where publishers make research papers accessible online immediately and researchers are eligible for reimbursement for article-processing charges from the Commission
- *green open access*: where researchers make their research papers available through an open access repository no later than six months after publication (or 12 months for articles in the social sciences and humanities).   Europa (2012)

UNESCO introduced an open access policy, which came to effect from 1 June 2013:

- UNESCO's Open Access Policy would grant an irrevocable worldwide right of access to copy, use, distribute, transmit, and make derivative works in any format within certain constraints.
- As one of the first steps, UNESCO will make these publications available online through a multilingual Repository.

UNESCO (2013)

The World Bank introduced a similar open access policy for all the works carried out by Bank staff members as part of their official duties and outside research funded by the Bank. The policy document defines the open access works of the World Bank as follows:

- For work carried out by Bank staff, the policy applies to manuscripts and all accompanying data sets (a) that result from research, analysis, economic and sector work, or development practice; (b) that have undergone peer review or have been otherwise vetted and approved for release to the public; and (c) for which internal approval for release is given on or after July 1, 2012.
- For external research funded by the Bank, for which funding was approved on or after July 1, 2012, the policy applies to the final report provided by the researchers to the funding unit within the Bank.

World Bank (2012)

The ARC has introduced an open access policy for ARC-funded research, which took effect from 1 January 2013. It requires that any publications arising from an ARC-supported research project must be deposited into an open access institutional repository within a 12-month period from the date of publication (ARC, 2013).

The open access policy of the US NIH requires that:

> all investigators funded by the NIH submit or have submitted for them to the National Library of Medicine's PubMed Central an electronic version of their final, peer-reviewed manuscripts upon acceptance for publication, to be made publicly available no later than 12 months after the official date of publication.

US NIH (2013)

The Wellcome Trust has introduced a similar open access policy guideline which:

> requires electronic copies of any research papers that have been accepted for publication in a peer-reviewed journal, and are supported in whole or in part by Wellcome Trust funding, to be made available through PubMed Central (PMC) and Europe PubMed Central (Europe PMC) as soon as possible and in any event within six months of the journal publisher's official date of final publication.

Wellcome Trust (2013)

RCUK has gone a step further and not only shown a preference for the gold open access route, but also proposed a funding mechanism for it. The policy document states:

- The policy applies to peer-reviewed research papers, which acknowledge Research Council funding, that are submitted for publication from 1st April 2013, and which are published in journals or conference proceedings (p.2)
- The RCUK Policy on Open Access aims to achieve immediate, unrestricted, on-line access to peer reviewed and published scholarly research papers, free of any access charge (p.2)
- The Research Councils UK (RCUK) policy supports both 'Gold' and 'Green' routes to Open Access, though RCUK has a preference for immediate Open Access with the maximum opportunity for re-use (p.1)
- Funding for Open Access arising from Research Council-supported research will be available through a block grant awarded directly to research organisations (p.1).

RCUK (2013)

The RCUK supports the idea of not only free access to research materials but also free re-use of research content:

> Our vision is for all users to be able to read published research papers in an electronic format and to search for and re-use (including download) the content of published research papers, both manually and using automated tools (such as those for text and data mining), provided that any such re-use is subject to full and proper attribution (p.2).

RCUK (2013)

Describing access provided to research papers produced using RCUK funding, the policy states,

> RCUK recognises a journal as being compliant with this policy if:

> The journal provides, via its own website, immediate and unrestricted access to the final published version of the paper, which should be made available using the Creative Commons Attribution (CC BY) licence. This may involve payment of an 'Article Processing Charge' (APC) to the publisher.
> Or,
> The journal consents to deposit of the final Accepted Manuscript in any repository, without restriction on non-commercial re-use and within a defined period. No APC will be payable to the publisher. In this latter case, RCUK will accept a delay of no more than six months between on-line publication and the final Accepted Manuscript becoming Open Access. In the case of papers in the arts, humanities and social sciences (which will mainly be funded by the AHRC [Arts & Humanities Research Council] and the ESRC [Economic and Social Research Council]), the maximum

embargo period will be twelve months. In some circumstances, where funding for APCs is unavailable during the transition period, longer embargo periods may be allowable (see section 3.6) (2).

RCUK (2013)

In a policy memorandum released in February 2013, the Office of Science and Technology Policy of the US Government directed all US federal agencies with more than US$100 million in R&D expenditure to develop plans to make the published results of federally funded research freely available to the public within one year of publication. It required researchers to better account for and manage the digital data resulting from federally funded scientific research (Stebbins, 2013).

Institutional repositories

One of the most significant outcomes of the green route to open access has been the establishment of several specialized open access digital libraries like PubMed Central, and thousands of institutional repositories. The first institutional repository in the UK was set up in Southampton in 2001 (Cullen and Chawner, 2011). The first institutional repository in the USA was set up in 2002 at MIT 'as a new strategy that allows universities to apply serious, systematic leverage to accelerate changes taking place in scholarship and scholarly communication' (Lynch, 2003). Over the past decade new technologies, software and standards have emerged that facilitate the creation and management of institutional repositories. Details of such developments are available on the Open Archives Initiative website (www.openarchives.org/) and in numerous publications.

In the UK, Jisc has played a key role in promoting the development, management and use of institutional repositories (Jacobs, Amber and McGregor, 2008; Jisc, 2011a, 2011b, 2011c). The OpenDOAR database at the University of Nottingham (www.opendoar.org) records a significant worldwide growth in the number of repositories over the past few years, from just over 300 in mid-2006 to 2553 by the end of 2013. Typically these repositories hold a mix of journal articles, theses and dissertations, unpublished working papers, conference papers, books and book chapters, and multimedia and other audiovisual materials. Availability of research datasets is still not common in institutional repositories.

The total of over 2553 databases in the OpenDOAR database are from 2135 institutions from all over the world. Some organizations have two or more repositories, and over 20 in some cases. Out of the total 2553 repositories, 1810 are in English, the predominant language of content, followed by 319 in Spanish, 203 in German, 158 in French, 144 in Japanese, 134 in Portuguese, 107 in

Chinese, 80 in Polish, 76 in Italian, 51 in Norwegian, 50 each in Russian and Ukrainian, 46 in Swedish, 30 in Dutch, 29 in Greek, 26 in Arabic, and so on. Most large institutions effectively hold all subjects in their repositories (1522 out of 2553); specialist institutions (e.g. engineering and agricultural colleges) and disciplinary repositories only cover a few subjects, for example, only 40 repositories contain materials in civil engineering, 50 in electrical engineering, 61 in mechanical engineering, 86 in management and planning, and 133 in arts and humanities.

The development of institutional repositories has not been uniform in different parts of the world. Out of the 2604 repositories in the OpenDOAR database 440 (16.9%) repositories are in the USA, 221 (8.5%) in the UK, 169 (6.5%) in Germany, 144 (5.5%) in Japan, 111 (4.3%) in Spain, 84 (3.2%) in Poland, 83 (3.2%) in Brazil, 82 (3.1%) in France, 75 (2.5%) in Italy, 69 (2.6%) in India, and 43.2% in the rest of the world. Content of the repositories varies. For example, 1742 out of 2553 repositories contain journal articles, 1387 contain theses and dissertations, 919 contain book chapters and sections, 916 contain unpublished works, 882 contain conference and workshop papers, 606 contain multimedia and audiovisual materials, 430 contain bibliographic references, 95 contain datasets, 80 contain patents, 38 contain software, and so on. The majority of institutional repositories – 41.5% – use DSpace software, 14.5% use EPrints, 4.7% use Digital Commons and 2.8% use OPUS; over 36% use other (or unknown) software. Only 8.1% of the repositories have a defined preservation policy.

Many researchers believe that institutional repositories have not grown as fast as they should have for various reasons, including:

- lack of understanding and commitment of faculty members regarding participation in the initiative (an issue of social sustainability)
- various challenges associated with faculty members and repository managers understanding and managing copyright issues (an issue of social and economic sustainability)
- lack of a continuous funding stream to support the development, management and preservation of content and data at institutional level, exacerbated by rapidly changing technologies and standards (an issue of economic sustainability and technological or environmental sustainability)
- lack of proper and acceptable evidence of better citation and academic rewards resulting from institutional repositories (an issue of social and economic sustainability)
- the additional workload on faculty members associated with the process of self-archiving of information (an issue of economic and social sustainability).

Many institutional repositories contain open access (non-commercial) and unpublished content, but progress in introducing open access policies is restricted to a large extent by the prevailing practices for assessment of research output and social or institutional recognition of open access publications. Major national research assessment exercises like the Research Excellence Framework (REF) in the UK and Excellence of Research in Australia (ERA) are still very much guided by the assessment of quality of research in journals and conferences with high impact factors. Although it is generally recognized that open access research output is more widely accessed, and therefore receives more citations, than research output that is not available on open access, there is still a lack of evidence as to how the academic and research community worldwide perceives the research impact of open access output compared with commercially produced journals and conferences. Anecdotal evidence shows that journal impact factors and the reputation of journal publishers still play a major role in the academic recognition of scholarly output in academic promotions, grant applications, and so on. This is a major factor affecting the social sustainability of open access information and open scholarship.

The implications of institutional repositories

While currently each individual institution takes on the stewardship of its repository, some specific services now facilitate access across a range of repositories, such as OpenDOAR, discussed earlier in this chapter. Some national bodies are promoting one-stop access to all the institutional repositories in a country, for example the CORE project from Jisc (2011a, 2011b, 2011c) and the DRIVER project (Peters and Lossau, 2011). Various tools and protocols like SWORD (Allinson, François and Lewis, 2008; Lewis, de Castro and Jones, 2012) have emerged to facilitate the interoperable deposit of resources into repositories. Services like OpenDOAR allow users to search across a large number of institutional repositories, and thereby facilitate free access to the scholarly and research output of several countries.

With the appearance of new institutional repositories and their integration with existing repositories, it is possible not only to provide access to a large international pool of scholarly output, but also to produce a variety of business intelligence reports showing who uses what, how frequently, for what purpose, and so on. This can facilitate other kinds of research ranging from linking of data and research to semantically linking scholarly output and integrating such semantic links with social networks, thereby creating a semantic network of digital data and content. A number of sustainability issues are associated with green open access and the resulting institutional repositories.

The economic sustainability of institutional repositories

A study commissioned by Jisc in the UK suggested that there are potential economic savings for universities where research output is made available on open access. If universities in the UK continue to pay journal subscriptions, as they do now, and also make their research output available through open access repositories, the amount of saving for universities, accrued from increased efficiencies in research and library handling processes, could range from £0.1 million to £1.32 million per annum, though there are costs associated with running institutional repositories. The Jisc study further noted that:

- annual operating costs for institutional repositories, including the cost of depositing items, range from around £26,000 to almost £210,000
- the cost of depositing a single article varies from around £6.50 to £15.40, and the annual cost of depositing into a repository all articles produced by each university ranges from just over £4,000 to over £75,000.   Swan (2010)

The costs of institutional repositories vary significantly depending on the size and nature of the universities, their research income and activities, the number of research papers produced per year, and so on. Even if one takes an average of these two extremes – an average of £135,000 per annum to run an institutional repository – the total costs for 166 higher education institutions would be £22.4 million per year, which is nearly 15% of the annual journal subscription budget of UK universities, estimated to be £150 million (Finch, 2012).

The overall cost of managing institutional repositories is higher when digital preservation costs are included. These are additional costs on top of article-processing charges proposed by the RCUK gold open access policy. Thus there are three parallel streams of cost:

- journal subscription costs (assuming that universities continue to subscribe to journals)
- costs of article-processing charges (for gold open access)
- institutional repository costs (for green open access).

These issues, and especially how these costs can be reduced, are discussed in the next chapter.

The social sustainability of institutional repositories

The social benefits of open access are enormous because it promotes free and equitable access to scholarly information, which is currently restricted by the subscription-only model. Therefore institutional repositories significantly improve the overall social sustainability of information systems and services in general, and scholarly information in particular. However, the social sustainability of institutional repositories can be affected by a number of factors, such as the differences in embargo periods of journals, efforts required for self-archiving, and search and access facilities offered by institutional repositories. These are discussed in the following sections.

Embargo periods

As mentioned earlier in this chapter, the open access policies of research funding and regulatory bodies relating to the embargo period – the period of time between the publication of a paper and its availability on the open access repository – vary. Some open access regulations impose a 12-month embargo period. For example, the ARC requires free public access to research papers within a 12-month period from the date of publication (ARC, 2013), and the US NIH requires open access within a 12-month period from the date of publication (Stebbins, 2013). Overall, open access regulations require free access within six months or within a year, but do not distinguish between disciplines. The RCUK regulations have proposed a different embargo period for different modes of open access and different disciplines:

> 3.6 (i) Ideally, a research paper should become Open Access as soon as it is published on-line. However, RCUK recognises that embargo periods are currently used by some journals with business models that depend on generating revenue through journal subscriptions. Therefore, where a journal does not offer an immediate Open Access option, RCUK will accept a delay between on-line publication and a paper becoming Open Access of no more than six months.
> (ii) Because six-month embargo periods can be particularly difficult in the arts, humanities and social sciences (which are mainly funded by the AHRC and the ESRC), RCUK will accept a delay of up to twelve months for such articles (6).
>
> RCUK (2013)

The RCUK open access policy recognizes that one embargo period may not be feasible in all cases, especially in non-STEM disciplines, stating that 'we would expect the paper to be published in a journal with maximum embargos of 12 months, for STEM disciplines, or 24 months in the arts, humanities and social sciences (which will mainly be funded by the AHRC and the ESRC)' (RCUK,

2013, 6). RCUK also proposes a decision tree for researchers (Figure 7.1) to help them decide the path for publication and the corresponding embargo period.

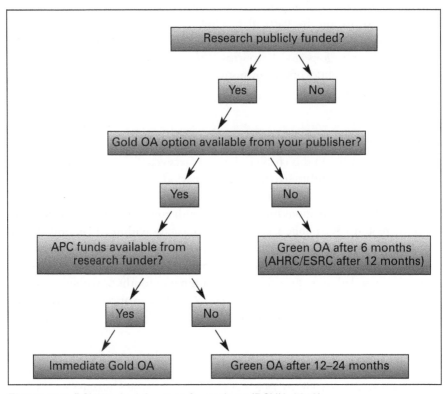

Figure 7.1 RCUK's decision tree for authors (RCUK, 2013)

The RCUK open access guidelines for the embargo period are different from others discussed here, as it recommends:

- a six-month embargo period for green open access for some publications and 12 months for others, especially in the arts, humanities and social science disciplines
- a 12–24 month embargo period for green open access where the chosen journal offers gold open access through article-processing charges, but the authors cannot pay them.

So, RCUK policies support different embargo periods depending on the gold and green route to open access, and in a way favour journals that have article-processing charges in place. There is a hidden risk here: if authors or their institutions cannot afford the required article-processing charges for a given paper, and choose to go through the green route, then the publisher may enforce a longer embargo period of up to 24 months. Contrarily, if the author chooses a journal that does not have article-processing charges then the resulting paper may be made freely available after 12 months.

Although some guidelines have been formulated for the purpose (see the SHERPA/RoMEO database; www.sherpa.ac.uk/romeo/) this may be confusing for authors. Moreover, there are some indirect impositions on authors for selection of their publication outlets, which may have a negative influence on the authors' choice of publication outlets for dissemination of their research results.

The environmental sustainability of institutional repositories

The way institutional repositories are implemented now is clearly not environmentally sustainable. For example, each of the 166 higher education institutions in the UK with at least one server running an institutional repository full time consumes a substantial amount of energy.

The total energy costs for computing equipment may be estimated by combining embodied energy costs, sometimes also called emergy costs, and socket energy costs (Raghavan and Ma, 2011). Emergy costs of a device can be obtained by considering the total energy used during the manufacturing of the device, and then taking a proportion of that depending on the share of the device's full life used in a specific operation. It can be estimated by taking the following three factors into account:

- the manufacturing energy costs
- the lifetime – the replacement cycle of the device; for example a laptop may be replaced every three years
- the fraction of the life of the device used in an operation, which may be based on the actual time used and the capacity in which it is used, for example 25% capacity or in 100% capacity.

Assuming that the total embodied energy cost of a server is 5 gigajoules (GJs), it works at 50% capacity and is replaced every three years, the embodied power cost of a server will be $(5/2) \times 10^9) / (3 \times 365 \times 24 \times 60 \times 60) = 26$ W. The other energy cost is the actual socket energy cost, which can be estimated by the required power to run the device and the amount of time the device is used for an operation or a specific activity. According to the SusteIT toolkit (SusteIT, n.d.), the socket energy cost of a server is 300 W. So, the total annual energy costs for each server will be 326 W × 4380 hours or 1.4 MW (assuming that the server works at 50% capacity). At this rate the total annual energy costs for all the institutional repositories in the UK will be substantial.

This is just one aspect of the environmental costs of institutional repositories. A number of others need to be considered to estimate their overall energy costs, for example, the actual number of servers and other devices used to host and manage repositories – server-side costs, plus the amount of time and number and type of computing devices used by users – and an estimate of the fraction of the internet time and energy used for self-archiving and access and use of the repositories.

Open access content and data

Open access content can be obtained through specific institutional repository sites or specific services like OpenDOAR, which provides one-stop access to the world's major institutional repositories. However, as stated earlier in this chapter, institutional repositories use a number of different, largely open source, types of software. There is also duplication in institutional repositories, which can be caused by multiple copies of the research papers and reports, etc. being maintained in several institutions where more than one author is involved. This can be avoided by building national repositories that reduce management costs, and improve access. The White House directive for open access policies in the USA recommends that repositories should be funded at agency level rather than institutional level, so funding bodies like the National Science Foundation (NSF) propose specific measures to develop a national infrastructure for access to open access publications. During the financial year 2014 NSF will 'design and test system architecture to manage a subset of NSF-supported research products (at a minimum, journal articles, conference proceedings, and book chapters)' (NSF, n.d.). The NSF also proposes to develop the capability to provide seamless access to other open access repositories like PubMed.

Such efforts will result in a few national repositories being created by national funding bodies, which will be economically sustainable because they will reduce the need to create and manage repositories at institution level, and socially sustainable because the central repository service provider will offer uniform search and access facilities.

One of the main goals of open access initiatives is to promote research and development activities through free access to research information. Although most open access guidelines considered in this chapter only talk about research papers, the RCUK guidelines cover access to research data:

As part of supporting the drive for openness and transparency in research, and to ensure that the researcher thinks about data access issues, the policy requires all research papers, if applicable, to include a statement on how any underlying research materials, such as data, samples or models, can be accessed. However, the policy does not require that the data must be made open. If there are considered to be good or compelling reasons to protect access to the data, for example commercial confidentiality or legitimate sensitivities around data derived from potentially identifiable human participants, these should be included in the statement.

RCUK (2013, 4–5)

In order to meet the objective of open access initiatives and guidelines, open access content should be made accessible to everyone, posing a significant challenge to those managing user interfaces, information access and usability issues. Currently institutional repositories are designed for academic and scholarly communities, so extending them to the general public, especially those outside academia or specific disciplines, may require a substantial re-design of the search and retrieval features and facilities of repository services. The intention to provide open access, as stated specifically in the RCUK open access guidelines, is to facilitate data and text mining and various data analytics, which would facilitate access to and use of research content and data for different purposes. This will require more research in linking content and research data, as discussed further in this book.

Long-term access and preservation

Most specific institutional repositories do not have a long-term preservation plan, and only about 8% of the 2553 institutional repositories contained in the OpenDOAR database have a clear preservation policy. This is a cause for concern for the economic and social sustainability of the institutional repositories. The costs of long-term preservation can be significantly reduced if preservation tasks are performed by a central agency, and the Fair Access to Science and Technology Research Act, introduced in the US Congress in March 2013, makes a specific recommendation for preservation. It states that the federal funding agency should ensure that an electronic copy of a submitted manuscript is preserved in a stable digital repository maintained by the agency or in another suitable repository that ensures free long-term access, interoperability and long-term preservation (Price, 2013).

Content access and re-use: the CC BY licence

As stated above, the main goal of open access is to promote free access to and use of research content by anyone. The RCUK open access guidelines specifically recommend the use of a Creative Commons (CC) BY licence:

> 3.7 (i): Where Research Council funds are used to pay the APC for an Open Access paper, we require that the publisher makes the paper freely available under a Creative Commons Attribution (CC BY) licence. This is the standard licence used by open access journals, and supports the maximum dissemination and re-use of published papers, whilst protecting the moral rights of authors. It allows others to distribute, remix, manipulate, and build upon a paper, including commercially, as long as they credit the authors for the original paper. The use of CC BY where an APC is paid is also the policy of the Wellcome Trust.
>
> (ii) The CC BY licence opens up exciting possibilities for new areas of research by the re-use of papers, and the content of papers through text and data mining, and for new ways of disseminating research by being able to re-present papers in innovative and potentially value-adding ways. Crucially, the CC BY licence removes any doubt or ambiguity as to what may be done with papers, and allows re-use without having to go back to the publisher to check conditions or ask for specific permissions (7).
>
> RCUK (2013)

Thus, in order to maximize the opportunities for access to, and re-use of, repository content, the research councils would like research papers in repositories to be made available using the most liberal and enabling licences, ideally CC BY. While in principle this will promote better use of research content and data, and sustainable development in a knowledge economy, there are some concerns. From the economic point of view, such a licence may disadvantage some authors and researchers as their work could be re-used for commercial benefit without requiring users to pay a share of those benefits to the original creators of the idea or knowledge. From a social sustainability point of view, there may be concerns related to research ethics and data protection. Currently research ethics and data protection guidelines require that a researcher or team obtains permission to create and use research datasets under specific circumstances for a specific research purpose. How the research findings and corresponding research datasets could be used by others for a different purpose, or for commercial purposes, is not clear. More research needs to be carried out and specific guidelines are to be formulated in this area. This is recognized in the RCUK guidelines:

3.7 (iv): RCUK will ensure that the 2014 review includes an assessment of the impact of the use of CC BY especially within the Arts, Humanities and Social Science disciplines, and this will be monitored through active engagement with the various academic communities and their publishers (p.8).

3.7 (v): RCUK will work with JISC and the UK Open Access Implementation Group to produce guidance on the use of CC BY licences, including how to identify effectively third-party material included within a paper licensed under CC BY (p.8).

RCUK (2013)

Gold open access and the sustainability of information

As discussed earlier in this chapter, the gold route to open access allows free access to published papers immediately, and the publishing cost is recovered through article-processing charges. The RCUK open access guidelines have clearly indicated their preference for the gold open access model through article-processing charges. This model and proposed funding mechanisms to support article-processing charges will have significant implications on the sustainability of the scholarly communication process in general, and for scholarly information services in particular. Specific RCUK open access guidelines, and some recommendations of the Finch Group (Finch, 2012), which forms the basis of the UK Government's and RCUK's positions on gold open access, are examined in the following sections with specific reference to their implications for sustainability.

The gold open access model

Many journals have adopted the gold open access model as they have introduced article-processing charges, and now some hybrid journals follow both the subscription and article-processing-charge-based open access model. Some funding bodies now include article-processing charges within their research funding models. For example, the open access policy of the Wellcome Trust states that the Trust, where appropriate, will provide research grant holders with additional funding through their institutions, to cover open access charges. The European Commission recommends the gold open access model as one of the options for open access: 'where research papers will be made immediately accessible online by the publisher and the researchers will be eligible for reimbursement of the article-processing charges from the Commission' (Europa, 2012).

Overall, the main challenge of the gold open access model arises from the lack of a sustainable business model that can support scholarly communication practised within the information industry, and at the same time make research information easily available to everyone free at the point of use.

The Finch Group report

Realizing the importance of open access to research publications, and the lack of a reliable funding model and policy framework to support it, a special working group was formed in the UK in October 2011, sponsored by BIS, the Higher Education Funding Council for England, RCUK and the Publishers Association. The report of the working group, chaired by Professor Dame Janet Finch, recommended that everyone should have open access to scholarly publications (Finch, 2012). It specifically recommended the gold route to open access, based on article-processing charges. The recommendations of the Finch report were discussed and debated through a series of submissions made to special committees in the House of Lords and House of Commons, and were finally accepted by the UK Government (Sample, 2012).

The report has been guided by four major principles: access, usability, quality and costs, and sustainability. The report recommends article-processing charges as the main vehicle for supporting open access, and that research councils and other public sector bodies funding research in the UK should establish more effective and flexible arrangements to meet the costs of publishing in open access and hybrid journals (Finch, 2012, 7). It proposed there should be funding of £50–60 million per year to support open access to research publications in the UK, with the following breakdown:

- £38 million on publishing in open access journals
- £10 million on extensions to licences for the higher education and health sectors
- £3–5 million for one-off transition costs.   (2012, 11)

The report describes how this model for open access will provide free access to scholarly publications not only to those in the higher education and health research sectors in the UK, but also to every person in the UK and virtually everyone in the world. It pointed out that some changes are required in the policies and culture of the government, funding bodies, universities and researchers to implement the proposed open access model. The UK Government announced on 16 July 2012 that it accepted the recommendations of the Finch report.

The Finch report did not provide any specific model or architectural framework to manage open access content and data. Chapter 8 provides a conceptual model and generic architecture for an open access research content and information management system for the UK, which could be linked with similar systems in other countries, as and when they implement a similar open access model.

Gold open access and RCUK policies

As stated earlier, the RCUK open access policy prefers the gold open access model paid for through article-processing charges:

- From 1st April 2013 the payment of APCs and other publication charges related to Research Council-funded research are supported through RCUK OA block grants provided to eligible research organisations. APCs and other publication charges relating to peer-reviewed research papers can no longer be included within research grant applications (p.2).
- Eligible research organisations in receipt of RCUK OA block grants are expected to establish institutional publication funds, and the processes to manage and allocate the funds provided. Institutions have the flexibility to use the block grant in the manner they consider will best deliver the RCUK Policy on Open Access in a transparent way that allocates funds fairly across the disciplines. RCUK expects that the primary use of the block grant will be for payment of APCs. We expect research organisations in receipt of an RCUK OA block grant to comply with the monitoring arrangements that will be put in place by the RCUK for this policy (p.3).

RCUK (2013)

It also states that the funds to support article-processing charges will be increased over the next five years until all published peer-reviewed papers, derived from RCUK funding, are open access.

The economic sustainability of gold open access

The costs and benefits of open access publishing models have been discussed widely in literature (for example Cullen and Chawner, 2009, 2010, 2011; Houghton et al., 2009; Houghton, 2011). The essence of the gold route to open access is that the cost of publication of journal articles is recovered from sources other than user subscriptions, and users do not pay any fees to access scholarly content. Over the past few years the most common route to pay for gold open access has been through the imposition of article-processing charges. The fees charged to authors vary from US$1000 to US$3000 (Bird, 2010), or can be as high as US$3900 (Zoubir, 2012). Bjork (2012) notes that the number of hybrid journals

– those following the commercial and gold open access model through article-processing charges – has doubled during 2010 to 2011, rising to 4300; and about 12,000 open access articles were published through article-processing charges in 2011. Bjork found that on average only about 12% authors take this option because of the very high article-processing charges associated with the publishing of research papers, and the lack of an established institutional framework and funding models to support these charges. These are the main reasons for the slow progress in establishing the gold open access model. Bjork and Solomon (2012) suggested that open access publishing funded through article-processing charges is likely to continue to grow. Lewis (2012) suggests that the gold open access model could be used for 50% of scholarly journal articles sometime between 2017 and 2021, and 90% of articles between 2020 and 2025.

A Jisc-funded study modelled the open access options for publication of scholarly papers in the UK:

- If universities switch from the current subscription-based system to publishing all their articles in Open Access journals that charge an article-processing fee, there would be savings for all universities when the article-processing fee is 700 GBP per article or less. Where article-processing fees (APCs) are 500 GBP per article, even the largest university would save, in this case around 1.53 million GBP *per annum*. The maximum savings found in our modelling, accruing to a medium-sized university, were 1.7 million GBP *per annum* when the article-processing fee is 500 GBP per article.
- If article-processing fees are 1000 GBP, all but the largest university in the study would save. Savings for three of the four universities in the study range from 0.17 million GBP to 1.4 million GBP *per annum*. The largest university studied would, however, face extra costs of around 1.86 million GBP *per annum* for this option.
- When article-processing fees for Open Access journals are 2000 GBP per article, there would still be savings for two of the four universities studied. When APCs are more than 2000 GBP per article, it is likely that most universities would spend more money than for the current subscription-based system. As with all other article-processing fee price points under this option, though, the direct costs of APCs would not all fall to the universities: some of the costs may be covered by external research grants as is current practice.

Swan (2010)

The RCUK policies on gold open access will have several implications. For example the policy document states that the RCUK block grant for article-processing charges is based on estimates:

- The RCUK block grant is not to be considered the only public funding that research organisations may use to support Open Access: it is legitimate, for example, to use funding received through Funding Council QR [quality related] allocations and fEC [full economic costing] indirect costs on research grants to pay APCs (pp.5–6).
- The RCUK OA Block Grant is principally to support the payment of APCs. However, Research Organisations have the flexibility to use the block grant in the manner they consider will best deliver the RCUK Policy on Open Access, as long as the primary purpose to support the payment of APCs is fulfilled (p.5).
- Institutions should work with their authors to ensure that a proper market in APCs develops, with price becoming one of the factors that is taken into consideration when deciding where to publish (pp.5–6).
- Therefore, institutions and bodies such as JISC Collections, Research Libraries UK and the Society of College, National and University Libraries (SCONUL) should work together to negotiate appropriate APCs with publishers (pp.5–6).
- The choice of route to Open Access remains with the author and their research organisation, and in some circumstances, where funding for APCs is unavailable during the transition period, longer embargo periods may be allowable. Where an author's preference is 'pay-to-publish' and their first choice of journal offers this option, but there are insufficient funds to pay for the APC, in order to meet the spirit of the RCUK policy, the Councils prefer the author to seek an alternative journal with an affordable 'pay-to-publish' option or with an option with embargo periods of six or twelve months (p.6).

RCUK (2013)

The above extracts show that article-processing charges and the corresponding RCUK policies will have significant implications for the overall scholarly communication process. For example, the RCUK policy is that the block grant should be managed at institution level to support authors for payment of article-processing charges to a chosen journal. The local institutional policies and overall ability of authors and institutions to pay article-processing charges will be an important factor when selecting appropriate journals for research publications. In future scholarly communication will be decided by not only the quality of a research paper, but also the ability of the researcher to pay the article-processing charges of target journals.

The social sustainability of the gold open access model

The RCUK has a clear policy for the selection of journals and article-processing charges:

- Journals which are not compliant with RCUK policy must not be used to publish research papers arising from Research Council funded work apart from in the special cases during the transition period, as noted in section 3.6 on embargos (p.4)
- Institutions and bodies such as JISC Collections, Research Libraries UK and the Society of College, National and University Libraries (SCONUL) should work together to negotiate appropriate APCs with publishers. In this context, it is important to recognise that the Research Councils fund only part of the total research effort in the UK (pp.5–6).

RCUK (2013)

These and similar policies may restrict researchers' choice of journals, with implications for the scholarly communication process and collaborative research and publication activities. They may affect collaborative publication decisions where several authors from different universities and institutions are involved, and they do not have the same resources to pay article-processing charges. The situation will be worse when there is international collaboration, especially when authors from developing countries are involved in research and publishing with UK authors.

RCUK recommends the use of a CC BY licence for open access publication so users can access scholarly information for any purpose including commercial use. This may disadvantage some researchers and their institutions as they may not be able to exploit their knowledge commercially because of the CC BY licence.

Summary

Analysis of open access guidelines proposed by various funding bodies show that they implement open access policies differently. The institutional repositories that now exist because of green open access initiatives promote the mission of open access by providing free access to research information, but the way they are currently implemented raises some economic and social sustainability issues. More importantly, this chapter observes that institutional repositories in their current form – one institutional repository for each higher education institution – are neither economically nor environmentally sustainable.

The foundation of the gold open access policy of RCUK is based on providing funding for researchers to support article-processing charges. While from the social sustainability point of view open access policies promote better and more equitable access to scholarly information, the gold open access policy and government or institutional funding for scholarly communications raise fundamental questions of sustainability. For example, is it sustainable that a handful of research-intensive entities – universities, institutions and even countries – subsidize knowledge creation and access for the whole country or the entire world? The gold open access model and the funding model based on article-processing charges will have a negative impact on economic sustainability, and to some extent on social sustainability and scholarly communication processes because there is a danger that the funding needed to support article-processing charges will reduce overall funding for research, which is becoming more and more scarce anyway.

Many new open access journals are coming up in an alternative model to the gold and open access models, such as the institution-supported model, sometimes called the platinum open access or universal open access model (Hunter, 2012). Under this model, journals are online and open access, and use open source software, hosted by institutions. Such open access journals are run voluntarily by academics and only time will tell how many survive in the long run in competition with commercial journals.

Overall, the green and gold open access models, and even the platinum open access model, have long-term implications for the scholarly communication process, and more importantly there is a paradigm shift in the access and management of scholarly information – research content and data. These issues are discussed in more detail in the following chapters.

References

Allinson, J., François, S. and Lewis, S. (2008) SWORD: Simple Web-service Offering Repository Deposit, *Ariadne*, **54**, www.ariadne.ac.uk/issue54/.

ARC (2013) ARC Open Access Policy, Australian Research Council, www.arc.gov.au/applicants/open_access.htm.

Bird, C. (2010) Continued Adventures in Open Access: 2009 perspective, *Learned Publishing*, **23** (2), 107–16.

Bjork, B. C. (2012) The Hybrid Model for Open Access Publication of Scholarly Articles: a failed experiment?, *Journal of the American Society for Information Science and Technology*, **63** (8), 1496–504.

Bjork, B.-C. and Solomon, D. J. (2012) Publication Fees in Open Access Publishing: sources of funding and factors influencing choice of journal, *Journal of the American Society for Information Science and Technology*, **63** (1), 98–107.

Cullen, R. and Chawner, B. (2009) Institutional Repositories in Tertiary Institutions: access, delivery and performance. In Griffiths, J. R. and Craven, J. (eds), *Access, Delivery, Performance: the future of libraries without walls: a festschrift to celebrate the work of Professor Peter Brophy,* 113-44, Facet Publishing.

Cullen, R. and Chawner, B. (2010) Institutional Repositories: assessing their value to the academic community, *Performance Measurement and Metrics*, **11** (2), 131–47.

Cullen, R. and Chawner, B. (2011) Institutional Repositories, Open Access and Scholarly Communication: a study of conflicting paradigms, *Journal of Academic Librarianship*, **37** (6), 460–70.

Europa (2012) Scientific Data: open access to research results will boost Europe's innovation capacity, press release, http://europa.eu/rapid/press-release_IP-12-790_en.htm.

Fair Access to Science and Technology Research Act of 2013 (2013) http://doyle.house.gov/sites/doyle.house.gov/files/documents/2013%2002%2014%20 DOYLE%20FASTR%20FINAL.pdf.

Finch, J. (ed.) (2012) *Accessibility, Sustainability, Excellence: how to expand access to research publications*, report of the Working Group on Expanding Access to Published Research, www.researchinfonet.org/wp-content/uploads/2012/06/Finch-Group-report-FINAL-VERSION.pdf.

Houghton, J. H. (2011) The Costs and Potential Benefits of Alternative Scholarly Publishing Models, *Information Research*, **16** (1), http://informationr.net/ir/16-1/paper469.html.

Houghton, J. W., Rasmussen, B., Sheehan, P. J., Oppenheim, C., Morris, A., Creaser, C. et al. (2009) *Economic Implications of Alternative Scholarly Publishing Models: exploring the costs and benefits*, Joint Information Systems Committee, www.jisc.ac.uk/media/documents/publications/rpteconomicoapublishing.pdf.

Hunter, R. (2012) Why We Oppose Gold Open Access: editorial, *feminists@law*, **2** (2), http://journals.kent.ac.uk/index.php/feministsatlaw/article/view/59/179.

Jacobs, N., Amber, T. and McGregor, A. (2008) Institutional Repositories in the UK: the JISC approach, *Library Trends*, **57** (2), 124–41.

Jisc (2011a) *Open Access*, Joint Information Systems Committee, www.jisc.ac.uk/openaccess.

Jisc (2011b) *Open Access for UK research: JISC's contributions – summary of achievements*, Joint Information Systems Committee, www.jisc.ac.uk/publications/programmerelated/2009/openaccesscontributions.aspx.

Jisc (2011c) *UK's Open Access Full-text Search Engine to Aid Research*, Joint Information Systems Committee, www.jisc.ac.uk/news/stories/2011/09/openaccess.aspx.

Lewis, D. W. (2012) The Inevitability of Open Access, *College & Research Libraries*, **73** (5), 493–5.

Lewis, S., de Castro, P. and Jones, R. (2012) SWORD: facilitating deposit scenarios, *D-Lib Magazine*, **18** (1/2), www.dlib.org/dlib/january12/lewis/01lewis.html.

Lynch, C. (2003) *Institutional Repositories: essential infrastructure for scholarship in the digital age*, Association of Research Libraries, *ARL Bimonthly Report*, **226**, www.arl.org/resources/pubs/br/br226/br226ir.shtml.

NSF (n.d.) NSF Public Access Initiative, National Science Foundation, www.nsf.gov/about/budget/fy2014/pdf/45_fy2014.pdf.

Peters, D. and Lossau, N. (2011) DRIVER: building a sustainable infrastructure for global repositories, *Electronic Library*, **29** (2), 249–60.

Price, G. (2013) OA: Fair Access to Science and Technology Research Act (FASTR) legislation introduced in US Congress, InfoDocket, *Library Journal*, 14 February, www.infodocket.com/2013/02/14/fair-access-to-science-and-technology-research-act-fastr-legislation-introduced-in-u-s-congress/.

Raghavan, B. and Ma, J. (2011) The Energy and Emergy of the Internet. In *Proceedings of the ACM Workshop on Hot Topics in Networks (Hotnets)*, Cambridge, MA, November, www.cs.berkeley.edu/~jtma/papers/emergy-hotnets2011.pdf.

RCUK (2013) RCUK Policy With Open Access and Guidance, www.rcuk.ac.uk/documents/documents/RCUKOpenAccessPolicy.pdf.

Sample, I. (2012) Free Access to British Scientific Research Within Two Years, *Guardian*, 15 July, www.guardian.co.uk/science/2012/jul/15/free-access-british-scientific-research.

Stebbins, M. (2013) Expanding Public Access to the Results of Federally Funded Research, blog, 22 February, Office of Science and Technology Policy, The White House, www.whitehouse.gov/blog/2013/02/22/expanding-public-access-results-federally-funded-research.

SusteIT (n.d.) Resources: ICT energy and carbon footprinting tool, www.susteit.org.uk/files/category.php?catID=4.

Swan, A. (2010) Modelling Scholarly Communication Options: costs and benefits for universities, report to the JISC, February, http://repository.jisc.ac.uk/442/2/Modelling_scholarly_communication_report_final1.pdf.

UNESCO (2013) Open Access Policy Concerning UNESCO Publications, www.unesco.org/new/fileadmin/MULTIMEDIA/HQ/ERI/pdf/oa_policy_en_2.pdf.

US NIH (2013) National Institutes of Health Public Access: NIH public access policy details, US National Institutes of Health, http://publicaccess.nih.gov/policy.htm.

Wellcome Trust (2013) Open Access Policy: position statement in support of open and unrestricted access to published research, www.wellcome.ac.uk/About-us/Policy/Policy-and-position-statements/WTD002766.htm.

World Bank (2012) World Bank Open Access Policy for Formal Publications, April, www-wds.worldbank.org/external/default/WDSContentServer/WDSP/IB/2012/04/03/000406484_20120403130112/Rendered/PDF/6783000PP00OFF0icy0Approved0April2.pdf.

Zoubir, A. (2012) Open Access Publications: more than a business model?, *IEEE Signal Processing*, **29** (6), 2–6.

Sustainable management of open access information: a conceptual model

Introduction

Chapter 7 discussed how the various open access policies of funding bodies and government agencies stipulate that research publications should be freely accessible to the public either immediately when they are published through the payment of article-processing charges, as part of the gold open access model, or after the expiry of the embargo period, as part of the green open access model, which can vary between 6 and 12 months, in general, and in some cases between 12 and 24 months after the publication date. Thus it can be expected that through the implementation of open access policies, more and more scholarly content and data will be available in the public domain. This will have significant implications for scholarly communication processes in general, and various information access and management activities in particular.

At the moment there are two major ways to access scholarly information resources: through commercial publishers or aggregator databases, or through the institutional repositories that began to appear over the past few years as a result of open access initiatives. However, with the implementation of the open access policies of various government and funding agencies, discussed in Chapter 7, increasingly more and more scholarly papers will be available through open access databases, thereby reducing users' reliance on commercial publisher or aggregator databases. This will bring a paradigm shift in the way we access and use scholarly information because only a small proportion of publicly funded research output, which is not published through gold open access and is within the embargo period of 6–12 months (or up to 24 months in some circumstances), will be with commercial publishers, and other scholarly publications will be in the public domain. This will not only promote free access to knowledge, but also open up new vistas for research and professional practices in information.

At the moment a variety of different services and channels exist that provide access to open access scholarly publications. For example, open access publications arising out of NIH funding in the USA can be accessed through PubMed. Similarly, open access publications arising out of an institution can be accessed through its institutional repository, or through a portal like OpenDOAR (www.opendoar.org). Chapter 7 noted that the current design and implementation of institutional repositories are not economically or environmentally sustainable.

It is expected that as more and more scholarly information and data become available in the public domain, institutions and businesses, including search engine services like Google Scholar and Microsoft Academic Search, will be able to generate a variety of citation reports, data analytics and value-added information services using textual and other information such as images, tables and charts in research papers and research datasets. It is necessary to design and implement an appropriate model to manage open access content and data, and a conceptual model for this is proposed in this chapter. How such a model can achieve economic, social and environmental sustainability and promote further research in information is also discussed.

Managing open access information

This book, especially Chapter 7, has examined the main challenge of open access, which comes from the lack of sustainable business models that can support the publication of scholarly information practised within the information industry and academic and research institutions, and at the same time make research information easily available to everyone free at the point of use. The recently introduced open access policies of RCUK and other funding bodies aim to provide easy and equitable access to the output of research – information and data – that has been publicly funded. In order to provide access to such information and data, it is necessary to make them available for free, and appropriate mechanisms need to be built in order to manage, and provide easy access to, such information and data. Some institutions and government bodies have made specific proposals or recommendations for this purpose. For example, the recently introduced open access policy of UNESCO proposes to build an open access repository for the purpose, with an interface in six different languages: 'Hosted within the UNESDOC system, the Open Access Repository will provide digital publications in full text to the public without cost or other restrictions (other than embargos and specific clauses restricting use). Its interface will be in six languages' (UNESCO, 2013).

The World Bank has also opened an open knowledge repository (https://openknowledge.worldbank.org/) to host all its open access publications.

US government directives to the federal funding agencies on open access recognize the need for appropriate systems and policies to manage, and provide future access to, open access information. The US Government specifically asks funding agencies to formulate:

- a strategy to improve the public's ability to locate and access digital data resulting from federally funded scientific research
- an approach to optimize search, archival and dissemination features that encourage innovation in accessibility and interoperability, while ensuring long-term stewardship of the results of federally funded research.

Executive Office of the President (2013)

Open access policies of other funding bodies such as those of the ARC or RCUK do not specifically make recommendations for the design and implementation of an appropriate open access information management system. Chapter 7 noted that the current models of institutional repositories, which are likely to grow fast with the implementation of green open access policies, are not economically and environmentally sustainable.

Therefore in order to reap the full benefits of recently introduced open access policies of funding bodies it is necessary to design and implement an appropriate information management system. The conceptual design of an information management system to manage open access, while providing access to commercial and other types of information, is proposed in the following sections. Design principles and discussions are based on the state of scholarly communications in the UK, but may be adopted for use in any other country.

Attributes of a new open access content and data management system

Access, usability and sustainability are some of the major guiding principles of good information management system design, and they should also be the guiding principles for designing an open access research content and data management system.

Free access for all

In line with the open access policies of various funding bodies discussed in Chapter 7, the first defining characteristic of a new conceptual model to manage open access content and data should be providing free and equitable access to publicly funded research information for all. So far, all commercial databases and information management systems have been designed specifically for a defined group of users – academics, scholars, researchers and students in higher education and health or research sectors. They have also been guided by the business model and profits of the publisher or aggregator providing the service. The new model is intended to make research publications available not only to people associated with the higher education and health sector but to everyone: such access should be free and not driven by the goal of making a profit. This will have significant implications for the design principles of the proposed new system because the nature, characteristics and expectations of user communities will vary significantly. The new information management system should have a sustainable business model to support its design and the management of its current and future operations. These issues are considered below.

Access to linked research content and data

Various national and international bodies that support higher education and research, like Jisc in the UK and the European Commission, and various researchers (Berners-Lee, 2009; Borgman, 2011; Chowdhury, 2012a), consider that scholarly activities and research can be facilitated and improved significantly by integrating research content – journal and conference papers, theses and research reports, and so on – with research datasets. The new model should have a mechanism to link, and integrate wherever possible, research publications and research data. The research issues and challenges associated with this are discussed later in the chapter.

Usability and user-centred design

'Know thy user' is the mantra of user-centred design (Chowdhury and Chowdhury, 2011). Pearrow comments that user-centred design is both a 'design and a philosophy that puts the user's needs ahead of anything else' (2007, 61). Several international standards, notably ISO 9241 part 11 (ISO 9241-11:1998) and ISO 9241 part 210 (ISO 9241-210:2010), prescribe guidelines for user-centred design and usability metrics. ISO 9241-210 provides guidelines to identify the requirements and recommendations for user-centred design principles and activities that can be applied to any information product or service (Chowdhury and Chowdhury, 2011, 95). Since the proposed open access content and data management system is to be designed to meet the requirements of a large variety of users (researchers and expert users in the higher education and the health sector and members of the public) with different levels of information need, expertise and experience, a variety of specific design measures may have to be undertaken. For example, there may be a simple and easy-to-use interface for every user, with more specific access features and data analytics for specialist users. Some such services are now available in scholarly databases like ISI Web of Knowledge and Scopus, and search engines like Google Scholar and Microsoft Academic Search. Similarly the proposed open access information system should be designed to support platform and device-independent access and use so people with any computing device or software platform can access it with equal ease and benefit.

In order to support sustainable access to open access research content and data, we also need to design an information management system that is sustainable. All the three forms of sustainability – economic, social and environmental – should remain at the core of the design decisions for an open access content and data management system. Specific issues of sustainability of open access content and data management models are examined in this chapter.

The conceptual model

Figure 8.1 on the next page shows the conceptual model and generic architecture of an open access content and data management system. It is based on the assumption that the model will be created for the UK market while other countries may adopt this or build similar models in coming years. Overall, the proposed model is designed to provide access to scholarly information and research data of all kinds – open access content and data, commercial content, and content and data available on numerous digital libraries and information services on the web. Thus the model will be primarily suitable for higher education institutions, but will also facilitate free access to research content and data for the general public in the UK and elsewhere in the world as envisaged in the Finch report (2012) and the RCUK open access policy document discussed in Chapter 7.

In the proposed model, it is assumed that publishers will continue to provide access to scholarly content through commercial publisher or aggregator databases in the UK and international market. It is obvious that dependence on the commercial databases will reduce significantly as the world moves towards the open access model.

This model proposes a central repository for published research papers, and therefore individual institutional repositories need not store and manage such open access publications. However, institutional repositories also store and manage other kinds of institutional scholarly output such as theses and dissertations, research reports and research data. Chapter 7 discussed how preliminary studies show that

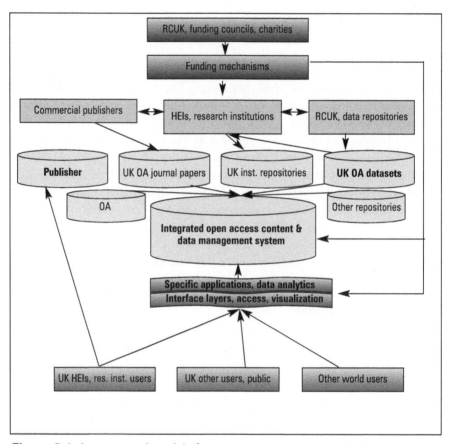

Figure 8.1 A conceptual model of an open access content and data management system

individual institutional repositories are not sustainable. Further research and empirical data will show whether such institutional repositories are sustainable, and whether a central repository of all kinds of institutional output – theses, project reports, special collections, and so on – will be better than having institutional repositories at each specific institution.

Research councils or their designated centre(s) may store research data centrally but they will make the open access research datasets available to the new system through appropriate interfaces and protocols. In accordance with RCUK policies discussed in Chapter 7, it may be assumed that specific universities and research institutions will put appropriate frameworks and policies in place to promote and manage open access publications by their researchers.

The architecture

The open access content and data management system will have a central storage system for open access journal papers, open access research datasets and institutional repositories. The interface will interact with the storage systems and other open access repositories and digital libraries to produce search results and data analytics. The cloud-based architecture will facilitate effective use of storage and processing requirements and thus be economically and environmentally sustainable (as proposed for example in Chowdhury, 2012a; Mell and Grance, 2011). This is considered further in this chapter, and in the discussion on green information service design in Chapter 9.

While keeping their own database for commercial (subscription-based) access, journal publishers will make the full text of open access journal papers available to an open access content repository as soon as the paper is published if article-processing charges are involved, or after the expiry of the embargo period. This will avoid duplication and reduce the workload of higher education institutions and scholars if they are self-archiving their papers and checking metadata and so on. Anyone can access a paper as soon as it is made available on the system.

Each institution will deposit its institutional repository collection – research and project reports, theses, dissertations, and so on – to a central institutional repository as soon as they are submitted to the institution. This is addressed in more detail later on.

Then each institution and research council, wherever appropriate, will make all the open access research datasets available to the central data repository and management system. Any user will be able to access research data as soon as they are deposited through the open access content and data management system. The applications built within the open access content and data management system will facilitate creation of different linked datasets and data analytics. This is discussed further in the section 'Linked open access research content and data'.

Figure 8.1 shows that the open content and data management system will provide integrated access to open access content, open access data, institutional repositories and various open access subject repositories and digital libraries. Users in higher education institutions will have access to both the open content and data management system and various commercial databases that their institution, or a consortium, subscribes to. It is expected that over time as open access publishing becomes common around the world, users will be less dependent on commercial databases. The model shows the UK scenario, but it is expected that over time, as similar systems are built in other countries, systems can be linked, so providing users with access to a virtual global digital library of linked research content and data. Overall, the integrated open access content and data management framework will be more environment-friendly through reductions in computing and ICT storage and management costs, as considered by Chowdhury (2012a, 2012b). This is discussed further later on.

Opportunities and challenges

As acknowledged in the Finch report, there will be a transition time for moving to a complete open access model (Finch, 2012). Success of this model will depend on continuing funding to support the gold open access model or strict adherence to the process of submission of research publications after the expiry of the embargo period. It is expected that as more and more countries adopt the proposed open access model, reliance on commercial databases will reduce and the savings made from journal subscriptions may be channelled to fund article-processing charges in the gold open access model. The proposed conceptual model of the open access research content and data management system (Figure 8.1) will promote more research and scholarly activities and therefore a digital economy in a number of ways. It will:

- provide access to linked research content and data created by UK researchers to everyone whether in the UK or elsewhere in the world
- create a global distributed digital library of scholarly research content and data by linking integrated open access content and data management systems worldwide as and when they are built in other countries
- facilitate creation of a variety of data analytics linking research data and content and linking content to people, and people to people.

There are various challenges associated with the design and implementation of the proposed model. According to the principles of open access, open access data and content will be accessed by experts – researchers, staff and students in the higher education and health sector – and members of the general public in the UK and anywhere in the world. Thus different interfaces and access mechanisms and services may have to be built to facilitate domain-, context-, user- and community-specific and general information access and interactions. Other opportunities and challenges of the proposed system are discussed in the following sections.

Linked open access research content and data

The world of information retrieval is moving fast from simple word- and search-based models to meaning- and connection-based models. The new open access content and data management system proposed in this chapter will provide new opportunities for information researchers. They will be able to build a variety of tools and applications to link data to content, content to content, content to scholars and scholars to scholars, thereby moving to the paradigm of linked big scholarly data. They will also build special applications and data analytics for specific users and/or disciplines; for example, it may be possible to build specific applications for university and funding council management to generate reports showing the research funding, output, researcher networks and overall research environment created by members of a given research team or a specific stream of research funding, or to build comparable figures for research developments in different areas or disciplines. Similar analytics and reports can be produced for researchers in specific disciplines at specific universities or for all the higher education institutions in the entire country. Currently some such data analytics are produced by specific databases and search services. For example commercial databases like ISI Web of Knowledge or Scopus produce citation reports, and search engine services like Google Scholar and Microsoft Academic Search generate author citations, co-author graphs and co-citation graphs in specific fields. Currently these are primarily based on citation analysis and do not link research content and datasets. The new system will enable researchers to do this.

Although the conceptual model shown in Figure 8.1 proposes a generic interface for all higher education users, a 'one-size-fits-all' approach will not be appropriate for every user in every discipline, in every institution and in every country. As widely addressed in literature (for example, Bawden and Robinson, 2012; Chowdhury and Chowdhury, 2011; Ruthven and Kelly, 2012), cultural, political and linguistic and other factors play a prominent role in the development and use of information services. In order for the open access content and data management service to succeed for a variety of local needs, local culture and standards need to be adopted in the design of the system and interfaces (Xia, 2012). Thus more user- and context-specific access and usability features need to be added on top of the generic interface of the new system in order to support directed and accidental (or opportunistic) discovery of information (Erdelez and Makri, 2011), and specific information access and use requirements of experts and non-expert users – members of the general public.

The sustainability of the proposed open access content and data management system

The three forms of sustainability – economic, social and environmental – of the proposed open access content and data management system are discussed in the following sections.

Economic sustainability

The economic sustainability of this model will depend on the funding available from higher education funding councils in the UK or other bodies to support the article-processing charges, where applicable, and also the costs of building and maintaining the service. There are a number of economic sustainability questions associated with the open access funding model proposed in the Finch report (Finch, 2012). The following are some obvious questions:

- Is the recommended amount of funding enough to cover the article-processing charges required to maintain the current level and future growth of research publications of UK academics and researchers?
- The Finch report noted that the Wellcome Trust paid an average £1422 article-processing charge for the first three months of 2011, and the University of Nottingham paid on average £1216 in the academic year 2010–11 (Finch, 2012, 69). At this rate the recommended amount of funding to cover article-processing charges for UK researchers – £38 million – will not be enough. In 2011 UK researchers published over 123,000 peer-reviewed journal articles (Finch, 2012, 59). At £1216 per article (the lower of the two article-processing charges mentioned above), the total amount required to cover article-processing charges would be £149,568 million (more than three times the recommended amount). Or if the processing charge is £1216 per article, only 31,250 journal articles can be published, a quarter the number of papers published in 2010. This leads to a related question: will this mechanism reduce the overall output of UK researchers, which now stands at over 6% of all the scholarly publications produced in the world per year (Finch, 2012, 62)? An optimistic view could be that article-processing charges for different journals will vary and some journals may charge less than £1216 per article, so more journal papers could be funded. The other likely outcome is the co-existence of both the green and gold open access models.
- How long will the funding be required and available? The Finch report acknowledges that during the period of transition to open access publishing worldwide, there will be additional costs, and funds should be found to extend and rationalize current licences to cover all the institutions in the higher education and research sectors (Finch, 2012, 7 and 10). As noted earlier in this book, some researchers estimate that it may take about a decade for the majority of journals to move into the full open access mode (Lewis, 2012). So, it is not clear at this stage how long funding authorities in the UK will have to provide this additional funding and how fast the rest of the world will move in order to reduce this additional cost. An optimistic view may be

that the rate of transition will be faster with the new model and other countries may follow suit soon.
- Where will the additional money come from? The amount of additional funding of £50–60 million requested for the open access model is a very small amount compared with the overall research costs of the UK Government (£10.4 billion) or even of the expenditure of research councils and higher education funding councils (£5.5 billion) (Finch, 2012, 38). However, there is still genuine concern, especially during the current crisis facing the UK economy, and the higher education sector in particular, over where the additional funding will come from. Will it reduce the overall research budget, so there will be a little less money to carry out the actual research? An optimistic view may be that in the long run the open access system and various associated information services of the proposed model will benefit everyone and promote more research and support the overall digital economy.

There are other issues relating to economic sustainability. The Finch report notes that UK researchers produce just over 6% of the peer-reviewed papers published each year, and nearly half of them are produced in collaboration with colleagues from overseas (Finch, 2012, 18). In the increasingly scarce funding environment, it will be interesting to see whether UK funding bodies will be able to pay the article-processing charges for 50% of the publications produced by overseas researchers.

Notwithstanding the aforementioned issues and challenges, the proposed open access content and data management system will reduce the long-term costs of information access and management in a number of ways, for example, through the centralized content storage and management systems for all types of content and data. This will reduce the infrastructure and management costs of individual higher education institutions that are currently spent in building and managing institutional repositories and data storage (discussed in Chapter 7). It will promote one-stop access to heterogeneous content and data on research and scholarship.

The conceptual model in Figure 8.1 shows that the open access content and data management system will provide access to open access content from various open access digital libraries, subject repositories and institutional repositories from around the world. It may be hoped that over time, as open access becomes common in other countries, and similar national repositories of open access journal publications are built nationally (because they will be supported by the funding bodies in the respective countries), the institutional repositories in those countries will also be smaller just like those in the UK, in accordance with the changes proposed above in relation to UK open access.

Social sustainability

Because the new model is designed to meet the requirements of recently introduced open access policies discussed in Chapter 7, the proposed model will improve the equity of access to research content and data and thus meet one of the major requirements of social sustainability. So far scholarly research publications have been accessible only to a small number of people who are affiliated with higher education or research institutions, and even then the proportion of scholarly output that these people can access is increasingly reducing because of the rising subscription charges of journals and databases, leading to falling acquisition in libraries. The new system will make all kinds of research information and data freely available not only to scholars but to everyone in society. This will promote the concepts of an information society and digital economy in the UK and eventually in other parts of the world.

Better access to and use of research information and data can be facilitated by automatic structuring and linking of research data and content, and by developing various text mining and data analytic tools (Clark et al. 2012; Kirk, 2012; McMahon et al., 2012; Witten et al., 2004). Appropriate data analytics within the proposed system will facilitate automatic creation of a social network of UK researchers with their global counterparts by linking their research output and thus promoting collaboration. The conceptual model shown in Figure 8.1 extends this goal by making it possible to provide linked open access research content and data to everyone. It will support the development and promotion of new research and an academic culture by moving from the paradigm of search and access to the new paradigm of connection, linking research content and research data; and by facilitating an environment for the creation of semantic links of different kinds: content to content, content to data, content to researcher, and researcher to researcher. Thus the new framework for management of open access research content and data will facilitate the creation and management of rich linked datasets, which will show not only the research output of a country, funding body or institution, but also the social structure of research in the higher education and health sectors in the UK and around the world.

However, there are risks associated with the proposed funding model and research culture, and some of these have already been considered in Chapter 7. Under the current subscription-based models, creation of knowledge through the publication of journal articles is judged by the merit of the publication while access to published research is restricted by economic affordability. The new open access model brings a paradigm shift: access will be free, but production of knowledge – publication of research papers – may be restricted by financial affordability. The risk of such a situation may be that researchers, under specific circumstances, may have to publish their research in journals that have lower article-processing charges, or – worse – the researcher may not be able to publish at all if no funds are available to pay the article-processing charges.

As pointed out in the Finch report, the proposed open access model will require a change in the culture of all the stakeholders ranging from publishers to government funding bodies, research councils, universities and researchers. Activities of all these stakeholders should be geared towards the overall goal of open access, to make the research content and data available to everyone free at the point of use. All the stakeholders need to move to a new paradigm of open access research content and data. New measures for assessing research output need to be built based on the proposed model, and the universities and funding bodies should also move from the traditional journal-based measures of research impact to article-based and social-network-based measures of research quality, collaboration and impact.

Environmental sustainability

As discussed earlier, especially in Chapter 4, the environmental impact of information is becoming a major area of concern, especially because of the excessive use of ICT infrastructure and services by modern information systems and services. Figure 8.1 shows that the proposed model has centralized storage of open access publications, an institutional repository of content and open access data. This will reduce the energy costs of ICT infrastructure and thus the overall environmental impact of the service (Chowdhury, 2012a, 2012b).

The proposed model should be based on the basic principles of green information service design, which aims to reduce duplication of storage and routine services, and focuses on more user- and context-specific services (Chowdhury, 2012a). Features of a green information service are examined in Chapter 9. The Finch report recommends that 'the infrastructure of subject and institutional repositories should be developed so that they play a valuable role complementary to formal publishing, particularly in providing access to research data and to grey literature, and in digital preservation' (Finch, 2012, 8). While the conceptual model proposed here complies with this recommendation, it also includes some changes in the nature of the institutional repositories. At the moment institutional repositories manage open access journal papers (self-archived by authors or harvested by the institution) and other institutional (local) resources such as theses, dissertations, research reports and special collections. According to the new architecture, institutional repositories need not store open access journal and conference papers. They will continue to collect other institutional research and scholarly output and research information, but a central institutional repository will harvest such institutional repository collections from all the UK higher education and health institutions. This will reduce the need for additional computing and infrastructure at specific higher education institutions, and will create a one-stop shop for all the institutional repositories. This may be accomplished through a service like CORE (http://core-project.kmi.open.ac.uk/), which was designed to provide access to institutional repository collections from the UK and elsewhere. However, over the years, as other countries adopt the open access model, and the conceptual model and design architecture of the system proposed here, there will be a national node for each country's institutional repository, which will be responsible for managing their collection. The information management system proposed here will access them for institutional resources of specific countries. This will reduce the workloads and resource requirements of specific higher education institutions and health institutions. In fact, as the new system matures, the institutional repositories at specific institution level may not be required any longer. Instead, institutional research content such as theses, research and project reports and special collections, may be directly deposited in the central repository of the new open access content and data management system.

The cost and effort of institutional repositories to preserve research content can be reduced significantly if items are stored at a central institutional repository. Using the platform as a service (PaaS) layer of the cloud architecture (Mell and Grance, 2011) (discussed in Chapter 9) different applications can be built on various storage services in order to build the information management layer. The cloud service will centrally store and preserve open access publications and the institutional repository collection. This will reduce the workload and ICT infrastructure and energy requirements of individual repositories with regard to the preservation of content and data. Cloud-based preservation research is at an early stage (for some directions see Askoj, Sugimoto and Nagamori, 2011), but as it matures new solutions will appear.

Summary

As Buckland (2012) suggests, enabling people to become better informed should be the central concern of information studies. The open access content and data management system proposed in this chapter will make value-added research content and data available to everyone free at the point of use. Such value-added, free and easy access to linked research content and data will benefit everyone, and this will help us build a better and more informed society.

The proposed open access content and data management system will promote new research to link various web and social networking technologies with scholarly content and data. McMahon et al. (2012) comment that 'social networks facilitate scientific progress by mixing people and ideas; social networking tools bring this mixing online'. By making appropriate use of the rapidly increasing social networking tools and technologies researchers can connect more people, create more paths for ideas to travel, and subsequently create many more opportunities to seed new research ideas (Banciu et al., 2012; Li, Liao and Lai, 2012). The new open access content and data management model proposed in this chapter will also enable information managers to integrate a variety of Web 2.0 and social networking technologies with research data and scholarly output, and analysis of these links will provide valuable information in promoting better use, sharing and re-use of research information and data.

References

Askoj, J., Sugimoto, S. and Nagamori, M. (2011) A Metadata Framework for Cloud-Based Digital Archives Using METS with PREMIS. In Xing, C., Crestani, F. and Rauber, A. (eds), *Digital Libraries: for cultural heritage, knowledge disseminations and future creation*, 13th International Conference on Asia-Pacific Digital Libraries, ICADL2011, Beijing, 24–27 October, Springer, 118–27.

Banciu, D., Pitic, A. G., Volovici, D. and Mitea, A. C. (2012) Using Social Networking Software to Promote Digital Libraries, *Studies in Informatics and Control*, **21** (2), 221–6.

Bawden, D. and Robinson, L. (2012) *Introduction to Information Science*, Facet Publishing.

Berners-Lee, T. (2009) Linked Data, www.w3.org/DesignIssues/LinkedData.html.

Borgman, C. L. (2011) The Conundrum of Sharing Research Data, *Journal of the American Society for Information Science and Technology*, **63** (6), 1059–78.

Buckland, M. (2012) What Kind of Science Can Information Science Be?, *Journal of the American Society for Information Science and Technology*, **63** (1), 1–7.

Chowdhury, G. G. (2012a) Building Sustainable Information Services: a green IS research agenda, *Journal of the American Society for Information Science and Technology*, **63** (4), 633–47.

Chowdhury, G. G. (2012b) An Agenda for Green Information Retrieval Research, *Information Processing and Management*, **48** (6), 1067–77.

Chowdhury, G. G. and Chowdhury, S. (2011) *Information Users and Usability in the Digital Age*, Facet Publishing.

Clark, M., Kim, Y., Kruschwitz, U., Song, D., Albakour, D., Dignum, S., Beresi, U. C., Fasli, M. and De Roeck, A. (2012) Automatically Structuring Domain Knowledge From Text: an overview of current research, *Information Processing and Management*, **48** (3), 552–68.

Erdelez, S. and Makri, S. (2011) Introduction to the Thematic Issue on Opportunistic Discovery of Information, *Information Research*, **16** (3), http://informationr.net/ir/16-3/odiintro.html.

Executive Office of the President (US) (2013) Memorandum for the Heads of Executive Departments and Agencies, Office of Science and Technology, 22 February, www. whitehouse.gov/sites/default/files/microsites/ostp/ostp_public_access_memo_2013.pdf.

Finch, J. (ed.) (2012) *Accessibility, Sustainability, Excellence: how to expand access to research publications*, report of the Working Group on Expanding Access to Published Research www.researchinfonet.org/wp-content/uploads/2012/06/Finch-Group-report-FINAL-VERSION.pdf.

ISO 9241-11:1998 *Ergonomic Requirements for Office Work with Visual Display Terminals (VDTs), Part II: guidance on usability*, International Organization for Standardization.

ISO 9241-210:2010 *Ergonomics of Human-System Interaction, Part 210: human-centred design for interactive systems*, International Organization for Standardization.

Kirk, H. (2012) Discovering Digital Library User Behavior with Google Analytics, *Code4Lib Journal*, **17**, 1–10, http://journal.code4lib.org/articles/6942.

Lewis, D. W. (2012) The Inevitability of Open Access, *College & Research Libraries*, **73** (5), 493–5.

Li, Y.-M., Liao, T.-S. and Lai, C.-Y. (2012) A Social Recommender Mechanism for Improving Knowledge Sharing in Online Forums, *Information Processing and Management*, **48** (5), 978–94.

McMahon, T. M., Powell, J. E., Hopkins, M., Alcazar, D. A., Miller, L. E., Collins, L. and Mane, K. K. (2012) Social Awareness Tools for Science Research, *D-Lib Magazine*, **18** (3/4), www.dlib.org/dlib/march12/mcmahon/03mcmahon.html.

Mell, P. and Grance, T. (2011) *The NIST Definition of Cloud Computing: recommendations of the National Institute of Standards and Technology*, http://csrc.nist.gov/publications/drafts/800-145/Draft-SP-800-145_cloud-definition.pdf.

Pearrow, M. (2007) *Web Usability Handbook*, 2nd ed., Charles River Media.

Ruthven, I. and Kelly, D. (eds) (2012) *Interactive Information Seeking, Behavior and Retrieval*, Facet Publishing.

UNESCO (2013) Open Access Policy Concerning UNESCO Publications, www.unesco.org/new/fileadmin/MULTIMEDIA/HQ/ERI/pdf/oa_policy_en_2.pdf.

Witten, I. H., Don, K. J., Dewsnip, M. and Tablan, V (2004) Text Mining in a Digital Library, *International Journal on Digital Libraries*, **4** (1), 56–9.

Xia, X. (2012) Diffusionism and Open Access, *Journal of Documentation*, **68** (1), 72–99.

Green information services: a conceptual model

Introduction

Earlier in this book there was a discussion about how the nature of information services has changed over the past few decades with the emergence of new ICTs, and their adaptation in different information services. Internet, web and mobile technologies have become major drivers behind the creation of a new era of digital information systems and services. These new technologies have significantly changed the ways in which we create, distribute, seek, access, use, share and re-create information.

The unprecedented growth in the volume and variety of digital information has significantly increased the demand for ICT and networking facilities, and the increasing use of ICT in the creation, management and use of information has significant economic and environmental implications. Individuals, institutions, governments, businesses, and so on, are making increasing use of ICT, which requires more economic resources for acquiring, managing and upgrading technologies because of the relatively short lifespan of computer and communications equipment. This makes the task of planning, managing and implementing projects that require substantial use of ICT more and more difficult. Increased use of ICT also makes more demands on energy consumption, which has adverse environmental impacts.

Globally ICTs contribute about 2% of current GHG emissions, and this figure will increase rapidly over coming years (Chapter 4; Climate Group, 2008). However, it was noted in Chapter 4 that the Climate Group has estimated that improved and appropriate use of ICT can reduce 'annual man-made global emissions by 15% by 2020 and deliver energy efficiency savings to global businesses of over EUR 500 billion' (Climate Group, 2008). This may be achieved by using green IT and cloud computing technologies that facilitate shared use of computing and networking resources, thereby avoiding wastage of computing resources and the corresponding energy consumption, while at the same time providing round the clock access to resources – content, hardware, software, networking, and so on – by using advanced technological facilities for scheduling and optimization, and instant scaling up or scaling down as and when required. This chapter discusses the basics of cloud computing technologies and shows how they can be used to build environment-friendly green information services. Design issues of a green information service are addressed in this chapter in the context of higher education and research as proposed by Chowdhury (2012a).

Cloud computing

Cloud computing is an internet-based IT service development, deployment and delivery model enabling real-time delivery of information products and IT services (Vouk, 2008). There are many definitions of and synonyms for cloud computing such as 'on-demand computing', 'software as a service', 'information utilities', 'the internet as a platform', and so on (for example, Hayes, 2008; Vaquero, Rodero-Merino and Moran, 2011). The US NIST defines cloud computing as: 'a model for enabling ubiquitous, convenient, on-demand network access to a shared pool of configurable computing resources (e.g., networks, servers, storage, applications, and services) that can be rapidly provisioned and released with minimal management effort or service provider interaction' (Mell and Grance, 2011).

Cloud computing may be regarded as an internet utility service, which can be used to create, manage and use information without requiring individual users or institutions to invest in a massive IT infrastructure. In a way a cloud computing service may be regarded as a typical utility service like the electricity that we get in our homes, offices and shops, to build several applications to suit our personal and/or organizational needs without having to worry about the potential investment in electricity generation, and the associated equipment and infrastructure used to carry electricity from its source to our point of use. We pay for the amount of electricity consumed. In addition to the shared use of computing and network infrastructure, cloud computing services may provide several ready-made software applications like Google Mail or Facebook, and consumers can also build their own applications without having to invest in building the required computing and network infrastructure. The cost of building massive data centres with hardware and software can be amortized so consumers can benefit from a significantly reduced computing and infrastructure cost. The following major benefits of cloud computing have been identified by researchers:

- on-demand unlimited computing services from a service provider that does not require human intervention for securing the service
- broadband network access to support a large variety of consumer activities and applications on heterogeneous platforms
- optimization of the computing resources by dynamically assigning resources based on demand
- rapid elasticity to meet unlimited consumer demands round the clock
- a variety of services with provisions for automatic monitoring, charging and reporting.
    Baliga et al. (2011); Mell and Grance (2011); Open Cloud Manifesto (2009)

However, there are a number of disadvantages of cloud computing as well, for example:

- Data security and privacy of users in the cloud environment may be a major concern.
- Users may be dependent on cloud service providers, and thus there may be a risk of what is called 'vendor lock-in', which makes it difficult to move to another cloud service provider.
- Since the data, and even the applications, are managed by cloud service providers, users may have limited control and flexibility, which may create incompetency of users.
- Despite the best efforts of cloud service providers, there may be some unexpected downtime and technical difficulties.
- Data being on the cloud, users may be vulnerable to being targeted by malicious users and hackers, and sometimes data may get lost.
                    Jain and Bhardwaj (2010); Vaquero, Rodero-Merino
                    and Moran (2011); Yu et al. (2010)

Despite these disadvantages cloud computing has some great potential for information systems and services (Mell and Grance, 2011; Open Cloud Manifesto, 2009).

The deployment of cloud computing technologies

In order to understand how a green information service can be developed on the cloud computing model, it is important to understand the different kinds of cloud computing services that can be considered as layers, where each layer builds on services offered by the layer below, and in turn offers services to the layer above:

- *Software as a service (SaaS)*: where the consumer can access applications running on a cloud infrastructure through a thin client interface such as a web browser. Examples are web-based e-mail and social networking services. The consumer has minimum responsibility and control, except some basic client-end configuration, while the network, servers, operating systems, storage and specific applications are controlled by the cloud service provider.
- *Platform as a service (PaaS)*: where the consumer can deploy applications created by using specific software and tools that are supported by the cloud service provider. The consumer does not control the cloud infrastructure – the network, servers, operating system or storage – but has control over specific applications, software technology and the hosting environment configurations.
- *Infrastructure as a service (IaaS)*: where the consumer uses the processing, storage and other fundamental computing resources provided by the cloud service provider; Amazon EC2 is an example. The consumer does not have control over the infrastructure, but has control over operating systems, storage, specific applications and some networking components such as firewalls.

Chang et al. (2010); Mell and Grance (2011); Open Cloud Manifesto (2009)

How the layered architecture of cloud computing can be used to build a green information service for higher education and research is discussed later in the chapter. Cloud services can be deployed in different ways, including through a:

- *private cloud*: solely for an organization – a business, government or institution – and managed by the organization itself or a third party
- *community cloud*: shared by several organizations, supporting a specific community that has shared activities and interests, for example universities, research institutions, and so on
- *public cloud*: available to the general public or a large industry group and owned by an organization selling or providing cloud services, e.g. web mail and social networking services
- *hybrid cloud*: a composition of two or more clouds – private, community or public – bound together by standardized or proprietary technology.

Mell and Grance (2011)

Depending on the model and deployment, cloud computing provides a consumer – an organization or an individual – with more flexibility to satisfy their computing needs in a number of ways. For example, while storing data or running an application one does not need to own the physical hardware required for storing or processing the information. The storage space and computing power to run applications can be used on a pay-as-you-go basis (Cervone, 2010; Mell and Grance, 2011), and this results in significant environmental benefits (Anagnostopoulou, Saadeldeen and Chong, 2010). This also makes planning and management of IT services a lot easier. Depending on the model of the cloud service chosen, an organization can reduce the load of hardware and software at the client or user end, and if the data processing is performed centrally, then the client can afford to use low-end computing equipment or a thin client. Thus, overall there is significant potential for cost savings because the operational responsibilities are shifted to the cloud provider, who is then responsible for the ongoing maintenance of the hardware and network security, control and performance (Cervone, 2010; Leavitt, 2009). However, Garg, Versteeg and Buyya (2013) argue that although there are a number of cloud service providers, customers often find it difficult to decide whose services they should use and on what basis to select them. They propose a framework that measures the quality and accordingly ranks cloud services based on user activities and preferences. Such a framework can help users choose a specific cloud service and at the same time will create healthy competition among cloud service providers.

Cloud computing and the environment

The environmental costs of cloud computing depend on the following factors:

- *server energy consumption*: can be reduced by optimizing the use of computing resources – using full computing power only when required; this can be achieved by techniques such as sleep scheduling and virtualization of computing resources (Baliga et al., 2011; Liu et al., 2009)
- *network energy consumption*: can be reduced by making optimum use of resources, e.g. by encouraging a very high volume of traffic, which will justify the energy consumption of the network (Baliga et al., 2011; Mell and Grance, 2011)
- *end-user energy consumption*: can be reduced by performing all the software and processing activities at the cloud data centre or service rather than at the user end, and thereby enabling users to use what is known as a 'thin client' – a computing facility with minimum processing capabilities (like the 'dumb terminal' used at the client end in the pre-PC era for online database searching) (Baliga et al., 2011; Cervone, 2010; Mell and Grance, 2011).

A study at Melbourne University observed that:

> The level of utilization achieved by a cloud service is a function of the type of services it provides, the number of users it serves, and the usage patterns of those users. Large-scale public clouds that serve a very large number of users are expected to be able to fully benefit from achieving high levels of utilization and high levels of virtualization, leading to low per-user energy consumption.
>
> Baliga et al. (2011)

Thus a cloud-based green information service should have a significant amount of traffic in order to make optimum use of the computing and network infrastructure, and energy. This justifies the direction for community cloud-based green information service as proposed by Jisc (see below). By performing all the processing – such as searching, filtering, sorting and formatting – centrally, the service can significantly reduce computing power and thereby energy consumption at the users' end, which will reduce economic and environmental costs. Better energy efficiency and therefore less pollution can be achieved by setting up the cloud data centre (for the green information service) in a place where more environment-friendly energy sources (alternative energy sources rather than coal-fired power stations, for example) and cooling facilities are available; and by using a federated cloud computing environment, the overall service can be made more environment-friendly (Andrew, 2010; Pawlish and Varde, 2010).

Cloud computing and information services

While cloud computing is a new area of research, some believe that it is simply an extension of the client server model that was introduced in the 1980s (for example, Fox, 2011). The model of cloud computing, where data are stored and processed centrally, has long been practised by OCLC in the library and information services world, for example, through the WorldCat service (Fox, 2011) and DuraCloud of Library of Congress (Chun, 2010). Reed Elsevier is working with hospitals to provide point-in-time information – books, papers, technical manuals, and so on – to medical technicians as and when they need it (Kho, 2009). Some researchers have proposed new models for cloud-based digital library and specific information retrieval services (Jordan, 2011; Kang, Li and Tang, 2007; Mishra et al., 2010; Teregowda, Urgaonkar and Giles, 2010; Wang and Xing, 2011; Yang and Liu, 2010).

In a typical higher or further education institution, large computing facilities are usually kept switched on round the clock, although their activities are significantly reduced at certain times of the day, week or month, for example, at nights, weekends and holiday periods. A significant amount of energy savings can be realized through cloud services by taking advantage of the variable transaction demands that most typical computing applications have and redistributing unused computing cycles during the slower periods of one application to more demanding applications running at the same time for the same or different clients.

Cloud computing is a relatively new technology, and standards for practices, protocol and management are still emerging. Issues of privacy, security and other barriers were noted earlier in the chapter. There are challenges when migrating large databases onto the cloud (Thakar and Szalay, 2010), and scepticism about the implications of the cloud computing model, especially where data are hosted internationally, because the application and data are then subject to the laws and policies of the host nation (Cervone, 2010). However, the Cloud Security Alliance has developed a set of guidelines and recommendations to help organizations make decisions for adoption of cloud computing (Cloud Security Alliance, 2013). There are also concerns about data loss in case of accident, inaccessibility or degradation of performance level due to unforeseen problems with the cloud service provider, which is beyond the remit of the organization(s) subscribing to the cloud service (Fox, 2011; Leavitt, 2009).

A framework for green information services for the higher education sector

Users in universities and colleges require a variety of information:

- *administrative or operational information*: required for day-to-day academic administration and management activities including faculty and student administration, marketing, student and staff support, and personnel and resource administration; this is stored in the library, department or faculty databases
- *scholarly information*: required to accomplish academic, scholarly and research activities, and information generated in the form of research data and scholarly output – unpublished or institutional reports, theses, dissertations, and so on, and published output such as books, journal and conference papers, and so on; this is stored in the databases of administrative departments or units.

Administrative information is generated and managed at different levels within the institution, and most administrative information systems and services in higher and further education institutions, especially in developed countries, have now been automated. Administrative data and information do not usually have a price tag or financial value, but they are of immense value for the day-to-day operation and management of activities within institutions. Some of these data – for example, financial data, student and staff personal information, and grade reports – are very sensitive and can be accessed only by authorized users, while other information, such as that related to various courses and subjects offered, research activities, staff contacts and other details, can be accessed by anyone. The volume and variety of such information grows very rapidly. Therefore a huge amount of resources and IT infrastructure and support is required to process, manage, access, use and preserve this information.

Scholarly information can be divided into various categories, for example:

- information generated within an institution as course or teaching materials, virtual learning environment resources, theses and dissertations, project and research reports, and scholarly output produced by staff and students
- published scholarly information acquired at institutional level – books, journals, and so on
- research data produced by staff and students in the course of academic and research activities.

The volume and variety of scholarly information from external producers or providers (as mentioned in the second point above) is significantly higher than the information generated in-house. Scholarly information generated in-house by members of staff and students (the first point above) is often stored in open access collections in one or more locations, such as within a library, a specific department or a research unit. Scholarly information generated externally and acquired from various sources and services can be commercial (priced or fee-based, e.g. books, journals, databases, and so on) or open access (free online book and journal resources, digital libraries and web resources). Research data generated within higher or further education institutions in the course of research projects can be enormous, and while some of these data are stored centrally, for example at a national level, others are stored locally, often within the servers of the specific research or project team or department. Often such data are not managed and preserved properly mainly because of the lack of resources and support after completion of the research project concerned.

Administrative information and use of IT

As discussed earlier in this chapter, higher or further education institutions currently make extensive use of IT and networks to manage their administrative information systems and services. This has significantly improved the tasks of management and access to operational and administrative information in higher education, and increased the use of computing resources and energy consumption. As already mentioned in Chapter 4, US institutions of higher education produce an equivalent of nearly 2% of total annual GHG emissions in the USA, or about a quarter of the entire State of California's annual emissions (Sinha et al., 2010). It was estimated that in the 2008–9 academic year universities and colleges in the UK alone used nearly 1,470,000 computers, 250,000 printers and 240,000 servers; the IT-related electricity bills to run this equipment was estimated to be around £116 million, and it was estimated that there would be 500,000 tonnes of CO_2 emissions from this electricity use (James and Hopkinson, 2009). The SusteIT toolkit produced through a Jisc-funded project in 2009 estimated that the annual energy required to run the ICT infrastructure at a research-intensive university (the University of Sheffield was used as an example) could be as high as 8.68 MWh, which generates 4661 tonnes of CO_2e (SusteIT, n.d.).

Chapter 4 discussed how green IT measures can reduce energy consumption and waste of computing resources by making optimum use of computing hardware, software and network utilities by consolidating servers using virtualization software, and reducing waste associated with obsolete equipment, and so on (Jenkin, Webster and McShane, 2011; Watson, Boudreau and Chen, 2010). Examples of software-based solutions now used in organizations include collaborative group software; remote video and teleconferencing; information systems to track and monitor environmental variables such as waste, emissions, toxicity and water consumption; and supply chain systems to optimize product routing and transportation with a view to reducing the amount of energy consumed in moving products (Jenkin, Webster and McShane, 2011; Watson, Boudreau and Chen, 2010).

Jisc recommends that there are many incentives for educational institutions to address green issues in the use of IT. While IT accounts for around 2% of global carbon emissions it can also play a key role in saving time, energy and money (Jisc, 2010). Increasingly green IT measures include establishment of remote data centres, use of alternative sources of energy, and natural cooling facilities for data centres (Chowdhury, 2012c). Cloud computing is now considered to be one of the most effective means of achieving a green IT and information service (Baliga et al., 2011; Open Cloud Manifesto, 2009).

A green information services model

A green information service should be environmentally sustainable: it should produce minimum, if not zero, GHG emissions throughout the lifecycle of an information product or service (Chowdhury, 2012a). Two major contributors for a green information service are dematerialization – replacement of content such as printed information resources, which generate more GHG, with digital content and services, which generate less GHG (Chowdhury, 2012b) – and use of green ICT and cloud computing facilities to optimize and share computing and network resources in order to reduce economic costs and energy consumption, which will result in reduced GHG emissions (Chowdhury, 2012a). A generic model of a green information service is presented in Figure 9.1. It may be noted that the goal of a green information service, as stated above, can be achieved through the use of green ICT. A green information service may comprise:

- one or more structured databases containing research and operational data relevant to one or more organizations or businesses
- one or more green digital libraries, and digital content services including e-book and e-journal services, online databases and search services, and web-based content services like Google Books and Google Scholar
- one or more green digital preservation services.

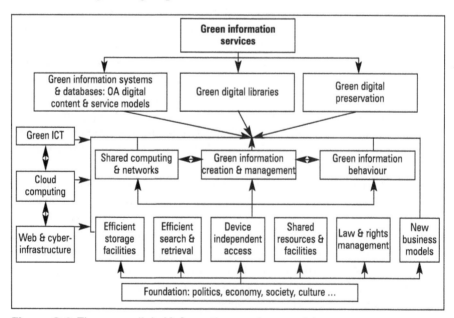

Figure 9.1 The green digital information services model

Each of these services should be based on the principles of:

- standard user-centred design and usability metrics, for example as proposed in ISO 9241 (ISO 9241-210:2010)
- shared and optimum use of computing and network resources
- green content creation and management techniques
- green information behaviour.

A green digital services information model should support efficient and device-independent access to information on demand (and in anticipation, if so desired) from heterogeneous systems and sources, and consequently new business models and regulatory frameworks have to be developed to support such activities.

Green information access and management

Chapter 6 discussed how printed content services are heavily dependent on massive industrial, transportation and physical storage and maintenance facilities for the production, transportation and storage of content, and together these activities produce a massive carbon footprint (Chowdhury, 2010, 2012b). Cloud-based real-time and on-demand access to information can be fully realized through dematerialization – by replacing printed content with their digital versions (Chowdhury, 2012b). While significant developments have taken place in the procurement and provision of e-books and e-journals in all sectors – especially the academic and research sector, with the help of Jisc and various other co-operative or centralized procurement and access services – the prevailing business models and copyright laws are not conducive for the optimum use of the potential of cloud computing and the green information services model proposed here. Luckily recommendations for change in copyright law and the development of suitable business models have been made at different levels, for example, in the Hargreaves report submitted to the UK Government (Hargreaves, 2011), and earlier in similar recommendations by others (for example, Chowdhury, 2009a, 2009b; Chowdhury and Fraser, 2011). Chowdhury (2009a, 2009b) and Hargreaves (2011) proposed there should be a digital copyright exchange, a special application built at the service level of the green information service model, which would deal with copyright detection and clearance automatically, with appropriate acknow-ledgement and/or payment or authorization of appropriate fees.

The cloud-based green information service model proposed here can reduce economic and environmental costs by adopting appropriate information management techniques. In the UK, Jisc recommends the adoption of the cloud computing model in the higher education and research sector, stating that it can:

1. Reduce environmental and financial costs – where functions are only needed for short periods, for example
2. Share the load – when a university is working with a partner organisation so that neither organisation need develop or maintain a physical infrastructure
3. Be flexible and pay as you go – researchers may need to use specialized web-based software that cannot be supported by in-house facilities or policies
4. Access data centres, web applications and services from any location
5. Make experiments more repeatable – write-ups of science experiments performed in the cloud can contain reference to cloud applications like a virtual machine, making the experiment easier to replicate.

Jisc (2011a)

In addition to these benefits, a range of new applications can be built more easily from a cloud-based green information service, for example:

• Several knowledge-mapping applications can be built on a green information service if it is based on the architecture proposed in this chapter. This will be possible because various databases – including those of open access and institutional repositories, commercial journals and conferences and funding agencies – can be linked through the cloud infrastructure; thus it will be easy to build semantic knowledge maps for specific domains to identify major areas of research, various leading publications, authors or researchers, funding bodies, and so on. This will facilitate further research and help in the management of research and scholarly activities.
• Various application programmes and data analytics similar to, or even better than, those currently produced by commercial databases and information services like Microsoft Academic Search and Scopus can be built to help researchers map the growth and development of a field of research over a period of time.
• With appropriate research and development, the cloud architecture of the green information service may give rise to a new knowledge creation platform where academics and researchers – individuals and groups or communities – will be able to create new knowledge by analysing existing data and research output, or running several parallel experiments.
• The cloud architecture, by virtue of linking various databases, funding bodies, and so on, will facilitate creation of various new measures of use and

impact of research knowledge, which can be used at national and institutional level for a research assessment exercise like the REF (formerly Research Assessment Exercise) in the UK, and ERA in Australia.
- A dynamic research and teaching or learning environment can be created based on the publicly available content and databases that are currently dispersed and require a lot of time and effort to find, access and extract required information. It is anticipated that various knowledge-intensive applications will be built on the cloud model to serve various niche markets and user communities, for example in the management of e-health.

Research shows that appropriate use of file and data management techniques, for example, a division between the most and the least frequently used files and storage of those files on servers of different performance capacities, can significantly reduce GHG emissions. In a Jisc-funded project called Planet Filestore, a Cardiff University research team developed an approach to storing data on disks with different energy consumption depending on the frequency with which the data is accessed; it is predicted that its application can save Cardiff University alone 87600 KWh (or approximately 51 tonnes of CO_2) per year which, at 2009 prices, would cost around £10,000 per annum (Jisc, 2011b). Thus, less frequently used content and data may be moved to less powerful servers to reduce energy consumptions. Green information services might distribute files to different servers based on file access frequency and server performance levels, as proposed by Planet Filestore, to save energy and reduce GHG emissions.

Further research is needed into information access, for example, for developing green information retrieval models for user- and context-specific searching, filtering and retrieval of data and information from heterogeneous systems and sources on the cloud (Chowdhury, 2012a), and in order for the green information service model to be successful, more green user awareness and green user behaviour studies need to be undertaken in all sections of our society, especially in the education and research sectors (Chowdhury, 2012a, 2012b, 2012c).

Summary

Cloud computing, being based on the principles of green IT, promises a number of economic and environmental benefits, and consequently there is a move towards developing cloud-based services in various sectors (Jisc, 2011a). Measures are also being taken by various universities and national agencies, like Jisc in the UK, to introduce cloud computing in the higher education and research sectors. Chowdhury has discussed the characteristics and potential benefits of a green information service in the past (Chowdhury, 2012a), but no one has examined the architecture of a cloud-based green information service.

The green information service architecture proposed in this chapter can provide institutions and users with access to information at anytime from anywhere at a reduced economic and environmental cost. In order to realize these benefits, a number of applications, protocols and standards have to be built by cloud service providers and institutions. This opens up a myriad of new research areas ranging from specific user-, community- and context-based information design and usability studies to green information retrieval and green user behaviour studies, which will bring a paradigm shift in the way we create, access, manage and use information at institutional and individual levels. Some changes in user information behaviour have already taken place due to the emergence of a range of new web, social networking and mobile technologies. Green information services and green information retrieval can help us develop economically, environmentally and socially sustainable information services. However, a number of research and development activities need to be undertaken in order to build and manage sustainable information systems and services (see chapters 10 and 12).

References

Anagnostopoulou, V., Saadeldeen, H. and Chong, F. T. (2010) Quantifying the Environmental Advantages of Large-scale Computing, paper given at the *International Conference on Green Computing*, Chicago, IL, 15–18 August.

Andrew, A. M. (2010) Going Green, *Kybernetes*, **39** (8), 1392–5.

Baliga, J., Ayre, R. W. A., Hinton, K. and Tucker, R. S. (2011) Green Cloud Computing: balancing energy in processing, storage, and transport, *Proceedings of the IEEE*, **99** (1), January, http://ieeexplore.ieee.org/stamp/stamp.jsp?arnumber=05559320.

Cervone, H. F. (2010) An Overview of Virtual and Cloud Computing, *OCLC Systems and Services*, **26** (3), 162–5.

Chang, B. R., Tsai, H. F., Huang, C.-F. and Huang, H.-C. (2010) Private Small-Cloud Computing in Connection with Linux Thin Client, paper given at the *1st International Conference on Pervasive Computing, Signal Processing and Applications*.

Chowdhury, G. (2009a) Towards the Conceptual Model of a Content Service Network. In *Globalizing Academic Libraries Vision 2020: proceedings of the International Conference on Academic Libraries*, Delhi, 5–8 October, Delhi Mittal Publications, 215–20.

Chowdhury, G. (2009b) Towards a New Service Model for the Content Supply Chain, plenary speech, *Seventh Book Conference*, University of Edinburgh, 16–18 December.

Chowdhury, G. G. (2010) Carbon Footprint of the Knowledge Sector: what's the future?, *Journal of Documentation*, **66** (6), 934–46.

Chowdhury, G. (2012a) An Agenda for Green Information Retrieval Research, *Information Processing and Management*, **48** (6), 1067–77.

Chowdhury, G. (2012b) How Digital Information Services Can Reduce Greenhouse Gas Emissions, *Online Information Review*, **36** (4), 489–506.

Chowdhury, G. (2012c) Building Sustainable Information Services: a green IS research agenda, *Journal of the American Society for Information Science and Technology*, **63** (4), 633–47.

Chowdhury, G. and Fraser, M. (2011) Carbon Footprint of the Knowledge Industry and Ways to Reduce It, *World Digital Libraries*, **4** (1), 9–18.

Chun, Y. (2010) Tactics for the Library Service Based on the Cloud Service, *Proceedings of the International Conference on E-Business and E-Government*, 4683–5.

The Climate Group (2008) *SMART2020: enabling the low carbon economy in the information age*, www.theclimategroup.org/publications/2008/6/19/smart2020-enabling-the-low-carbon-economy-in-the-information-age/.

Cloud Security Alliance (2013) https://cloudsecurityalliance.org/.

Fox, R. (2011) Digital Libraries: systems analysis perspective – the golden mean, *OCLC Systems and Services*, **27** (1), 10–17.

Garg, S. K., Versteeg, S. and Buyya, R. (2013) A Framework for Ranking of Cloud Computing Services: future generation computer systems, *International Journal of Grid Computing and Escience*, **29** (4), 1012–23.

Hargreaves, I. (2011) *Digital Opportunity: a review of intellectual property and growth*, www.ipo.gov.uk/ipreview-finalreport.pdf.

Hayes, B. (2008), Cloud Computing, *Communications of the ACM*, **51** (7), 9–11.

ISO 9241-210:2010 *Ergonomics of Human-System Interaction, Part 210: human-centred design for interactive systems*, International Organization for Standardization.

Jain, L. and Bhardwaj, S. (2010) Enterprise Cloud Computing: key considerations for adoption, *International Journal of Engineering and Information Technology*, **2** (2), 113–17.

James, P. and Hopkinson, L. (2009) *Green ICT: managing sustainable ICT in education and research*, www.jisc.ac.uk/publications/programmerelated/2009/sustainableictfinalreport.aspx.

Jenkin, T. A., Webster, J. and McShane, L. (2011) An Agenda for 'Green' Information Technology and Systems Research, *Information and Organization*, **21** (1), 1–24.

Jisc (2010) *Managing Sustainable ICT in FE and HE: strategic overview*, Joint Information Systems Committee, www.jisc.ac.uk/publications/programmerelated/2009/sustainableictoverview.aspx.

Jisc (2011a) Cloud Computing Increasingly Attractive to Universities, Says JISC, Joint Information Systems Committee, www.jisc.ac.uk/news/stories/2011/05/cloud.aspx.

Jisc (2011b) *Moving Files, Saving Energy*, Joint Information Systems Committee, www.jisc.ac.uk/news/stories/2011/01/filestore.aspx.

Jordan, J. (2011) Climbing Out of the Box and Into the Cloud: building web-scale for libraries, *Journal of Library Administration*, **51** (1), 3–17.

Kang, H.-Y., Li, Y.-F. and Tang, S.-P. (2007) Application of Cloud Models in Digital Libraries. In *Proceedings of the Sixth International Conference on Machine Learning and Cybernetics*, Hong Kong, 19–22 August, 3876–9.

Kho, N. D. (2009) Content in the Cloud, *EContent*, **32** (2), 26–30.

Leavitt, N. (2009) Is Cloud Computing Really Ready for Prime Time?, *Computer*, **42** (1), 15–20.

Liu, J., Zhao, F., Liu, X. and He, W. (2009) Challenges Towards Elastic Power Management in Internet Data Centers. In *Proceedings of IEEE International Conference on Distributed Computer Systems*, IEEE CS Press, 65–72.

Mell, P. and Grance, T. (2011) *The NIST Definition of Cloud Computing: recommendations of the National Institute of Standards and Technology*, http://csrc.nist.gov/publications/drafts/800-145/Draft-SP-800-145_cloud-definition.pdf.

Mishra, S., Gorai, A., Oberoi, T. and Ghosh, H. (2010) Efficient Visualization of Content and Contextual Information of an online Multimedia Digital Library for Effective Browsing. In Institute of Electrical and Electronics Engineers, *Web Intelligence/IAT Workshops*, 257–60.

Open Cloud Manifesto (2009) Introduction, www.opencloudmanifesto.org/opencloudmanifesto1.htm.

Pawlish, M. and Varde, A. S. (2010) Free Cooling: a paradigm shift in data centers. In *Proceedings of the 2010 Fifth International Conference on Information and Automation for Sustainability*, Colombo, 17–19 December, 1–28.

Sinha, P., Schew, W. A., Sawant, A., Kolwaite, K. J. and Strode, S. A. (2010) Greenhouse Gas Emissions from US Institutions of Higher Education, *Journal of Air and Waste Management Association*, **60** (5), 568–73.

SusteIT (n.d.) Resources: ICT energy and carbon footprinting tool, www.susteit.org.uk/files/category.php?catID=4.

Teregowda, P. T., Urgaonkar, B. and Giles, C. L. (2010) Cloud Computing: a digital libraries perspective. In *2010 IEEE 3rd International Conference on Cloud Computing*, 115–22.

Thakar, A. and Szalay, A. (2010) Migrating a (Large) Science Database to the Cloud, HPDC 2010. In *Proceedings of the 19th ACM International Symposium on High Performance Distributed Computing*, Chicago, IL, 21–25 June, 430–4.

Vaquero, L. M., Rodero-Merino, L. and Moran, D. (2011) Locking the Sky: a survey on IaaS cloud security, *Computing*, **91** (1), 93–118.

Vouk, M. A. (2008) Cloud Computing: issues, research and implementations, *Journal of Computing and Information Technology*, **16** (4), 235–46.

Wang, Y. C. and Xing, R. (2011) The Application of Cloud Computing in the Digital Library, *Advanced Materials Research*, **187**, 647–51.

Watson, R. T., Boudreau, M. C. and Chen, A. J. (2010) Information Systems and Environmentally Sustainable Development: energy informatics and new directions for the IS community, *MIS Quarterly*, **34** (1), 23–38.

Yang, J. and Liu, W. (2010) Cloud Computing in the Application of Digital Library. In 2010 International Conference on Intelligent Computation Technology and Automation, **1**, 939–41.

Yu, S. C., Wang, C., Ren, K. and Lou, W. (2010) Achieving Secure, Scalable, and Fine-grained Data Access Control in Cloud Computing, *Proceedings of INFOCOM 2010*, San Diego, CA, 19–25 March, www.ece.iit.edu/~ubisec/cloud/papers/INFOCOM10-sharing.pdf.

Information access and sustainability issues

Introduction

Traditionally information retrieval systems and services have been used by a select few, especially those engaged in knowledge-intensive professions and related activities, such as education and research, law and medicine. However, with the proliferation of web, social networking and mobile technologies, far more people than just those in knowledge-intensive professions now retrieve information. Every time we search for a specific message in our e-mail box, or look for information on the web, in a digital library or on a database of some kind, we use an information retrieval tool like a search engine, which allows us to discover, access, use and share information.

Although use of information retrieval tools has proliferated over the past two decades since the advent and proliferation of web and digital libraries, an information retrieval research community and industry has existed for nearly five decades, engaged in building tools and techniques 'to improve the process of finding information not only on the web, but also within a single computer ("desktop search") or a set of computers ("enterprise search"), as well as within very large databases, such as libraries ("database search"). Further, information retrieval techniques have been used to identify key links within, for example, legal records, genomics data, and spam' (Rowe et al., 2010, 19). Nowadays many researchers prefer to use the term information access instead of information retrieval. Information access includes all the typical information retrieval processes and activities ranging from content and data selection, processing and indexing, to search and retrieval, and use of information and data by users in order to meet their information requirements (Chowdhury and Foo, 2012, 47).

Nowadays we conduct billions of searches every day to find information on the web, library catalogues and databases, digital libraries, institutional repositories, e-books, e-journals, and so on. For example, Google handled 1.2 trillion searches in 2012 (Google, 2013). Behind every search there is a search engine that collects, processes and manages information from a variety of information sources in order to give us access to the information that we seek. In order to keep pace with the rapidly growing volume and variety of information on the web, digital libraries, databases and information retrieval systems have to work constantly behind the scenes in order to collect, organize and manage information in a manner that facilitates easy access and retrieval.

Information retrieval systems and services make extensive use of ICT at every stage of their creation, management and use, and this has an adverse environmental impact (Chowdhury, 2010, 2012a). As discussed in Chapters 4 and 7, the creation and destruction of ICT equipment creates a significant amount of GHG. Again, in order to run ICT equipment and facilities we need to use energy, which also generates a substantial amount of GHG. Thus in our daily life as we are becoming more and more reliant on information retrieval systems and services to access and use digital information in a variety of forms, we are creating more environmental damage because of our increased use of ICT and energy. Consequently, it may be argued that we need to find a way to develop information retrieval systems and services that are environmentally sustainable.

In order to be sustainable, information access should be green, and should generate minimum GHG, in all its activities. Chowdhury (2012b) comments that it is difficult to estimate the carbon footprint of all the various forms of information retrieval systems and services that we use every day in accessing a variety of information. He also adds that information retrieval systems are often embedded within a broader service portfolio, for example, as a web search service or within a digital library, social networking service, library management system or online database. Therefore it may not always be easy to determine the carbon footprint of information access separately from the entire digital information system or service.

The lifecycle analysis approach (ISO 14040:2006) may be used to identify the various stages and components of information access, and thus to identify the corresponding factors and their contributions to overall GHG emission figures. This approach may be taken for conducting case studies on information access systems and services designed for specific digital libraries and institutional repositories, for specific online databases, and so on, in order to determine the main contributors to GHG emissions. This will tell us the measures that need to be taken in order to reduce GHG emissions in relation to information access. The lifecycle analysis will also identify where and how the use of ICT can be optimized by using green IT and green information services that may help us reduce overall GHG emissions from information access, leading to the development of green information access. However, given the resource requirements and complexities of the underlying processes, an alternative and relatively simple process to estimate energy consumption and GHG emissions of information access, proposed by Raghavan and Ma (2011), is discussed in this chapter. It examines how to estimate GHG emissions for information access based on this approach and the concept of green information behaviour, which is an essential requirement for green information retrieval systems and services.

Cloud computing and information retrieval research

A simple search conducted on 10 May 2013 on 'cloud computing' and 'information retrieval' returned 191 hits from the Scopus database. This area of research is very new – the earliest result returned from Scopus was from 2008. The overall distribution of results from Scopus was 3 papers published in 2013 (up to 10 May), 77 papers published in 2012, 72 papers in 2011, 32 papers in 2010, 6 papers in 2009 and only 1 in 2008. Not all these papers were on cloud computing and information retrieval in the strict sense of the terms. They covered different issues of cloud computing, information management, information retrieval, business models for information and resource sharing, and so on. However, some research focused specifically on different aspects of information retrieval and access in the cloud computing environment, and the following are some typical examples:

- new technologies for information retrieval in the cloud environment:
  — Bradford (2011) examined large-scale semantic indexing for cloud computing applications.
  — Jiang, Watanabe and Yokota (2011) discussed XArp, an XML data allocation algorithm, to reduce power consumption in cloud computing.
  — Liu et al. (2012) described a new model for efficient information retrieval for ranked query (EIRQ), to reduce querying costs incurred in the cloud.
  — Miyano and Uehara (2012) proposed the design and implementation of cloud search engine as a service.
  — Maiorana and Fazio (2012) looked at a text mining framework and its applications to bioinformatics into a cloud architecture.
  — Rose (2012) discussed how Amazon CloudSearch can facilitate better information access on the cloud.
- retrieval of specific types or genres of information:
  — Nandzik et al. (2013) proposed a new set of technologies for managing multimedia digital libraries on the cloud.
  — Alonso-Calvo et al. (2012) discussed a new biomedical image retrieval system on the cloud.

— Hsu et al. (2012) examined the indexing and retrieval of spatial data in the cloud.

— Raj and Mala (2013) described Cloudpress 2.0, a news retrieval system on the cloud.

— Shih, Tseng and Yang (2011) discussed the fuzzy index creation problem for learning content retrieval on the cloud.

— Teregowda, Urgaonkar and Giles (2010) proposed that cloud implementation can improve the performance of CiteSeer, a service that provides citation indexing, full-text indexing and extensive document metadata from documents crawled from the web across computer and information sciences and related fields.

- new information retrieval models and approaches based on cloud computing:
  — Bales, Sohn and Setlur (2011) discussed information access behaviour using mobile and other computing devices, especially smartphones and computers.

  — Chowdhury (2012b) looked at various issues and challenges associated with a cloud-based green information service model.

  — Ibrahim et al. (2012), and Chiueh et al. (2012) discussed new indexing and information retrieval techniques for the encrypted cloud data.

  — Osinka, Bala and Gawarkiewicz (2012) described new techniques to develop information retrieval interfaces for visualization and semantic information retrieval using cloud computing.

  — Wang (2012) looked at how some lessons from music information retrieval can be used in the medical domain in patient treatments using cloud computing technologies.

- pattern recognition, image retrieval, and so on:
  — Basirat and Khan (2010) proposed that data storage and retrieval on the cloud can be performed using a distributed pattern recognition approach.

  — Yang, Kamata and Ahrary (2009) proposed an open source cloud computing-enabled content-based image retrieval system called NIR.

  — Langer (2011) examined how cloud computing can help researchers in the storage and retrieval of large medical image databases.

  — Zhang et al. (2011) investigated a new content-based image retrieval (CBIR) based on visual content and watermarking protocol for cloud computing environment.

These examples show that information retrieval researchers are now engaged in addressing various challenges associated with information retrieval in the cloud computing environment. However, as discussed earlier in the chapter, there is a lack of research on the environmental impact of information retrieval systems and services in general, and more specifically how green information retrieval systems and services can be developed to promote the idea of environmental sustainability in the context of access to and use of digital information in different forms and application environments – education and research, business, government, and so on (Chowdhury, 2012b). The main challenge comes from the lack of an established methodology to calculate GHG emission figures for an information retrieval system or service, which is often embedded within a bigger product or service. Research is needed to estimate the energy consumption and environmental impact of various ICT equipment, network and activities involved in information access, including all the activities from processing of input information – digital content – to searching, accessing and using information.

Measuring the environmental impact of information access: the lifecycle analysis approach

Although green IT and cloud computing research has progressed rapidly over the past few years, to date there are no authoritative research data on the environmental impact of information retrieval systems and services, nor have there been studies that can help us understand which factors contribute to the carbon footprint of information access. As discussed earlier, this is partly because of the complexities involved in making estimates, especially because there are different ICT equipment and technologies to develop information retrieval systems, and they are used as part of larger systems like the internet, digital libraries and databases.

The GHG emissions of a product or service are calculated by using what is known as the lifecycle assessment or lifecycle analysis (Finnveden et al., 2009; ISO 14040:2006). This method takes into account the energy inputs and emission outputs throughout the production chain from exploration and extraction of raw materials to different stages of processing, manufacturing, storage, transportation, use and disposal. Lifecycle assessment is accredited by the ISO 14000 series standards, which reflect 'international consensus on good environmental and business practices that can be applied by organizations all over the world in their specific context' (ISO, 2009).

Although the software development lifecycle can be modified to achieve environmental sustainability, this is a relatively new area of research and there is little research literature that specifically discusses how the lifecycle analysis approach can be used to assess GHG emissions from a software lifecycle. The International Workshop on Software Research and Climate Change (WSRCC) addressed the environmental sustainability of software engineering (WSRCC,

2011). Galster noted that the lifecycle analysis approach may be used to determine environmental sustainability by measuring the carbon footprint (an alternative term to denote GHG emissions) of:

- a particular software product
- a software development process for an organization or a suite of consumer activities
- the whole software product life cycle (development, usage, maintenance, and so on).   Galster (2010)

Each stage in the software development lifecycle should be analysed to determine how much energy is used, and the corresponding GHG emissions for production and use of every physical item involved in the process, plus the energy cost of all the activities in the design, development, testing and implementation of the software, including the energy consumption for the office space used, any travelling, and future maintenance (debugging, upgrading, and so on).

Before conducting a lifecycle analysis it is important to define the scope of a product or service being studied. At one level, an information retrieval system may be considered to be a piece of software or a search engine that allows users to search and retrieve digital information. Those managing an information retrieval service as part of an information search service or database such as a digital library, open archive, institutional repository or commercial database of content have the same goal as those managing information retrieval systems or search engines – to provide access to information – but the lifecycle analysis of an information retrieval service has a broader scope because it has to have a collection of digital content and a target user community that accesses and uses the digital information. Therefore the lifecycle of information retrieval as a tool and information retrieval as a service is different and each produces different GHG emissions throughout its lifecycle. One may also argue that a search service may provide access to digital information but may not have a collection of digital content, as with search engines. So, for a search engine the process starts from identifying and indexing digital content as opposed to content creation or harvesting, storing, preserving, and so on.

For the purpose of lifecycle analysis, it is important to consider three different classes of information retrieval:

- information retrieval as a software or tool – a software product
- information retrieval as a search service or a search engine that uses software to provide search and retrieval facilities

- information retrieval as an integral part of an information service, for example a digital library, which uses a search engine that comprises an information retrieval tool or software in order to facilitate access to and use of one or more collections of digital content for a designated user community.

This classification is not always distinct and mutually exclusive, because information retrieval as a piece software or a search service, while playing the part of an information access service like an online database, open archive or institutional repository, is always evaluated and modified or improved as part of a usability testing cycle. Similarly there is a significant overlap in the scope of specific features of search engine and database search services, but when conducting the lifecycle analysis to estimate GHG emissions it is useful to have this classification, because for each class there may be several different factors contributing to the GHG emission. These need to be identified and appropriate measures taken to reduce GHG emissions from each component, which will then lead to the development of green information retrieval.

Measuring the environmental impact of information retrieval: an alternative approach

The lifecycle analysis approach is resource intensive and, depending on the level of analysis, the process of estimating the energy consumption of an information retrieval system or service can be complex. An alternative, and relatively less complex and less expensive, approach similar to that adopted for estimating the energy consumption of the internet in a study by Raghavan and Ma (2011), already discussed in Chapter 7, may be taken when estimating the energy consumption, and consequently the GHG emission figures, of an information retrieval system or service.

In this approach, the energy cost of information access should be based on the estimation of two types of energy:

- *the embodied energy* of the different the devices – servers, desktops, laptops, networks, routers, modems, and so on, used in different activities associated with information access on the server side – and emergy on the client side – devices such as desktops, laptops, iPads, e-book readers and mobile devices used to access information
- *the socket energy* consumed by various devices on the client side for the creation, storage and maintenance of databases and search engines, and devices used to access and use digital information.

In this approach, estimation of the energy consumption of information access, measured in GHG emissions, involves server-side energy costs:

- embodied energy costs of the various computing equipment and network facilities, such as servers, desktops or laptops, wi-fi or local area network, Telecom switches, modems and routers, for different server-side activities for search engine software development and management, input selection and preparation, indexing and file management, and so on
- estimation of the socket energy consumption of all the computing and network devices for all the above-mentioned activities

and client-side energy costs:

- embodied energy costs of various client-side computing equipment and network devices for various information access activities including search and retrieval, online use of information, downloading and offline use of information and printing
- socket energy costs of all the above-mentioned client-side equipment and network devices for all the above-mentioned information access activities.

As already discussed in Chapters 4 and 7, the embodied energy costs of a device can be obtained by using a 'factor' of the total energy used during the manufacturing of a specific computing or network device. The 'factor' is the proportion of a device's full life that has been used in a specific operation or activity. This can be estimated by taking into account three parameters:

- the manufacturing energy costs of a specific computing device or network equipment
- the lifetime (replacement cycle) of that device, for example a server may be replaced every two years, a laptop may be replaced every three years, and so on
- the fraction of its life used in an operation, which may be based on the actual time used and the capacity in which the device is used, for example 50% usage (used only about half of its time for information access activities) and 100% capacity (used to its full capacity).

The socket energy costs for server and client-side computing devices are easy to estimate based on the energy consumption rate of the devices and the actual time of their usage for various information access activities. Together these figures will give an estimation of the energy and the corresponding environmental cost of information access. Chapter 4 considered how the embodied energy and socket energy costs can be calculated, but some assumptions may have to be made in these calculations. For example, the estimate of the apportionment of internet energy costs for various activities ranging from input preparation (e.g. uploading and verification of research papers in an institutional repository) to search and retrieval of information by the clients may have to be based on transaction logs. It is estimated that on average people in the UK use the internet for 16.8 hours per week or 2.4 hours per day (European Travel Commission, 2013). According to Internet World Stats it is estimated that as of June 2012 there were 52,731,209 internet users in the UK (84.1% of the population) and 2,405,518,376 people in the world (Internet World Stats, 2013). Using these figures and the annual internet energy costs produced by Raghavan and Ma (2011) it may be possible to estimate the average internet energy costs per person. There are many other estimations of the energy usage of the internet (see Chapter 4). For example one estimate shows that the internet generates 830 million tonnes of CO_2e per year (ACS News Service, 2013). Using this figure it may be estimated that the average emission per person for use of the internet is 0.345 tonnes per year. This figure may also be used to estimate the environmental cost of internet use for information access by a given user. However, all these calculations will only produce a gross or an approximate figure because the actual internet energy cost per person will depend on the frequency and duration of their usage.

Similarly, the time used by clients when using information in offline mode, or through printing, will have to be estimated. Again, the energy and the environmental costs will vary depending on the nature of the digital information service; they will be different for commercial database services like Scopus, large digital libraries like PubMed or institutional repositories. There is a need for more research in this area, and an appropriate methodology and reliable figures can only be produced through empirical research.

Raghavan and Ma (2011) noted that embodied energy accounted for about 53% of the total energy consumption of the internet, and that desktops and laptops account for about half of the total energy consumption of the internet. This may very well be the case for information access and thus the energy consumption by desktops and laptops used for information access may be the major contributor to overall energy consumption figures. While sharing computing and network resources may reduce embodied energy consumption for the server-side costs of information access, user information behaviour also plays a major role. Client-side energy consumption depends on the duration of a search session and the type of computing facilities used, the source of energy used, and the overall search behaviour of the user, for example whether the user reads the content and interacts with it online, or whether this is done offline still using a computing device, or through printed content, and so on.

Green user behaviour

As discussed earlier in this chapter, many researchers have proposed new models and approaches for information retrieval for cloud environment (for example, Chiueh et al., 2012; Ibrahim et al., 2012; Jiang, Watanabe and Yokota, 2011). Whichever approach is taken the overall energy consumption, and thus the GHG emission figures, of information access can be reduced by:

- making information retrieval systems more efficient so the overall time for generation and processing of digital content by the information retrieval system and their retrieval time is reduced
- making it possible for users to access information using a thin client, which has low energy consumption
- reducing the socket energy consumption of end-user devices.

It should be noted that for the first option, there is a trade-off between the retrieval time and simultaneous use of multiple servers. For example, Google uses multiple servers simultaneously in order to reduce retrieval time. While it has a significant impact on the efficiency of an information retrieval service, very efficient retrieval (measured by the fraction of a second) may not always be a specific requirement for every information retrieval system. The second option is more important, and indeed many information services are moving towards the use of thin clients at the user end so overall energy consumption at the user end can be reduced significantly. The third option is related to the second option, but creation and processing of digital content by information retrieval systems can play a major role. For example, the time for access and use can be reduced by using granular content and providing targeted information services through specific applications. This depends on the trends in the content and IT industry.

Some generic measures may be taken to facilitate the development of green information retrieval (Chowdhury, 2012b). Human information behaviour has remained a major area of research within the information community and for many this is an integral part of information retrieval research, because the success or failure of any information retrieval system or service depends on how it meets user information needs, which depends on a number of user behaviours and character-istics. Green user behaviour is an important component of green IT or green information services (Jenkin, Webster and McShane, 2011), and several projects have looked at user behaviour with regard to energy consumption and user perceptions of their environmental impact (for a list of projects see Jisc, 2011).

Green user behaviour in the context of climate change may mean several things, which include a range of behaviour changes in energy usage, business practices, lifestyle, and so on. This also relates to social sustainability which, as discussed before, is an important enabler for environmental sustainability. At the very basic level, green user behaviour in the context of green ICT may lead to changes in users' printing and photocopying activities, which have a significant adverse effect on the environment. It is estimated that printing and copying at UK universities account for 10–16% of ICT-related electricity consumption, and the total printing and copying costs in larger universities can be well over £1 million per year (James and Hopkinson, 2009). Proper user education supported by appropriate measures for easy access to information through the cloud can lead to the development of green user behaviour, which is a key enabler for green ICT. It is expected that copying and printing will decrease with increasing use of sophisticated devices like iPads, e-book readers and various mobile devices, and specific measures taken by information retrieval systems and services where users can store, use and share content of their choice, for example, content they have accessed before, where and when they want.

In addition to reducing printing and copying, those working in information-intensive businesses, such as teaching and research, may need to change their overall cultural and business practices – education and learning activities, research and innovation, business and administration, and so on – in such a way that digital content and data are created, accessed and used with low-end computing devices. Research shows that significant reductions in GHG emissions can be achieved only when users access and use data from the cloud using low energy computing devices (Baliga et al., 2011). More research and user education is needed to promote the idea of green information user behaviour, and thus achieve the social sustainability of information retrieval systems and services.

Summary

Information retrieval has become an integral part of many, if not most, of our daily activities where we generate, access and use digital information in a number of ways for a number of our day-to-day activities. Given the new developments and promises of cloud computing, such as the recent Jisc cloud computing initiatives in the UK described earlier in this book, and related developments such as recent initiatives prompted by RCUK's policies, the Finch report and the Hargreaves review (also discussed earlier in the book) will no doubt open new opportunities for new and more rigorous information retrieval research. It is expected that these developments will encourage information retrieval researchers to undertake research and develop new domain- and context-specific information retrieval tools and applications, including new data or text mining and visualization applications to facilitate access to integrated data and content from heterogeneous platforms and services. This increased research, and more frequent use of information retrieval should be coupled with environmental research in order to develop sustainable information retrieval systems and services.

Green information retrieval that produces minimum GHG emissions in facilitating access to and use of digital information can significantly help in achieving sustainable development. Although a considerable amount of research has been undertaken in the recent past on green IT, green information services and cloud computing, to date there has been hardly any research on green information retrieval per se. In order to develop green information retrieval systems and services we first need to know which components of an information retrieval system and service produce how much GHG; then we need to find appropriate ways of optimizing those operations to reduce the corresponding emissions. This calls for detailed research and analysis because information retrieval systems vary significantly and often form an integral part of a database, a digital library or an information search service.

Concerted efforts from the information retrieval research community are needed to promote green information retrieval as a major research agenda to build sustainable digital information and communication services, which are increasingly becoming an integral part of our daily life and activities (Chowdhury, 2012b). Green information retrieval research will help us find better ways to standardize, share and re-use digital content and data and tools and technologies related to information retrieval systems and services leading to environmental sustainability. It will also promote green user behaviour, which will lead to the social sustainability of green information retrieval systems and services. Appropriately designed digital information systems and services can play a key role in sustainable development, and appropriate green information retrieval research can play a big role in that.

References

ACS News Service (2013) Toward Reducing the Greenhouse Gas Emissions of the
    Internet and Telecommunications, Weekly PressPac, 2 January,
        www.acs.org/content/acs/en/pressroom/presspacs/2013/acs-presspac-january-23-2013/

toward-reducing-the-greenhouse-gas-emissions-of-the-internet-and-telecommunications.html.

Alonso-Calvo, R., Crespo, J., Munoz-Marmol, M., Intriago, M. and Jimenez-Castellanos, A. (2012) A Cloud Computing Service for Managing Biomedical Image Collections. In *Proceedings of CBMS 2012: the 25th IEEE International Symposium on Computer-Based Medical Systems*, Rome, 20–22 June, 1–6.

Bales, E., Sohn, T. and Setlur, V. (2011) Planning, Apps, and the High-End Smartphone: exploring the landscape of modern cross-device reaccess. In Lyons, K., Hightower, J. and Huang, E. M. (eds), *Pervasive Computing: 9th International Conference, Pervasive 2011, San Francisco, USA, June 12–15, 2011, Proceedings*, Lecture Notes in Computer Science, **6696**, 1–18.

Baliga, J., Ayre, R. W. A., Hinton, K. and Tucker, R. S. (2011) Green Cloud Computing: balancing energy in processing, storage, and transport, *Proceedings of the IEEE*, **99** (1), January, http://ieeexplore.ieee.org/stamp/stamp.jsp?arnumber=05559320.

Basirat, A. H. and Khan, A. I. (2010) Evolution of Information Retrieval in Cloud Computing by Redesigning Data Management Architecture from a Scalable Associative Computing Perspective. In Wong, K. W., Mendis, B. S. U. and Bouzerdoum, A. (eds), *Neural Information Processing: models and applications, 17th International Conference, ICONIP 2010, Sydney, Australia, November 22–25, 2010, Proceedings, Part II*, Lecture Notes in Computer Science, **6444** (2), 275–82.

Bradford, R. B. (2011) Implementation Techniques for Large-scale Latent Semantic Indexing Applications. In *Proceedings of the 20th ACM Conference on Information and Knowledge Management*, Glasgow, 24–28 October, 339–44.

Chiueh, T.-C., Simha, D. N., Saxena, A., Bhola, S., Lin, P.-H. and Pang, C.-E. (2012) Encryption Domain Text Retrieval. In *2012 IEEE 4th International Conference on Cloud Computing Technology and Science (CloudCom)*, Taipei, 3–6 December, 107–12.

Chowdhury, G. G. (2010) Carbon Footprint of the Knowledge Sector: what's the future?, *Journal of Documentation*, **66** (6), 934–46.

Chowdhury, G. G. (2012a) Building Sustainable Information Services: a green IS research agenda, *Journal of the American Society for Information Science and Technology*, **63** (4), 633–47.

Chowdhury, G. G. (2012b) An Agenda for Green Information Retrieval Research, *Information Processing and Management*, **48** (6), 1067–77.

Chowdhury, G. G. and Foo, S. (eds) (2012) *Digital Libraries and Information Access: research perspectives*, Facet Publishing.

European Travel Commission (2013) Usage Patterns and Demographics, www.newmediatrendwatch.com/markets-by-country/18-uk/148-usage-patterns-and-demographics.

Finnveden, G., Hauschild, M., Ekvall, T., Guinée, J., Heijungs, R., Hellweg, S., Koehler, A., Pennington, D. and Suh, S. (2009) Recent Developments in Life Cycle Assessment, *Journal of Environmental Management*, **91** (1), 1–21.

Galster, M. (2010) Life-cycle Assessment in Software Engineering, position paper, *Workshop on Software Research and Climate Change*, www.cs.toronto.edu/wsrcc/WSRCC2/papers/wsrcc2010-Galster.pdf.

Google (2013) *Zeitgeist 2012*, https://www.google.co.uk/zeitgeist/2012/#the-world.

Hsu, Y.-T., Pan, Y.-C., Wei, L,-Y., Peng, W.-C. and Lee, W.-C. (2012) Key Formulation Schemes for Spatial Index in Cloud Data Managements. In *IEEE 13th International Conference on Mobile Data Management*, Bengaluru, India, 23–26 July, 21–6.

Ibrahim, A., Jin, H., Yasin, A. A. and Zou, D. (2012) Secure Rank-Ordered Search of Multi-Keyword Trapdoor Over Encrypted Cloud Data. In *7th IEEE Asia-Pacific Services Computing Conference*, Guilin, China, 6–8 December, 263–70.

Internet World Stats (2013) *Internet Usage Statistics: the internet big picture – world internet users and population stats*, www.internetworldstats.com/stats.htm.

ISO (2009) *Environmental Management: the ISO 14000 family of international standards*, International Organization for Standardization, www.iso.org/iso/theiso14000family_2009.pdf.

ISO 14040:2006 *Environmental Management – Life Cycle Assessment – Principles And Framework*, International Organization for Standardization.

James, P. and Hopkinson, L. (2009) *Green ICT: managing sustainable ICT in education and research*, www.jisc.ac.uk/publications/programmerelated/2009/sustainableictfinalreport.aspx.

Jenkin, T. A., Webster, J. and McShane, L. (2011) An Agenda for 'Green' Information Technology and Systems Research, *Information and Organization*, **21** (1), 1–24.

Jiang, X., Watanabe, Y. and Yokota, H. (2011) Data Allocation Based on XML Query Patterns to Reduce Power Consumption. In *DASC 2011: 2011 IEEE Ninth International Conference on Dependable, Autonomic and Secure Computing*, Sydney, NSW, 12–14 December, 532–9.

Jisc (2011) *Green ICT: managing environmentally sustainable ICT in education and research: energy dashboard and user behaviour*, Joint Information Systems Committee, http://greenict.jiscinvolve.org/wp/2011/06/30/energy-dashboards-and-user-behaviour/.

Langer, S. G. (2011) Challenges for Data Storage in Medical Imaging Research, *Journal of Digital Imaging*, **24** (2), 203–7.

Liu, Q., Tan, C. C., Wu, J. and Wang, G. (2012) Efficient Information Retrieval for Ranked Queries in Cost-Effective Cloud Environments. In *Proceedings of the IEEE Conference on Computer Communications*, Orlando, FL, 25–30 March, 2581–5.

Maiorana, F. and Fazio, G. (2012) Knowledge Discovery from Text on a Cloud

Architecture and its Application to Bioinformatics. In *Proceedings of the 9th IASTED International Conference on Biomedical Engineering*, Innsbruck, Austria, 15–17 February, 557–64.

Miyano, T. and Uehara, M. (2012) Proposal for Cloud Search Engine as a Service. In *Proceedings of the 5th International Conference on Network-Based Information Systems*, Melbourne, Australia, 26–28 September, 627–32.

Nandzik, J., Litz, B., Flores-Herr, N., Lohden, A., Konya, I., Baum, D., Bergholz, A., Schonfuss, D., Fey, C., Osterhoff, J., Waitelonis, J., Sack, H., Kohler, R. and Ndjiki-Nya, P. (2013) CONTENTUS–technologies for next generation multimedia libraries: automatic multimedia processing for semantic search, *Multimedia Tools and Applications*, **63** (2), 287–329.

Osinka, V., Bala, P. and Gawarkiewicz, M. (2012) Information Retrieval Across Information Visualization. In *Proceedings of the Federated Conference on Computer Science and Information Systems*, Wroclaw, Poland, 9–12 September, 233–9.

Raghavan, B. and Ma, J. (2011) The Energy and Emergy of the Internet. In *Proceedings of the ACM Workshop on Hot Topics in Networks (Hotnets)*, Cambridge, MA, November, www.cs.berkeley.edu/~jtma/papers/emergy-hotnets2011.pdf.

Raj, A. A. and Mala, T. (2013) Cloudpress 2.0: a new-age news retrieval system on the cloud, *International Journal of Information and Communication Technology*, **5** (2), 150–66.

Rose, D. E. (2012) CloudSearch and the Democratization of Information Retrieval. In *Proceedings of the 35th Annual ACM SIGIR Conference on Research and Development in Information Retrieval*, Portland, OR, 12–16 August, 1022–3.

Rowe, B. R., Wood, D. W., Link, A. N. and Simoni, D. A. (2010) *Economic Impact Assessment of NIST's Text REtrieval Conference (TREC) Program*, http://trec.nist.gov/pubs/2010.economic.impact.pdf.

Shih, W.-C., Tseng, S.-S. and Yang, C.-T. (2011) Due Time Setting for Peer-to-Peer Retrieval of Teaching Material in Cloud Computing Environments. In *Proceedings of the 2011 International Conference on Information Science and Applications*, Jeju Island, 26–29 April, 965–70.

Teregowda, P. T., Urgaonkar, B. and Giles, C. L. (2010) Cloud Computing: a digital libraries perspective. In *2010 IEEE 3rd International Conference on Cloud Computing*, 115–22.

Wang, Y. (2012) When Music, Information Technology, and Medicine Meet. In *Proceedings of the 2nd International ACM Workshop on Music Information Retrieval with User-centered and Multimodal Strategies*, Nara, Japan, 2 November, 43–4.

WSRCC (2011) Overview and Motivation, *3rd International Workshop on Software Research and Climate Change, European Conference on Object-Oriented Programming (ECOOP) 2011*, https://sites.google.com/site/wsrcc2011.

Yang, Z., Kamata, S.-I. and Ahrary, A. (2009) NIR: content based image retrieval on cloud computing. In *Proceedings of the 2009 IEEE International Conference on Intelligent Computing and Intelligent Systems*, Shanghai, 20–22 November, 556–9.

Zhang, J., Xiang, Y., Zhou, W., Ye, L. and Mu, Y. (2011) Secure Image Retrieval Based on Visual Content and Watermarking Protocol, *Computer Journal*, **54** (10), 1661–74.

The sustainability of information models

Introduction

Sustainable developments rely on the three pillars of sustainability – economic, social and environmental sustainability – and this chapter discusses various aspects of sustainable communication processes in today's digital age. It proposes an integrated model for study of the sustainability of scholarly communication processes in general, and sustainability of information services in particular. First a generic framework for study of the sustainability of information systems and services is proposed. The model is then used to investigate various factors responsible for the economic, social and environmental sustainability of information systems and services. It is shown that the conceptual model can be used to study the sustainability of the scholarly communication processes in general. The proposed model can also be used to identify factors responsible for the sustainability of any digital library or information service.

The three pillars of sustainable information services

In today's world typical scholarly information systems and services comprise library and information services, commercial journal and database services, open access journals and database services, digital libraries and repositories, and even various search engine services. These services deal with different types of content and data in order to meet the information needs of different types of users and communities. They may be offered or controlled by various institutions, funding bodies and business models; and governed by institutional, national and international regulations and policies. However, as argued throughout this book, in order to achieve sustainability, information systems and services should be economically, socially and environmentally sustainable. Various research issues in information science and their implications for the three forms of sustainability are discussed in this chapter.

Scholarly communication processes

Scholarly communication is a process through which research and scholarly outputs are created, peer reviewed and disseminated, and preserved for future use (ARL, 2013). Traditionally a large part of the scholarly communication process is publicly funded. For example, the research and scholarly activities that generate scholarly output are funded by governments or research funding agencies. Such funding usually comes either directly through research and/or dissemination grants or indirectly through staff remuneration in education and research institutions where academics and researchers produce research output as part of their activities. Similarly, the library and information services that facilitate the management of, and access to, scholarly outputs are also funded publicly through institutions that own them. Figure 11.1 is a schematic diagram showing the different activities involved in typical scholarly communication processes, which range from the

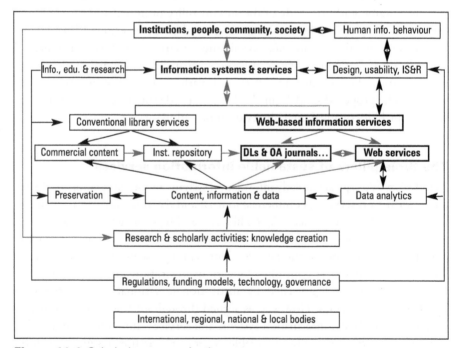

Figure 11.1 Scholarly communication processes

creation of scholarly content and data to access and use of scholarly output. This in turn facilitates creation of new content and data.

As Figure 11.1 shows, various local, regional, national and international bodies and a number of regulations, funding models, technologies and governance policies support and control the knowledge creation process through research and scholarly activities. These activities generate content that can appear through commercial publishers (in the form of books, journal and conference papers), as open access publications (books, journal articles and conference papers) or as web information resources (open access reports, papers, and so on). The policies, funding models and ICT supporting the knowledge creation process have a significant influence on the overall scholarly communication processes; these issues are discussed later in this book in the context of sustainability and open access policies.

People from various institutions and communities now use a range of information systems and services in order to access the output of scholarly communications. In today's world these information systems and services can be grouped into two categories – conventional library services and web-based information services. Typical library-based services provide access to commercial content in hard copy or, increasingly, in soft copy through various commercial databases and subscription-based services, and institutional repositories comprising various institutional output, special collections, and so on. Libraries also provide access to various information resources and services that are available on the web but users do not necessarily need to go through a library in order to access and use such services. Web-based services can be divided into two categories: digital libraries, institutional repositories and open access resources (books, journals, and so on) and a variety of web-based information sources and services (institutional resources such as research and project reports, papers, and so on; specific web-based reference services like Ask a Librarian or the Internet Public Library; and specific search engine services like Google Books, Google Scholar, Microsoft Academic Search).

Figure 11.1 can help us understand the characteristics of the entire scholarly communication process – from content creation to access and use. Increasingly library users are relying more on web-based information services than on conventional library services. Chapter 7 noted that recent open access policies are going to bring a paradigm shift in overall scholarly communication processes. This is shown in Figure 11.1 by using highlighted boxes for 'web-based information services', which will take precedence as more and more research content and data are made available through open access. Thus increasingly commercial content will move to open access repositories, open access journals, conferences and digital libraries, which have been shown using dark arrows in Figure 11.1. The figure also shows that information services will shift from conventional library-based services to web-based services. It is expected that open access repositories, digital libraries and web services will form the foundation of future scholarly information services and hence these boxes and their interactions have been highlighted in bold.

Figure 11.1 also shows that as more and more scholarly content and data are available through open access repositories, digital libraries and the web (shown through highlighted arrows), people will have better access to and use of research content and data, which will facilitate better research and knowledge creation processes (shown through highlighted arrows). The figure also shows that the sustainability of scholarly communications and information services will depend on appropriate funding models, regulations and governance for some key activities such as digital preservation, data analytics, design and usability studies of information systems and services, and information education and research.

The rest of this chapter proposes and discusses an integrated approach and a conceptual model, which can be used to study the sustainability of scholarly communication processes in general, and the sustainability of information in particular.

An integrated approach to research on the sustainability of digital information

As noted earlier, a number of factors are associated with the sustainability of digital information systems and services, and while some aspects of economic and social sustainability of information have been studied implicitly in the course of research in other areas such as in human information behaviour, evaluation and usability, the environmental research into the sustainability of information services has remained unexplored. Some major directions in information research, discussed in this chapter, suggest there are opportunities to bring about economic and social sustainability of scholarly information services, but such research activities should be integrated and the findings consolidated properly in order to achieve all three forms of sustainability.

Figure 11.2 lists some contemporary and emerging research topics, which can be mapped onto the different aspects of sustainability, giving rise to a new model for understanding of the various challenges and research issues in sustainability of digital information systems and services (Chowdhury, 2013).

A number of new developments are taking place that need to be studied closely to achieve economic sustainability of information. For example, new business models, which are different from the typical user or consumer pays model prevailing in the information industry, are being introduced with new services like

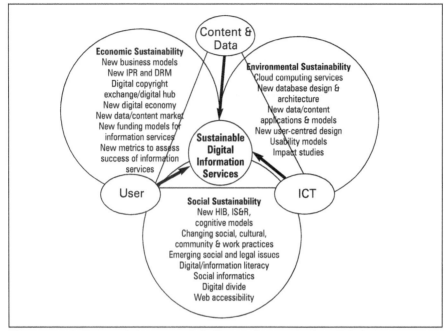

Figure 11.2 Research issues and challenges in sustainable digital information services (Chowdhury, 2013)

Google Books, Google Scholar and Microsoft Academic Search. Alternative funding models, which are somewhat different from the above, have also appeared for institutional repositories and open access digital libraries. Similarly, new models are being developed for specific services like e-books, e-journal and database services, for example, EBSCOhost, Gale Virtual Reference Library and Ebrary, 123Library, Dawsonera, EBL and MyiLibrary (Chapter 3). New open access publishing models for digital monographs in the humanities and social sciences are also being developed by specific publishers, for example, the Bloomsbury and Open Humanities Press. Side by side, research is under way into how to build special digital collections, for example Jisc Collections in the UK, with government initiatives, in order to support better access to, and management of, digital content by academic and research institutions.

While all these new developments and measures to attain economic sustainability of digital information services are very promising, they cannot succeed unless appropriate measures are taken to ensure environmental and social sustainability. For example, as shown in several Jisc studies and other research discussed in Chapter 9, the new digital data and content models, information services and the proposed digital copyright exchange can be better implemented and economically and environmentally sustainable by adopting the cloud computing model. However, a number of new research and development activities need to be undertaken in order to build appropriate data and content models, domain and client-centred applications for user- and context-specific access to digital information, and new models for data- and content-centred applications to meet specific user requirements, for example, for research and scholarship and the management of research data in specific disciplines and fields of activities in higher education and research. Again, these developments cannot succeed unless measures are taken to:

- accommodate new and emerging user information behaviour
- improve digital and information literacy
- improve web accessibility to accommodate all kinds of users, especially those who require special assistance (people with special needs)
- accommodate new and emerging social networking and the social informatics models in specific disciplines and application areas such as digital education, digital health and digital culture.

The principles and parameters used to measure the impact of scientific research are also changing, and digital information services will eventually come under these new evaluation schemes and metrics. A study on the impact of NSDL in the USA within the criteria set out by funding agencies like the NSF in the USA notes, 'if a proposal sets the expectations for judging a broad, societal impact, then researchers must, first, be careful in what they promise and, second, create and use the tools to measure the impact' (Mardis, Hoffman and McMartin, 2012, 14). Sustainability of digital information systems and services can be ensured only when information professionals and researchers can provide the positive and measurable impact of digital information services on a specific domain or sector, and society at large. Hence, determining how best to measure the broader institutional, sectoral and societal impact of digital information services is essential for sustainability.

The sustainability of specific information services

The issues of sustainability can be considered in the context of the major factors influencing the lifecycle of information – from creation to management, use or re-use, and disposal, when required, for example disposal of analogue information resources, or of computing infrastructure and equipment. The different factors affecting people's information seeking behaviour (Ingwersen and Järvelin, 2005; Järvelin and Wilson, 2003; Robson and Robinson, 2013; Ruthven and Kelly, 2011; Wilson, 1997) can be explained through the sustainability model in Figure 11.2. For example, the intervening variables in Wilson's model of information behaviour – psychological, demographic, role-related or interpersonal, nvironmental and source characteristic (Wilson, 1997) – can form part of the social sustainability of information but they have implications on economic and environmental sustainability because research in this area can inform better information system design leading to better and energy-efficient information systems supported by new business models.

Similarly, the major factors affecting information seeking and retrieval shown in Ingwersen's model such as the information objects themselves, the information retrieval system setting and interfaces, and users' cognitive space and social setting, can be explained through the links between different research themes in the sustainability model (Ingwersen, 1996). In today's digital world, user information behaviour in general, and information seeking and retrieval in particular, is significantly influenced by the internet and web technologies including mobile and social networking technologies (Bates, 2010; Bennett, Maton and Kervin, 2008; Cunningham, 2010; Hargittai, 2010; Rowlands et al., 2008; Williams and Rowlands, 2007). This can be explained through the sustainability model by the links between several emerging research themes involving the information industry and businesses, people and society, information systems and applications design, and so on.

Thus the sustainability model shows that a balance between those factors that are responsible for users' information seeking and retrieval needs to be maintained in order to achieve sustainability of information. Similarly the sustainability model can also support the principles of green information services and green information retrieval proposed in the literature (Chowdhury, 2012a, 2012b, 2012c). Overall, the sustainability model can be used in association with various other information models in order to study the issues and challenges associated with the sustainability of information.

The model serves to illustrate that a number of factors are responsible for, and contribute to, different forms of sustainability of digital information services. These factors may be related to digital content and data, discipline and domain, user information behaviour, society and culture, ICT infrastructure, information design, and so on. Again, these factors are inter-related, and none can be considered in isolation. For example, increasing use of advanced ICT infrastructure and information design to deal with digital content and data will have implications for all the three forms of sustainability of digital information services. Economic sustainability may be affected by the increasing costs, increasing levels of effort or the need for ICT equipment for access to information, and so on, but this may be compensated for by reduced costs for digital content compared with printed content, as demonstrated by several studies (Houghton, 2011; Houghton et al., 2009; Swan, 2010), and improved social sustainability.

The social sustainability of an information service may improve because of the increased access to and use of information. Studies show evidence of increased access to digital content compared with its printed counterparts (Estelle, 2011; Nicholas, Rowlands and Jamali, 2010; Nicholas et al., 2008). The environmental sustainability of information services may be affected by increased GHG emissions due to the increasing use of ICT infrastructure and equipment, but this may be compensated for by designing green information services as proposed in literature (Chowdhury, 2012a, 2012c). There are a number of external factors that form the foundations of digital information systems and services, such as the emerging ICT infrastructure; web, social networking and mobile technologies; and legal issues such as IPR and digital rights management (Hargreaves, 2011; Hooper and Lynch, 2012). Often these factors play a part in each area of sustainability, thus affecting the overall sustainability of digital information.

The sustainability model serves to illustrate the different parameters, their inter-dependence and their implications on the overall sustainability of information. This model can be adjusted for any specific type of digital library or information services in any sector. A typical example may be a digital library service like Europeana, which is designed to provide virtually every European citizen and other people in the world (Europeana does not make provision for people with special needs, nor for those lacking basic internet skills) with access to the digital culture of Europe. Such a digital library service will have a significantly different set of parameters for social sustainability, and somewhat different parameters for economic sustainability, compared with a digital library service that is designed for a specific sector like higher education and research, for example. The parameters for environmental sustainability will also change between these two scenarios primarily because of the issues of social sustainability, e.g. web accessibility and access to ICT equipment and infrastructure, which is relatively high for users in the higher education setting (at least in the western world) but cannot be taken for granted for every ordinary citizen of Europe who wants to access Europeana. Social sustainability may also be affected by the digital and information literacy of the user population. Economic sustainability depends on governments and institutions involved in and contributing to Europeana. A report by the Europeana Foundation points out that in the 2010-11 financial year Europeana had a funding gap of €1.2 million and obtaining renewed funding support has remained a challenge (Europeana Foundation, 2011). The increasing economic costs that might affect the economic sustainability of a digital library may be compensated by the increased social development that can be achieved in the long run through providing better access to, and use of knowledge, thereby creating a more educated and enlightened society. However, such measures are difficult to quantify, and one needs to wait for a number of years in order to see such intangible outcomes.

Summary

This book has discussed how sustainability is an extremely important issue for any institution and business, and since information forms an integral part of scholarly communications and innovations, sustainability should become a mainstream research topic within information studies. Figure 11.1 provides a model for scholarly communication processes in today's digital age. Figure 11.2 provides a model for understanding the research issues and challenges of sustainability of scholarly communication processes in general, and sustainability of information in particular. It illustrates how the various emerging research topics are inter-related, and how together they can help us build sustainable digital information services.

The model in Figure 11.2 shows that while specific studies need to be undertaken in achieving sustainability in each area of digital information, the underlying research topics and challenges are inter-related. Hence any new measure or development attempting to attain sustainability in one area may have a significant positive or negative influence on another area of sustainability. For example, while new business models of information coupled with the new digital copyright exchange and cloud computing technologies (discussed in Chapter 9) can promise better distribution, access and use of digital information and thereby promote digital economy, they may have a significant influence on a number of industries, especially the ICT and the content industry. These industries need to change their business models and practices. For example, the ICT industry, which plays a key role in today's economy, may be affected by decreasing demand for servers and end-user computing devices as more and more data, content and services move to cloud, and become apps based, thereby reducing the need to have elaborate ICT infrastructure at the individual institution level. Similarly, the content industry, which plays a key role in a country's economy (discussed in Chapter 7), may have to adjust its business models and practices as more open access is promoted, or new players and services like Google Books, Google Scholar and Microsoft Academic Search appear in the marketplace. There are social implications as well, because all these developments will influence the way people create, access, use and share content and data for various purposes. In order to reap the optimum benefits of digital information services, the work culture and practices and information behaviour of individuals and communities also need to change.

More research is needed to study how emerging web technologies and services – including social networking technologies coupled with various government and other (sectoral and institutional) initiatives, for example to make relevant information and data available on the web for governments and ministries, local councils, and specific sectors like health, education and research – are influencing and changing user behaviour and expectations. Further research will identify various measures that need to be taken to achieve the social sustainability of emerging digital information services. The rapid growth of data and information – scholarly and user-generated data and content – is adding more problems and challenges in attaining sustainability. Therefore, only a concerted effort and an integrated approach to study and research in information can help us build sustainable information systems and services that will be capable of meeting the information needs of all kinds of education, research, business and development activities.

References

ARL (2013) Scholarly Communication, Association of Research Libraries, www.arl.org/focus-areas/scholarly-communication.

Bates, M. J. (2010) Information Behavior. In Bates, M. J. and Maack, M. N. (eds), *Encyclopedia of Library and Information Sciences*, 3rd edn, CRC Press, 2381–91.

BBC News (2012) Millions in UK 'lack basic online skills', 8 November, www.bbc.co.uk/news/technology-20236708.

Bennett, S., Maton, K. and Kervin, L. (2008) The 'Digital Natives' Debate: a critical review of the evidence, *British Journal of Educational Technology*, **39** (5), 775–86.

Chowdhury, G. G. (2012a) Building Sustainable Information Services: a green IS research agenda, *Journal of the American Society for Information Science and Technology*, **63** (4), 633–47.

Chowdhury, G. G. (2012b) An Agenda for Green Information Retrieval Research, *Information Processing and Management*, **48** (6), 1067–77.

Chowdhury, G. G. (2012c) How Digital Information Services Can Reduce Greenhouse Gas Emissions, *Online Information Review*, **36** (4), 489–506.

Chowdhury, G. G. (2013) Sustainability of Digital Information Services, *Journal of Documentation*, **69** (5), 602–22.

Cunningham, J. (2010) New Workers, New Workplace? Getting the balance right, *Strategic Direction*, **26** (1), 5–6.

Estelle, L. (2011) E-books Models and Joint Purchasing, RLUK Members' Meeting, 24–25 November, www.rluk.ac.uk/.../Estelle_ebook%20models%20RLUK% 20members%2025.11.11.ppt.

Europeana Foundation (2011) *Europeana Funding Gap, 2012 and 2013*, http://pro.europeana.eu/documents/844813/851970/Funding+Gap+Paper.pdf.

Hargittai, E. (2010) Digital Na(t)ives? Variation in internet skills and uses among members of the 'net generation', *Sociological Inquiry*, **80** (1), 92–113.

Hargreaves, I. (2011) *Digital Opportunity: a review of intellectual property and growth*, www.ipo.gov.uk/ipreview-finalreport.pdf.

Hooper, R. and Lynch, R. (2012) *Copyright Works: streaming copyright licensing for the digital age*, UK Intellectual Property Office, www.ipo.gov.uk/dce-report-phase2.pdf.

Houghton, J. H. (2011) The Costs and Potential Benefits of Alternative Scholarly Publishing Models, *Information Research*, **16** (1), http://informationr.net/ir/16-1/paper469.html.

Houghton, J. W., Rasmussen, B., Sheehan, P. J., Oppenheim, C., Morris, A., Creaser, C. et al. (2009) *Economic Implications of Alternative Scholarly Publishing Models: exploring the costs and benefits*, Joint Information Systems Committee, www.jisc.ac.uk/media/documents/publications/rpteconomicoapublishing.pdf.

Ingwersen, P. (1996) Cognitive Perspectives of Information Retrieval Interaction: elements of a cognitive IR theory, *Journal of Documentation*, **52** (1), 3–50.

Ingwersen, P. and Järvelin, K. (2005) *The Turn: integration of information seeking and retrieval in context*, Springer.

Järvelin, K. and Wilson, T. D. (2003) On Conceptual Models for Information Seeking and Retrieval Research, *Information Research*, **9** (1), http://informationr.net/ir/9-1/paper163.html.

Mardis, M. A., Hoffman, E. S. and McMartin, F. P. (2012) Toward Broader Impacts: making sense of NSF's merit review criteria in the context of the National Science Digital Library, *Journal of the American Society for Information Science and Technology*, **63** (9), 1758–72.

Nicholas, D., Rowlands, I. and Jamali, H. (2010) E-textbook Use, Information Seeking Behaviour and its Impact: case study business and management, *Journal of Information Science*, **36** (2), 263–80.

Nicholas, D., Rowlands, I., Clark, D., Huntington, P., Jamali, H. R. and Ollé, C. (2008) UK Scholarly E-book Usage: a landmark survey, *Aslib Proceedings: New Information Perspectives*, **60** (4), 311–34.

Robson, A. and Robinson, L. (2013) Building on Models of Information Behaviour: linking information seeking and communication, *Journal of Documentation*, **69** (2), 169–93.

Rowlands, I., Nicholas, D., Williams, P., Huntington, P., Fieldhouse, M. and Gunter, B.

(2008) The Google Generation: the information behaviour of the researcher of the future, *Aslib Proceedings*, **60** (4), 290–310.

Ruthven, I. and Kelly, D. (eds) (2011) *Interactive Information Seeking, Behaviour and Retrieval*, Facet Publishing.

Swan, A. (2010) Modelling Scholarly Communication Options: costs and benefits for universities, report to the JISC, February, http://repository.jisc.ac.uk/442/2/ Modelling_scholarly_communication_report_final1.pdf.

Williams, P. and Rowlands, I. (2007) The Literature on Young People and their Information Behaviour, Work Package II, British Library and Joint Information Systems Committee, www.jisc.ac.uk/media/documents/programmes/reppres/ggworkpackageii.pdf.

Wilson, T. (1997) Information Behaviour: an interdisciplinary perspective, *Information Processing and Management*, **33** (4), 551–72.

Research on sustainable information

Introduction

Different issues of sustainability and the various factors related to the economic, social and environmental sustainability of information systems and services have been identified and discussed in this book. Sustainability issues relating to various recent developments in ICT, such as green IT and green information services, and several policy issues – such as the sustainable development policies of the United Nations, the open access policies of various research funding bodies, and legal and policy issues of some government- and institution-sponsored studies – have been addressed in the context of sustainability of information. Various models and frameworks for the study of sustainability of scholarly communications, information systems and services have also been considered.

However, appropriate research and manpower development activities are essential to develop and manage sustainable information systems and services – from the creation of recorded information to its distribution, management, access and use or re-use. This book has demonstrated that in order to achieve sustainability of information a variety of research and professional expertise and skills are required at different stages of the lifecycle of information systems and services. Some of these research directions have already been identified. This chapter looks at how these new trends in research can contribute to the sustainability of information, and at some new areas of research and development activities required to attain sustainability of information.

Open access and a paradigm shift in information management, education and research

Chapters 7 and 8 explored how implementation of open access policies can create virtually a global distributed digital library of scholarly research data and output of academic and research institutions. While continuous funding support and other resources like growing demands for ICT infrastructure currently stand in the way of the progress of open access research content and data (for details see Connell, 2011; Cryer and Collins, 2011; Cullen and Chawner, 2011; MacDonald, 2011; St Jean et al., 2011), the recently introduced open access policies of various funding agencies and institutions will bring a paradigm shift in information management, access and use, especially in the context of scholarly communication processes. The promises of cloud computing and green information systems, and further research in these areas, may provide solutions to some of the sustainability problems by reducing ICT infrastructure and energy consumption costs and thereby improving the economic and environmental sustainability of digital information systems and services (Chowdhury, 2012a, 2012b). As more and more scholarly content and data are available through open access repositories, open access journals, digital libraries and the web, people will have better access to research knowledge, which will facilitate further research and knowledge creation processes. Together these developments promise better and easier access to information on a global scale, which will improve the quality of education, research, business and productivity; this will lead to information being socially sustainable. However, the sustainability of scholarly communications and information services will depend on the appropriate funding models, regulations and governance for some key activities such as digital preservation, data analytics, design and usability studies of information systems and services, and information education and research.

Facilitating content-specific access and use

As the amount and diversity of open access content and data increase, leading to a global digital library of scholarly and popular information, the need for more user- and context-specific search and retrieval services will grow significantly. More user- and context-specific services need to be built in order to overcome the so called information overload problems created by a mixed information marketplace containing peer-reviewed and user-generated content. A single user interface may not be appropriate for every category of user in every discipline and in every institution. The information science field is witnessing a steady shift in digital information environments from information search to information discovery in a specific user, institutional and cultural context. While this trend shows more user-centred and targeted digital information services, sometimes information discovery can also be accidental – serendipitous or opportunistic (Erdelez and Makri, 2011). A collection of papers in *Information Research* (2011) provides a richer understanding of the opportunistic discovery of information in various research and everyday life contexts.

In the emerging global digital content and data marketplace, more user- and context-specific access and usability features need to be added on top of the generic interface in order to support directed and accidental (or opportunistic) discovery of information. Cultural, political and linguistic variations play a prominent role in the access to and use of information, and therefore a variety of local contexts, culture, standards and practices need to be adopted in the design of information access systems and services (Xia, 2012).

As more and more content and data become available through the open access digital library and open digital content marketplace, the usability of information and data services based on these developments will become more important. Studies show that the usability of digital information services depends on a number of factors, including the nature of users – digital native vs digital migrants (Dobreva and Chowdhury, 2010; Rowlands et al., 2008); the wider political, social and ideological agenda underlying a specific culture and community (Selwyn, 2009); and a variety of other social and technological factors (Chowdhury and Chowdhury, 2011). A review of literature on the usability and evaluation of digital libraries identified a number of challenges that need to be tackled, including a consensus on standard definitions of usability and usefulness, and adoption of appropriate study methods especially with regard to the size and selection of study samples, use of appropriate scales for data gathering, and employment of appropriate statistical methods, in order to be able to produce reliable and statistically significant findings (Heradio et al., 2012). Overall, a variety of information research skills need to be developed and/or updated where necessary, in order to provide better quality of digital information services at institutional and researcher or community level.

Information research directions
Information research direction 1: more research and professional practices in user- and context-specific access and usability of information
Implications for the sustainability of information systems and services

New research and professional practices leading to the provision of user- and context-specific digital information services for everyone in every sphere of our society and community will contribute to the ease and equity of access to information, which are the two essential criteria for the social sustainability of information (Chapter 5). This research direction will promote the use of digital information, and this in turn will create a better workforce and an informed society, which are the indicators of the economic sustainability of information (Chapter 3).

Standards and tools for seamless access, interoperability and analysis

As more and diverse kinds of data and content are made available through open digital libraries and new information services, as shown in Figure 11.1, there will be a more pressing need for seamless access to information by people and machines. However, as mentioned in the Hargreaves review (2011) and by other researchers, 'a major bottleneck in research in academic document mining and analysis is the unavailability of public datasets for use in evaluating and comparing proposed techniques with existing methods' (Bhatia et al., 2012). To address this issue, academic publishers, through the Brussels Declaration of STM Publishing (STM, 2007), 'have strongly endorsed the principle that research data relating to journal articles should be made freely available, to enable inspection of the data and validation of the claims made in the article, and to permit data reuse in other contexts' (Shotton, 2012). Chapter 7 discussed how open access policies of various funding agencies, especially those of RCUK, require that research content and datasets should be made available with a CC BY licence, so they can be accessed and used by anyone, including on computer software, for further analysis and use. This will require more research on traditional information management skills such as metadata and interoperability issues, and on a number of relatively new research areas like data and text mining, data analytics and intelligence. Some such research activities are already under way as reported in the first international workshop on mining scientific publications held during the Joint Conference on Digital Libraries in 2012, and the papers have been published in the July/August 2012 issue of *D-Lib Magazine* (2012).

Hjorland (2011) argues that knowledge organization in a variety of forms is an essential part of any information activity. In fact, knowledge organization activities including semantically mapping and linking of data and documents based on different subject or domain-, user- and context-specific attributes will be more important in the growing world of digital content and data. Digital technologies offer fantastic opportunities to link content and data semantically, which was not possible in the analogue information environment. A number of research initiatives have taken place in the recent past to explore how new and robust techniques and tools can be developed and used for text mining, automatic pulling of contextual information and semantic linking of documents on the web. Examples of many such research initiatives are discussed in Shotton (2012), and a detailed review of automatic techniques used to build domain knowledge structures is available in Clark et al. (2012).

Information research direction 2: more research and professional practices in metadata, interoperability, data and text mining, data linking and semantic knowledge mapping

Implications for the sustainability of information systems and services

New research and professional practices in knowledge organization, text mining and data analytics will facilitate better access to and use of digital information, and will promote the social sustainability of information. By facilitating better access to and use of digital information, this will contribute to the creation of a better workforce and an informed society thus promoting the economic sustainability of information.

New measures for quality assessment

The information profession has long been associated with quality assessment and quality assurance through a number of research and professional practices, for example collection development policies based on market analysis and user requirement analysis, quality and impact analysis of journals and publications based on citation analysis, and other related measures such as reviews. However, techniques of citation analysis and journal impact factor have been criticized because of a number of limitations inherent in these measures, including the narrow coverage and readership of specific journals and conferences, limited accessibility of readers to specific publications because of the high cost of subscription, and language issues. So far these measures have been applied to content that is formally published in a journal or a conference.

Recent research shows that subject repositories like arXiv and PubMed have come of age, making a significant impact on specific research communities, and open access institutional repositories are moving towards early adulthood (Nicholas et al., 2012). Some new research and data collection techniques have been developed to measure the impact of open access repositories. Asunka, Chae and Natriello (2011) report on a study of the use of an institutional repository and social networking website by the academic community using transaction log analysis, content analysis and grounded theory. As an open access global digital library of institutional repositories become more mature, further research is needed to measure usage patterns and impact measures of specific publications – journal papers, book chapters, and so on – in those repositories. This will allow information managers to create a variety of new usage statistics and thus to generate different quality measures based on access and use of content and data. In fact, a variety of usage statistics is now produced by specific institutional repositories and portal services like OpenDOAR, and with proper resources and new tools and technologies it will be possible to generate usage data for specific publications (research papers for example), authors, subjects or disciplines, institutions, countries, funding agencies, and so on. Such data will not only create new quality measures, but also produce a picture of the kind and quality of research and output produced by different types of researcher. Such data can be combined with the impact factors of specific journals and various conferences, providing a better and richer picture of research quality based on research content and data access and use.

Similar usage statistics and data analytics can be produced for specific social network data and user-generated content and data. At the moment some publicly accessible data are automatically generated for some user-generated content, such as the number of views for a YouTube video or number of times a site is accessed. However, special applications may be built in order to gather specific statistics and analytics from user-generated content and social network data, in order to generate a variety of rich datasets related to people's interests in a specific content – a picture, an image, a scholarly paper, for example – and the corresponding use and applications. Such aggregated data for a specific content or a content producer will be useful not only to boost their creativity, but also to produce other kinds of data aggregation such as by content type, domain or discipline, which will promote competitiveness in the market, and this will in turn boost creativity and promote research, innovation and business in specific fields.

All these new developments will play a big role in meeting Tim Berners-Lee's vision of linked open data in the context of academic and scholarly research and new innovations (Berners-Lee, 2009). Some research is already under way proposing different measures to assess the quality of open access content, for example the new factors, such as the five stars of online journal articles, proposed by Shotton (2012) for evaluating online journal articles. Open peer review, such as that encouraged by *BMJ Open* (http://bmjopen.bmj.com/) and *Semantic Web Journal* (www.semantic-web-journal.net/), may open up new models for quality assessment and evaluation of scholarly research.

Information research direction 3: more research and professional practices in generating usage statistics and new measures for quality or impact of research

Implications for the sustainability of information systems and services

New research and professional practices in generating new value indicators based on usage statistics will add value for information users and the information industry. These will in turn promote the social sustainability of information through value addition, and the economic sustainability of information by generating new indicators and business intelligence for the information industry.

More user- and context-specific services will emerge

Research and professional practices in information management have always focused on providing user-centred and context-specific information services. However, the need for user- and context-specific services will be more acute as the open data and content marketplaces emerge with the implementation of open access policies. Information professionals at institutional and even national levels need to build information services to meet the requirements of user communities in specific disciplines to accomplish specific tasks. As users are able to access the scholarly and research output of virtually every major academic and research institution in the world, better access, filtering and contextualization of information and data will be required. Research is under way on different fronts to develop new and user-centred digital library and information services. Mitchell and Suchy (2012) discuss the mobile digital library services of some selected libraries and other institutions. They note that 'offering mobile access to digital collections is still a relatively new endeavor for libraries and museums, and can be approached and developed in a variety of ways'. Borrego and Fry (2012) report on a study of researchers' use of scholarly information through social bookmarking data. These studies show the potential of research for more user- and context-specific services for users and appropriate use of these research findings will facilitate better access to and use of research content and data.

Social information retrieval and social tagging provide new approaches to information access and use. The conventional inverted indexes, which form the basis of any information retrieval system, consider only the binary relationship between terms and documents and not specific user contexts. Contrarily an index based on document terms and social tagging shows a ternary relationship among terms, documents and users. Lee, Kim and Kim (2012) propose a new social-tagging-based information retrieval based on a social inverted index, which retrieves information better than a conventional inverted index-based retrieval system. Various other new techniques and tools, such as recommendation systems, collaborative filtering (Rafeh and Bahrehmand, 2012) and social semantic tagging (Huang, Lin and Chan, 2012) are now being developed and experimented by researchers. More research based on social tagging, collaborative filtering and user-centric access mechanisms will promote better access to global research and scholarly output through the global open access digital library of institutional repositories, thus contributing to the vision of the digital economy and information society.

Information research direction 4: more research and professional practices in user- and context-specific services through social information retrieval and mobile technologies
Implications for the sustainability of information systems and services

New research and professional practices in building more user-context-specific services by using various social information retrieval and mobile technologies will help us build more value-added and context-specific information services. This in turn will promote better access to and use of digital information, promoting social and economic sustainability of information.

New tools and standards for the emerging information market

Institutions need to build tools and mechanisms to automatically harvest their repositories based on the research and scholarly activities of their staff and students. Chapter 7 discussed how a central institutional repository or open access digital library will be economically and environmentally sustainable, and this will also facilitate better and easier access to scholarly information and data, thereby achieving the social sustainability of information. Institutions, individual content and data creators can significantly benefit if their research and scholarly output are semantically linked with comparable data and content. Similarly, institutions and individuals can get better credits for their work if data on the access and use of scholarly output are gathered, analysed and presented systematically. As more and more data and content become accessible, the need for, and challenges of, integration of data and content to support specific user activities become essential.

Wolski, Richardson and Rebollo (2011) comment that at a national level government funding and policy guidelines are placing pressure on universities to increase the accessibility of their research output. The recently introduced open access policies of various government and other funding bodies are a testament to this. In order to make optimum use of these open access policies, there is a need to improve research data management, sharing and accessibility to research content and data.

Research for management of data to support research and scholarly activities had a tremendous boost with the establishment of *DataCite* (www.datacite.org/whatisdatacite), which was launched in 2009 in order to facilitate easier access and management of research data on the internet: 'DataCite plays a global leadership role promoting the use of persistent identifiers for datasets' (Wolski, Richardson and Rebollo, 2011). A special issue of *D-Lib Magazine* (2011) includes eight papers submitted to the first DataCite summer meeting in June 2010. With the realization that institutional repositories will not automatically link all kinds of data and content in the lifecycle of research, many researchers have attempted to build new architecture for integration of data and content in institutional repositories (for example, Lougee, 2009; Wolski, Richardson and Rebollo, 2011).

Although management of research data has not been an area of activity within the mainstream information profession, over the past few years the need for research data management and linking of research content and data has been recognized as an important step in the promotion of research and scholarship. However, as Borgman (2011) argues, data are not only numbers or symbols; they can be samples, software, field notes, code books, survey results, and so on. Borgman provides a detailed discussion of the complexities of data management and sharing in a research environment.

Information research direction 5: more research and professional practices in the integration of research data and content, and development of specific applications to support research, scholarship and innovation

Implications for the sustainability of information systems and services

New research and professional practices in linking research content and research data will bring a new dimension to scholarly information services. This in turn will promote better access to and use of research information and data; this will promote social and economic sustainability of information.

Integration of information services with web and social networking technologies

Many new information management tools, practices and services have appeared recently that make use of different kinds of web and social networking technologies. Examples range from social information retrieval and social network analysis (Goh and Foo, 2007; Theng et al., 2009) to social tagging (Lee and Schleyer, 2012; Ransom and Rafferty, 2011), social discovery tools (Spiteri, 2012) and crowd sourcing (Estelles-Arolas and González-Ladrón-de-Guevara, 2012; Holley, 2010). Most libraries now have incorporated social media tools like Facebook, Twitter and Flickr into their websites (for discussions of specific benefits and applications of these technologies see Rubin, Gavin and Kamal, 2011). Many research studies show how social tagging is emerging as the alternative indexing and social discovery tool (Spiteri, 2012; Woolwine et al., 2011).

The new open access policies and the global digital library of institutional repositories will facilitate better access, use, annotation and re-use of content and data in a shared environment. In order to facilitate this, new research needs to be undertaken to link various web and social networking technologies with scholarly content and data. McMahon et al. comment that 'social networks facilitate scientific progress by mixing people and ideas; social networking tools bring this mixing online' (2012). Research shows that Facebook can play a big role in the promotion of digital libraries (Banciu et al., 2012). By making appropriate use of rapidly increasing social networking tools and technologies researchers can connect with more people, create more paths for ideas to travel, and subsequently create many more new opportunities to seed new research ideas.

Digital libraries and information services nowadays make use of a variety of Web 2.0 and social networking technologies such as digital conferencing, chat, instant messaging, blogging, podcasts, social networking and wikis. Many people now use online forums to create and share digital information. Such online forum and social networks can provide valuable information for the creation of a personalized framework for each user in the online forum space, and such information can be used to create innovative recommendation mechanisms for users (Li, Liao and Lai, 2012). However, access to data on commercial databases often prohibits a reliable estimation of the relative frequency of implemented Web 2.0 services (Gardois et al., 2012). The new developments – the global digital library of open access content and institutional repositories – will enable information managers to integrate a variety of Web 2.0 and social networking technologies with research data and scholarly output, and analysis of these links will provide valuable information to promote better use, sharing and re-use of information.

Information research direction 6: more research and professional practices in the integration of information services with web and social networking technologies
Implications for the sustainability of information systems and services

New research and professional practices in linking research content and research data with social networking tools and technologies will bring various new and value-added features to digital information services. This in turn will promote better access to and use of research information and data, which will promote the social and economic sustainability of information.

Research to promote sustainability of information systems and services

While the emerging research directions in information management discussed so far in the chapter, and discussed in more details in Chowdhury (2013), can promote the overall sustainability of information systems and services in general, some specific research activities may be undertaken to promote specific aspects of sustainability. Some such research themes are considered below; these are just examples rather than an exhaustive list.

Design and usability issues

Although recent developments in ICT, especially web and mobile technologies, have improved the processes of creation, distribution and access to digital information, the information industry has not fully exploited the benefits that digital technologies can offer users. Compared with the music and games industries, the information industry still uses digital technologies largely to create a digital replica of the print world. As a result, users cannot take full advantage of digital technologies. This is partly because of design issues but there are also a number of usability and user training issues that affect the social sustainability of digital information systems and services. For instance, a recent study on the use of digital images by historians clearly illustrates this situation. Harris and Hepburn (2013) note that although images are easily available through digital libraries and archives, and image access facilities on the web such as Flickr and Google Images, there is still relatively little use of images in scholarly publications in history. As a result, the potential gains from the use of images in research and scholarly activities have not been realized: 'visual analysis in the historical literature remains stunted, as long as most images are used merely as illustration' (Harris and Hepburn, 2013, 283).

Several measures may be taken to increase the use of images in scholarly publications:

- Market and promote collections better, not only among regular users but to everyone using the websites and social networks, and through other means such as exhibitions and blog posts.
- Foster collaboration among librarians, archivists and historians that can better shape digitization efforts in order to embed the usage and work culture of the user community in the design of services.
- Build appropriate mechanisms to keep a balance between the cost of images (where a price is involved) and the benefits that they can bring to the researcher, to make them affordable for researchers, thereby facilitating their use.
- Build tools and applications so researchers can make better use of the images and associated research content and data.

Projects like the humanities workbench, which aims to build a suite of tools and technologies to facilitate the works of digital humanities researchers and scholars (Bia, 2012), aim to address some of these issues, especially the fourth one listed above.

Policy and management issues

In order to keep pace with the rapid developments in ICT, and changing social and user requirements, the information profession has focused on change management, either through innovation, organizational change or project management (Macevičiūtė, 2011). In addition to the scholarly research activities mentioned so far in this chapter, some policy and management research is needed in order to develop and deliver sustainable information systems and services. Such management and policy research should be directed to estimate:

- the environmental costs of physical library infrastructure – buildings, energy consumption for lighting, heating or air conditioning, and so on; some toolkits like SusteIT and data related to energy consumption is available at higher education institution level, but they need to be put into perspective, e.g. in comparison with the environmental costs of digital content and digital information services
- the environmental costs of physical information objects – printed books, journals, and so on; as discussed earlier in the book, some data are available on the costs of printed information sources, but they vary depending on the production and distribution of specific content types, and the sources of energy and raw materials used for the purpose; more research is needed to generate empirical data in order to estimate the energy and environmental costs of print vs digital information services in specific higher education institutions and disciplines
- the long-term environmental benefits of replacing physical content with its digital counterparts and long-term preservation and access
- the environmental costs of client-side ICT infrastructure, and their implications for the overall energy and environmental costs of specific information systems and services; more research is needed to generate empirical data in order to investigate the impact of ICT and information behaviour of users on the energy and environmental costs of accessing and using digital information systems services in different contexts.

In the UK some policy- and management-related research in information systems and services in higher education institutions is funded by Jisc, but to date very little research has been undertaken to study the environmental costs relating to the economic and social sustainability of digital information systems and services.

Building partnerships

Chapter 1 discussed how the need to share knowledge in order to achieve sustainability has been recognized in several UN policy documents (United Nations General Assembly, 2012, 20, 48; United Nations, 2013, 1, 3). Researchers have also shown the benefits of knowledge sharing among stakeholders and the community of practice in climate change (Etti et al., 2010) and the benefits of the actor network theory – a network of various actors (stakeholders), actions and information-related processes – in the management of climate change information (Sharifzadeh et al., 2013). MacDonald et al. argue that 'multidimensional thinking and analysis stimulated by an interdisciplinary perspective is essential for further understanding of the role of information at the science-policy interface' of environmental policy and decision making (2013, 61).

Governments and regulatory bodies, funding agencies, institutions, publishers and various search service providers should join hands in order to provide the best support for sustainable knowledge creation, distribution and access. Some developments have already taken place and lessons may be learnt, for example,

- The Google Books project has proven that massive digitization activities require huge resources that governments or specific institutions cannot afford; appropriate regulations and institutional participation are required to promote digitization and better information access for present and future generations.
- Large digital library projects like Europeana show that co-operative and shared resources and management of digital libraries are workable, but a sustainable funding model is required to support this.
- The open access movement is trying to find solutions for all the stakeholders, publishers, research funders, content creators and users, but this will require significant changes in the research and funding management and culture of universities and research institutions vis-à-vis researchers – both as creators and consumers of information.
- Sustainable digital preservation models require partnership of publishers, digitization agencies, institutions, funding bodies and various government agencies in order to develop sustainable funding support and sustainable design and usability features commensurate with emerging digital technologies and the changing user and community behaviour and practices to ensure long-term accessibility to digital information and data.

Green IT, green information behaviour and environmental literacy

In order to build and use environmentally sustainable information systems and services, it is essential that appropriate measures are taken at all levels to reduce GHG emissions throughout the lifecycle of information – from creation to management, access and use. Research shows that green IT and green information services can play a major role in building sustainable digital information systems and services (Chowdhury, 2012a, 2012b), and they help businesses implement a proactive environmental strategy (Benitez-Amado and Walczuch, 2012).

Discussions in Chapters 4, 9, 10 and 11 demonstrate that end-user computing and information behaviour can significantly improve the social and environmental sustainability of digital information systems and services. Empirical studies on end-user and institutional behaviour in information creation and information use in higher education and research can provide pointers for improved (green) design of information systems and services in order to achieve economic, social and environmental sustainability of information.

Research in green information behaviour can help us understand users' ICT behaviour when creating, accessing and using digital information. It can also help us develop appropriate environmental literacy programmes that can inculcate green behaviour in various stakeholders, especially end-users. Environmental literacy is an integral part of green information behaviour.

Environmental literacy can be defined as 'the capability for a contextual and detailed understanding of an environmental problem in order to enable analysis, synthesis, evaluation, and ultimately sound and informed decision making at a citizen's level' (CMU, n.d.). The Environmental Literacy Council provides a more detailed definition as follows: 'Environmental literacy requires a fundamental understanding of the systems of the natural world, the relationships and interactions between the living and the non-living environment, and the ability to deal sensibly with the problems that involve scientific evidence, uncertainty, and economic, aesthetic, and ethical considerations' (Environmental Literacy Council, 2008).

Abiolu and Okere argue that 'information professionals are strategically positioned to influence behaviour at different levels through information, awareness creation and education', and therefore 'the onus lies on them to contribute to building and maintaining an environmentally literate citizenry' (2012, 57). The development of environmental literacy programmes is a complex task, and can take many forms (McBeth et al., 2008). Research shows that environmental attitudes, environmental responsibility, environmental concern, environmental knowledge and the outdoor activities of university students are related to each other (Teksoz, Sahin and Tekkaya-Oztekin, 2012). In the context of higher education and research an environmental literacy programme can create environmentally literate students and staff who can routinely include the environment as one of their considerations in their work and daily living. However, only a concerted and systematic approach to environmental literacy grounded in people's lifestyle and work culture can help promote green information behaviour. Such environmentally literate people will exercise their green information behaviour and judgement in order to play their role in reducing the carbon footprint of the digital information systems and services that they use regularly.

Conclusion

As Buckland (2012) suggests, enabling people to become better informed should be the central concern of information studies. Sustainability of digital information systems and services can be ensured only when information managers can prove the positive and measurable impact of digital information systems and services on society. Hence, determining how best to measure the broader societal impact of digital information systems and services will become imperative to information science education and research.

The nature of digital information systems and services has been constantly changing over the past few years as a result of rapid developments in internet, web, social networking and mobile technologies and the economic, political, social and legal changes taking place in the information industry and society as a whole. New information services are appearing, and existing information services are changing their design and architecture in order to meet the growing demands of the consumer market, for example to provide access through handheld and mobile devices. Many such information services are accessed through what is known as referrals, where users are referred to services by search engines. While studying the mobile user behaviour of Europeana, Nicholas et al. (2013) noted that search engines – predominantly Google – are the key drivers of referrals; as much as 80% of Europeana's traffic is sent by Google. Fixed and mobile users do not differ much in their referral patterns to Europeana (Nicholas et al., 2013), suggesting that search engines are the first port of call for users, who are referred to respective digital information services by search engines in response to a query. This raises a number of questions for digital information systems and services. For example,

- Should digital information services merely be storehouses of digital information, leaving the access part of information retrieval to search engine services?

- What changes will be brought by the fast changing mobile technologies?
- Given the proliferation of the use of mobile technologies, how are the information industry and information services sector going to be influenced by the 'apps' industry?

Nicholas et al. predict that there might be 'a parting of the ways between a traditional website as a store of content and a more dynamically managed; "app"-based service: paid-for, personalized, paradoxically more actively engaging with a mercurial yet passive consumer' (Nicholas et al., 2013).

The internet and associated technologies have brought a paradigm shift in the digital information world, which will continue. In order to meet the demands of users and the dynamic information world, new research on more sophisticated and hitherto unexplored technologies for data and content storage and processing is essential. New and advanced technologies are constantly challenging and changing the information landscape and the information management profession. For example the use of a DNA structure to store digital data and content (Goldman et al., 2013) may call for more change management within the information profession.

The information profession needs constantly to shift and adjust its research focus and professional practices in order to make people better informed, thus validating its contribution and impact in general, and various information systems and services in particular. Sustainability will remain the central challenge for the information industry and information services sector in the rapidly changing digital world; only concerted efforts and integrated research and professional activities will find appropriate ways to ensure that information systems and services are as sustainable as possible.

References

Abiolu, O. A. and Okere, O. O. (2012) Environmental Literacy and the Emerging Roles of Information Professionals in Developing Economies, *IFLA Journal*, **38** (1), 53–9.

Asunka, S., Chae, H. S. and Natriello, G. (2011) Towards an Understanding of the Use of an Institutional Repository with Integrated Social Networking Tools: a case study of PocketKnowledge, *Library & Information Science Research*, **33** (1), 80–8.

Banciu, D., Pitic, A. G., Volovici, D. and Mitea, A. C. (2012) Using Social Networking Software to Promote Digital Libraries, *Studies in Informatics and Control*, **21** (2), 221–6.

Benitez-Amado, J. and Walczuch, R. M. (2012) Information Technology, the Organizational Capability of Proactive Corporate Environmental Strategy and Firm Performance: a resource-based analysis, *European Journal of Information Systems*, **21**, 664–79.

Berners-Lee, T. (2009) Linked Data, www.w3.org/DesignIssues/LinkedData.html.

Bhatia, S., Caragea, C., Chen, H.-H., Wu, J., Treeratpituk, P., Wu, Z., Khabsa, M., Mitra, P. and Giles, C. L. (2012) Specialized Research Datasets in the CiteSeer^x Digital Library, *D-Lib Magazine*, **18** (7/8), www.dlib.org/dlib/july12/bhatia/07bhatia.html.

Bia, A. (2012) The Digital Humanities Workbench. In *Proceedings of the 13th International Conference on Interacción Persona-Ordenador*, Miguel Hernandez University of Elche (Spain), 3–5 October 2012, http://dl.acm.org/citation.cfm?id=2379685.

Borgman, C. L. (2011) The Conundrum of Sharing Research Data, *Journal of the American Society for Information Science and Technology*, **63** (6), 1059–78.

Borrego, A. and Fry, J. (2012) Measuring Researchers' Use of Scholarly Information Through Social Bookmarking Data: a case study of BibSonomy, *Journal of Information Science*, **38** (3), 297–308.

Buckland, M. (2012) What Kind of Science Can Information Science Be?, *Journal of the American Society for Information Science and Technology*, **63** (1), 1–7.

Chowdhury, G. G. (2012a) Building Sustainable Information Services: a green IS research agenda, *Journal of the American Society for Information Science and Technology*, **63** (4), 633–47.

Chowdhury, G. G. (2012b) An Agenda for Green Information Retrieval Research, *Information Processing and Management*, **48** (6), 1067–77.

Chowdhury, G. G. (2013) Sustainability of Digital Information Services, *Journal of Documentation*, **69** (5), 602–22.

Chowdhury, G. G. and Chowdhury, S. (2011) *Information Users and Usability in the Digital Age*, Facet Publishing.

Clark, M., Kim, Y., Kruschwitz, U., Song, D., Albakour, D., Dignum, S., Beresi, U. C., Fasli, M. and De Roeck, A. (2012) Automatically Structuring Domain Knowledge From Text: an overview of current research, *Information Processing and Management*, **48** (3), 552–68.

CMU (n.d.) What is Environmental Literacy?, Environmental Decision Making, Science, and Technology, Carnegie Mellon University, http://telstar.ote.cmu.edu/environ/m2/s1/envlit.shtml.

Connell, T. H. (2011) The Use of Institutional Repositories: the Ohio State University experience, *College & Research Libraries*, **72** (3), 253–74.

Cryer, E. and Collins, M. (2011) Incorporating Open Access Into Libraries, *Serials Review*, **37** (2), 103–7.

Cullen, R. and Chawner, B. (2011) Institutional Repositories, Open Access and Scholarly Communication: a study of conflicting paradigms, *Journal of Academic Librarianship*, **37** (6), 460–70.

D-Lib Magazine (2011) papers submitted to first DataCite summer meeting held in

Hannover, Germany, June 2010, **17** (1–2).

D-Lib Magazine (2012) Special Issue on Mining Scientific Publications, **18** (7–8), July/August, www.dlib.org/dlib/july12/07contents.html.

Dobreva, M. and Chowdhury, S. (2010) A User-centric Evaluation of the Europeana Digital Library. In Chowdhury, G., Khoo, C. and Hunter, J. (eds), *The Role of Digital Libraries in a Time of Global Change*, Lecture Notes in Computer Science, **6102**, 148–57.

Environmental Literacy Council (2008) What is Environmental Literacy?, www.enviroliteracy.org/subcategory.php/1.html.

Erdelez, S. and Makri, S. (2011) Introduction to the Thematic Issue on Opportunistic Discovery of Information, *Information Research*, **16** (3), http://informationr.net/ir/16-3/odiintro.html.

Estelles-Arolas, E. and González-Ladrón-de-Guevara, F. (2012) Towards an Integrated Crowdsourcing Definition, *Journal of Information Science*, **38** (2), 189–200.

Etti, S., Perkinton, K., Cheuk, B. and Curtis, J. (2010) Growing the ERM Energy and Climate Change Practice Through Knowledge Sharing, *Journal of Information & Knowledge Management*, **9** (3), 241–50.

Gardois, P., Colombi, N., Grillo, G. and Villanacci, M. C. (2012) Implementation of Web 2.0 Services in Academic, Medical and Research Libraries: a scoping review, *Health Information and Libraries Journal*, **29** (2), 90–109.

Goh, H. L. D. and Foo, S. (2007) *Social Information Retrieval Systems: emerging technologies and applications for searching the web effectively*, Information Science Reference.

Goldman, N., Bertone, P., Chen, S., Dessimoz, C., LeProust, E., Sipos, B. and Birney, E. (2013) Towards Practical, High-capacity, Low-maintenance Information Storage in Synthesized DNA, *Nature*, **494**, 77–80, doi:10.1038/nature11875.

Hargreaves, I. (2011) *Digital Opportunity: a review of intellectual property and growth*, www.ipo.gov.uk/ipreview-finalreport.pdf.

Harris, V. and Hepburn, P. (2013) Trends in Image Use by Historians and the Implications for Librarians and Archivists, *College & Research Libraries*, **74** (3), 272–87.

Heradio, R., Fernandez-Amoros, D., Cabrerizo, F. J. and Herrera-Viedma, E. (2012) A Review of Quality Evaluation of Digital Libraries Based on Users' Perceptions, *Journal of Information Science*, **38** (3), 269–83.

Hjorland, B. (2011) Is Classification Necessary After Google?, *Journal of Documentation*, **68** (3), 299–317.

Holley, R. (2010) Crowdsourcing: how and why should libraries do it?, *D-Lib Magazine*, **16** (3/4), www.dlib.org/dlib/march10/holley/03holley.html.

Huang, S.-L., Lin, S.-C. and Chan, Y.-C. (2012) Investigating Effectiveness and User Acceptance of Semantic Social Tagging of Knowledge Sharing, *Information Processing and Management*, **48** (4), 599–617.

Information Research (2011) papers from First International Workshop on Opportunistic

Discovery of Information, University of Missouri, October 2010, **16** (3).

Lee, D. H. and Schleyer, T. (2012) Social Tagging is No Substitute for Controlled Indexing: a comparison of medical subject headings and CiteULike tags assigned to 231,388 papers, *Journal of the American Society for Information Science and Technology*, **63** (9), 1747–57.

Lee, K.-P., Kim, H.-G. and Kim, H.-J. (2012) A Social Inverted Index for Social Tagging-based Information Retrieval, *Journal of Information Science*, **38** (4), 313–32.

Li, Y.-M., Liao, T.-S. and Lai, C.-Y. (2012) A Social Recommender Mechanism for Improving Knowledge Sharing in Online Forums, *Information Processing and Management*, **48** (5), 978–94.

Lougee, W. (2009) The Diffuse Library Revisited: aligning the library as strategic asset, *Library Hi Tech*, **27** (4), 610–23.

MacDonald, B. H., De Santo, E. M., Quigley, K., Soomai, S. S. and Wells, P. G. (2013) Tracking the Influence of Grey Literature in Public Policy Contexts: the necessity and benefits of interdisciplinary research, *Grey Journal*, **9** (2), 61–8.

MacDonald, R. (2011) Starting, Strengthening, and Managing Institutional Repositories, *Electronic Library*, **29** (4), 553–4.

Macevičiūtė, E. (2011) Education for Digital Libraries: library management perspective, *World Digital Libraries*, **4** (1), 49–61.

McBeth, B., Hungerford, H., Marcinkowski, T., Volk, T. and Meyers, R. (2008) National Environmental Literacy Assessment Project: Year 1, National Baseline Study of Middle Grades Students, Final Research Report, www.oesd.noaa.gov/outreach/reports/Final_NELA_minus_MSELS_8-12-08.pdf.

McMahon, T. M., Powell, J. E., Hopkins, M., Alcazar, D. A., Miller, L. E., Collins, L. and Mane, K. K. (2012) Social Awareness Tools for Science Research, *D-Lib Magazine*, **18** (3/4), www.dlib.org/dlib/march12/mcmahon/03mcmahon.html.

Mitchell, C. and Suchy, D. (2012) Developing Mobile Access to Digital Collections, *D-Lib Magazine*, **18** (1/2), www.dlib.org/dlib/March12/mitchell/01mitchell.html.

Nicholas, D., Rowlands, I., Watkinson, A., Brown, D. and Jamali, H. R. (2012) Digital Repositories Ten Years On: what do scientific researchers think of them and how do they use them?, *Learned Publishing*, **25** (3), 195–206.

Nicholas, D., Clark, D., Rowlands, I. and Jamali, H. R. (2013) Information On the Go: a case study of Europeana mobile users, *Journal of the American Society for Information Science and Technology*, **64** (7), 1311–22.

Rafeh, R. and Bahrehmand, A. (2012) An Adaptive Approach to Dealing with Unstable Behaviour of Users in Collaborative Filtering Systems, *Journal of Information Science*, **38** (3), 205–21.

Ransom, N. and Rafferty, P. (2011) Facets of User-Assigned Tags and Their Effectiveness in Image Retrieval, *Journal of Documentation*, **67** (6), 1038–66.

Rowlands, I., Nicholas, D., Williams, P., Huntington, P., Fieldhouse, M. and Gunter, B. (2008) The Google generation: the information behaviour of the researcher of the future, *Aslib Proceedings*, **60** (4), 290–310.

Rubin, V. L., Gavin, P. T. and Kamal, A. M. (2011) Innovation in Public and Academic North American Libraries: examining white literature and website applications, *Canadian Journal of Information and Library Science*, **35** (4), 187–212.

Selwyn, N. (2009) The Digital Native: myth and reality, *Aslib Proceedings: New Information Perspectives*, **61** (4), 364–79.

Sharifzadeh, M., Hossein Zamani, G., Karami, E., Taghi Iman, M. and Khalili, D. (2013) Actor Network Theory Approach and its Application in Investigating Agricultural Climate Information System, *Journal of Information Processing & Management*, **28** (2), 433–54.

Shotton, D. (2012) The Five Stars of Online Journal Articles: a framework for article evaluation, *D-Lib Magazine*, **18** (1/2), www.dlib.org/dlib/january12/shotton/01shotton.html.

Spiteri, L. F. (2012) Social Discovery Tools: extending the principle of user convenience, *Journal of Documentation*, **68** (2), 206–17.

St Jean, B., Rieh, S. Y., Yakel, E. and Markey, K. (2011) Unheard Voices: institutional repository end-users, *College & Research Libraries*, **72** (1), 21–42.

STM (2007) Brussels Declaration, International Association of Scientific, Technical & Medical Publishers, www.stm-assoc.org/brussels-declaration/.

Teksoz, G., Sahin, E. and Tekkaya-Oztekin, C. (2012) Modeling Environmental Literacy of University Students, *Journal of Science Education and Technology*, **21**, 157–66.

Theng, Y. L., Foo, S., Goh, H. L. D. and Na, J. C. (2009) *Handbook of Research on Digital Libraries: design, development and impact*. IGI Global.

United Nations (2013) *Bridging Knowledge and Capacity Gaps for Sustainability Transition: a framework for action*, UN Office for Sustainable Development, 8 March, http://sustainabledevelopment.un.org/content/documents/1681Framework%20for%20Action.pdf.

United Nations General Assembly (2012) *The Future We Want*, resolution adopted by the General Assembly, A/RES/66/288, 11 September, http://daccess-dds-ny.un.org/doc/UNDOC/GEN/N11/476/10/PDF/N1147610.pdf?OpenElement.

Wolski, M., Richardson, J. and Rebollo, R. (2011) Building an Institutional Discovery Layer for Virtual Research Collections, *D-Lib Magazine*, **17** (5/6). www.dlib.org/dlib/may11/wolski/05wolski.html.

Woolwine, D., Ferguson, M., Joy, E., Pickup, D. and Udma, C. M. (2011) Folksonomies, Social Tagging and Scholarly Articles, *Canadian Journal of Information and Library Science*, **35** (1), 77–92.

Xia, X. (2012) Diffusionism and Open Access, *Journal of Documentation*, **68** (1), 72–99.

Index

123Library 41, 195
4C Project 50

abstracting databases 1
ACM Digital Library 47
actor network theory 215
aggregators 36, 37, 40, 41, 42, 107, 141, 144
AHRC 120, 125
Amazon 34, 42
Amazon EC2 160
AmazonCloudSearch 177
analogue collection 1
anthropogenic GHG 59 (*see also* GHG)
APCs 120, 121, 126, 130, 133, 134, 135, 136 (*see also* article-processing charges; author-pays model; gold open access)
ARC 91
article-processing charges 39, 46, 92, 124, 126, 127, 131, 132, 133, 134, 135, 136, 137, 141, 148, 150, 151, 153
arXiv 38, 117, 207
Ask a Librarian 193
Australian Computer Society 61
Australian Research Council *see* ARC
author-pays model 38, 51 (*see also* APCs; gold open access)

Barnes & Noble 34
bibliographic databases 1
big deal 42, 45
Blue Ribbon Task Force 49
British Library 72
Brundtland Commission 21
Brundtland report 3, 21, 26 (*see also Our Common Future*)
Budapest Open Access Initiative 39
business models
    digital information services 47
    e-books 41
    information and resource sharing 177
    open access journals 45

capital approach
    for measuring sustainability 17
carbon footprint 9, 22, 23, 63, 64, 67, 70, 72, 110, 112, 167, 176 (*see also* GHG)
    digital information systems and services 217
    digital libraries 69
    information access 179
    information infrastructure and services 62
    infromation retrieval systems 11

carbon footprint (*continued*)
  IT 60
  journals 107, 108
  printed and digital content 108
  printed books 105, 106, 107, 113
  printed content 104
  software 180
carbon neutrality 66, 67
CC BY 120 (*see also* Creative Commons)
  content access 130
  RCUK open access policies 130, 131,
    136, 206
chlorofluorocarbons 23 (*see also* GHG)
circulation 1, 23, 109
CiteSeer 178
client-side ICT 63,
  environmental costs 214
climate change 9, 22, 58, 60, 61, 64, 73,
    215 (*see also* GHG)
  debate 23-4
  green user behaviour 185
cloud computing 11, 72, 112, 157
  benefits 159; higher education 168
  definition 158
  deployment 159
  disadvantages 159
  environmental costs 161
  information retrieval research 177-9
  information services 162-3
  layered architecture 160
  technologies, deployment of 159-60
Cloud Security Alliance 163
Cloudpress 2.0 178
collaborative filtering 209
collaborative purchasing models 46
community cloud 160 (*see also* hybrid
    cloud; private cloud; public cloud)
copyright laws 113, 167 (*see also* Hargreaves
    Review)

CORE 123, 154
CourseSmart 41
Creative Commons 51, 120, 130 (*see also*
    CC BY)
cultural heritage 48, 69,
current awareness services 1

data analytics 129, 142, 145, 147, 148, 149,
    152, 168, 194, 204, 206, 207, 208
data linking 95, 207
data management services 8, 149
database search services 2, 181
DataCite 210
Dawsonera 41, 195
desktop search 175 (*see also* enterprise
    search)
digital content 51, 57, 69, 72
  access 2, 37, 195, 198
  and information retrieval 184, 185, 186
  business models 40
  creation and access, GHG emissions
    111
  environmental costs, 68, 214
  future access 49
  GHG emissions, factors 108, 109,
    111-13, 166
  linking 95
  marketplace 205
digital copyright exchange 90, 91, 167,
    196, 199 (*see also* Hargreaves Review)
digital curation 50
digital economy 27, 28, 148, 151, 152, 199,
    209
digital information
  access 41
  economics 46-7
  printed, economic sustainability 9
  research on sustainability, integrated
    approach 194

digital information services
    business models 47
    environmental costs 111
    green, model 166
    influencing policies 95
    research issues 195, 205-12
    sustainable, model 195
digital information systems and services
    86
    foundations 198
    impact 196, 217
    level of success 88, 89
    technology infrastructure and usability
        92
digital libraries
    carbon footprint, measuring of 69-72
    categories 69
    economic sustainability 47-8
    evaluation 205
    green 166
    social networking technologies 212
    social sustainability measure 88
    software, energy cost 72
    usability 82, 205
digital preservation
    costs 113
    economic sustainability 48-50
    green 166
    sustainable models 215
digital publishing 2
digital rights management 10, 90, 198
    intellectual property rights 90
DigitalPreservationEurope 49
Display Energy Certificates 110
DPimpact study 49
DSpace 72, 122
DuraCloud 162

EBL 41, 195

e-books 9
    business models 41-4
    GHG emissions, factors 109
    market 44, 46, 105
    readers 34, 104
    service providers 34
    use of 82
E-books Observatory project 82
eBooks.com 41
Ebrary 41, 195
EBSCOhost 41, 195
economic sustainability 4, 16-18
    content and data management system
        150-1
    criteria 16
    definition 16
    digital libraries 47-8
    digital preservation 48-50
    Europeana 198
    gold open access 133-5
    impact of/on environmental
        sustainability, social sustainability 26-7
    indicators 26
    information 33, 34
    institutinal repositories 124
    service sectors 18
    sustainability of information model 195
ecosystem 6, 7, 16, 17
e-journals 2, 9, 34, 41
    GHG emissions 109
embargo period (open access) 38, 117, 121,
        125-7, 141, 142, 147
    definition 125
embodied energy 68, 70, 71, 72, 127, 181,
        182, 183 (see also socket energy)
    definition 68
emergy see embodied energy
energy and environmental costs of libraries
        111

enterprise search 175 (*see also* desktop
    search)
environmental benefits
    cloud computing 169
    green information services 161, 214
environmental cost
    client-side ICT 214
    cloud computing 161-2
    data transfer 112
    digital content, factors 112-13
    digital information services 68, 72
    digital library 70
    digital preservation 68, 113
    digitization 69
    green information services 167
    ICT 61
    institutional repositories 128
    library and information services 150
    library infrastructure 241
    library storage and handling 113
    print vs online newspapers 104
    printed content 105, 214
    printed vs digital content 104, 108-10,
        214
    printing 68, 107, 109, 113
    reading 112
    software 70
environmental literacy
    definition 216
    programmes 216-17
Environmental Literacy Council 216
environmental performance 17, 23
environmental protection 4, 25
Environmental Protection Agency *see* EPA
environmental strategy 216
environmental sustainability 4, 21-2, 27
    definition 21
    green information retrieval 186
    impact on economy 27

institutional repositories 127-8
    open access 153-4
    origin 21-2
    research issues 23
    software 179-80
    sustainability of information model
        195
EPA 16, 21, 23
    mandatory reporting rule 22
    sustainability, definition 4
    US GHG emissions 106
EPrints 122
ERA 123
ESRC 120, 125
    research, embargo period 126
European Commission 7, 49
    open access policy 91, 118, 131
Europeana 41, 69, 83, 93, 198, 215
    funding 48
    metadata records 51
    mobile user behaviour 217
    usability study 82
Europeana Foundation 198
Excellence of Research in Australia *see*
    ERA

Facebook 158, 211, 212
Fedora 72
financial capital 17 (*see also* total capital)
Flickr 211, 213

Gale Virtual Reference Library 41
GDP 16, 17, 18 (*see also* GNP)
GHG 9, 22, 23 (*see also* carbon footprint)
    components 80
    definition 23
    emissions; digital content creation and
        access 111-13; digital libraries 69-72;
        global ICTs 165; Google 62;

GHG (*continued*)
 green information retrieval 186;
  information access 176, 179, 182, 184;
  IPCC report 58-60; journals 107-8;
  lifecycle analysis 176, 179; print vs
  digital books 104-6, 108-10; USA 63
 green information service (*see also* green
  information retrieval; green user
  behaviour); benefits 168-9; definition
  66-7; framework 163-5; model 166-7
 ICT infrastructure, universities 61
 impact of 23
 information services 67, 68
 Smart2020 report 61
Global Warming Potential 59
GNP 17 (*see also* GDP)
gold open access 38, 39 (*see also* green open
 access)
 economic sustainability 133
 European Commission policies 118
 meaning 117-35
 RCUK policies 120, 124, 133-6
 social sustainability 135-6
 sustainability of information 131-6
Google Books 34, 40, 90, 166, 193, 195,
 199, 215
Google Images 213
Google Scholar 34, 40, 44, 51, 142, 145,
 149, 166, 193, 195, 199
Google search
 environmental costs 112
green building certifications 111
Green Building Council
 Australia 110
 USA 110
green building technologies 110
 cloud computing 72
 information behaviour 216
green information access 11, 167-9 (*see also*

green infromation services)
green information behaviour 166, 167,
 177, 216, 217
green information retrieval 11, 169, 170,
 177, 179, 181, 184, 186, 197
green information service 9, 11, 72, 153,
 160, 169, 170, 176, 178, 186, 197,
 198, 203, 216 (*see also* green
 information retrieval; green user
 behaviour)
 applications 168-9
 benefits 168-9
 carbon neutrality 66-7
 definition 66-7
 framework for higher education 163-7
 model 166-7
green information systems 7, 9, 11, 58, 64,
 65, 204
 model 166
green IT 63-65
green library building rating systems 110
 LEED 110
 green library buildings 110-11
green open access 38, 136 (*see also* gold
 open access)
 embargo period 126
 European Commission policies 118
 institutional repositories 121-8
 model 38, 117
 RCUK policies 121, 126
 sustainability issues 123
 vs gold open access 39
Green Star Education rating system 110
green supercomputers 65
green user behaviour 66, 169, 170, 184-5
greenhouse gas *see* GHG
Greenstone 72
gross domestic product *see* GDP
gross national product *see* GNP

Hargreaves Review 90, 114, 206
HathiTrust Digital Library 50
Historypin 48
human capital 17 (*see also* total capital)
humanities workbench 213
hybrid cloud 160 (*see also* community
    cloud; private cloud; public cloud)
hydrofluorocarbons 23 (*see also* GHG)

IaaS 160 (*see also* PaaS; SaaS)
information access 10, 11, 85, 92, 129, 141,
    148, 149, 175, 176, 177
  behaviour 178
  energy consumption 167-9
  environmental impact, measuring of
    179-84
  sustainability issues 175
information behaviour 2, 10, 80, 81-4,
    87, 92, 94, 177, 183, 184, 194, 200,
    214
  green 166, 167, 216-17
  Wilson's model 197
information for sustainable development 5,
    6, 28, 29, 86
information industry
  business model 40
  sustainability 34
information literacy 80, 83, 84, 87, 93,
    196, 198
information overload 204
information retrieval 2, 11, 70, 82, 85, 95,
    148, 162 (*see also* information access)
  cloud computing 177-9
  environmental impact 179-84
  green 169, 170, 177
  green user behaviour 184-5
  sustainability 175
information science
  definition 8

information seeking and retrieval 2, 10, 80,
    94, 95, 96, 197
  Ingwersen's model 81
infrastructure as a service *see* IaaS (*see also*
    PaaS; cloud computing)
institutional repositories 39, 50, 51, 69, 83,
    88, 118, 121-8, 142, 143, 145, 146
  economic sustainability 124
  environmental sustainability 127-8
  history 121
  open access 128-9, 147
  preservation plans 129, 154
  social sustainability 124-7
Intergovernmental Panel on Climate
    Change *see* IPCC
Internet Public Library 41, 193
interoperability 74, 169, 185, 261, 262,
    263
IPCC 23
IPCC 2007 report 23, 57
  GHG emissions 58-60

Jisc collections 45, 135, 136, 195
Jisc model licences 45

Kindle 34, 42, 90, 113
Kyoto Protocol 22

LEED verification of green buildings
    110
library buildings 110-11
Library of Congress 162
lifecycle analysis 58, 66, 176
  information access 179-81
linked open access 148-9

Mendeley 34
metadata 51, 112, 147, 178, 206, 207
methane 59 (*see also* GHG)

Microsoft Academic Search 34, 51, 90, 142, 145, 149, 168, 193, 199
millennium development goals 5
multimedia digital libraries 177
MyiLibrary 41

National Institutes of Health *see* NIH
National Science Digital Library *see* NSDL
natural capital 17 (*see also* total capital)
NDLTD 69, 83
Networked Digital Library of Theses and Dissertations *see* NDLTD
NIH 11, 48, 91, 119, 125, 142
nitrous oxide 23 (*see also* GHG)
NSDL 41, 48, 69, 83, 196

OCLC 162
OECD 7, 23, 25
    capital approach 17
    economic growth 26
online databases 1, 2, 34, 51, 166, 176
open access 37, 39
    Budapest Open Access Initiative 38
    definition 38
    gold 38, 117
    green 38, 117
    history 38
    institutional repositories 121-8
    journals, business model 45-6
    models 38
    policies 91-2; ARC 119; European Commission 118; NIH, USA 119; RCUK 119-21; UNESCO 118; US Government 121; Wellcome Trust 119; World Bank 118-19
Open Archives Initiative 38, 117, 121
Open Data Conference 39
open peer review 208
open scholarship 46, 123

OpenDOAR 83, 121, 122, 123, 128, 129, 142, 207
OPUS 122
Our Common Future 3, 5, 21, 26
ozone 23 (*see also* GHG)

PaaS 154, 160 (*see also* IaaS; SaaS)
perfluorocarbons 59 (*see also* GHG)
Planet Filestore 169
platform as a service *see* PaaS
private cloud 160 (*see also* cloud computing; public cloud)
produced capital 17 (*see also* total capital)
public cloud 160 (*see also* cloud computing; private cloud)
PubMed 41, 48, 83, 91, 119, 121, 128, 142, 183, 207

Research Excellence Framework (REF) 123
Rio Declaration on Environment and Development 21, 26
Rio+20 5, 24, 88

SaaS 160 (*see also* cloud computing; IaaS; PaaS)
scholarly communications
    definition 192
    processes 192
Scopus 44, 145, 149, 168, 177, 183
selective dissemination of information 1
semantic knowledge mapping 207
SHAMAN 50
social bookmarking 209
social capital 17 (*see also* total capital)
social informatics 195, 196
social information retrieval 209, 210, 211
social inverted index 209
social network analysis 211

social networking 79, 81, 92, 94, 95, 103, 155, 160, 170, 175, 176, 196, 197, 198, 200, 207
    integration with information services 211-12
    social sustainability model 82
social semantic tagging 209
social sustainability 4, 7, 11, 12, 26, 96
    data protection 130
    definition 18
    gold open access 135-6
    green information retrieval 186
    indicators 20
    information 79; indicators 84-6; literacy 198; study of 86-7
    information services 88-9
    institutional repositories 122, 124-7, 129
    meaning 28
    model 87, 195
    open access 83; content and data management system 152-3
    relationship with economic sustainability 27-8
    relationship with environmental sustainability 27-8
    technology 92-3
    usability 213
    users 81; culture 94-6
social tagging 209, 211
socket energy 68, 70, 113, 127, 181, 182, 183 (*see also* embodied energy)
    calculation 71
software as a service *see* SaaS
software development lifecycle 65, 179, 180
Sony e-book reader 34, 90, 113
sulphur-hexafluoride 59 (*see also* GHG)
sustainability (*see also* economic sustainability; environmental sustainability; social sustainability)
    definition 3-4
    indicators 17
    three dimensions 16
sustainability of information 28
sustainable development 3, 4, 5, 7, 16, 17, 18, 80, 84, 86, 87
    definition 4-5
    green information retrieval 186
    indicators 19
    information systems and services 88
    integrated approach 26-8, 191
    IPCC 58-9
    three pillars 24
    UN Resolution 22
sustainable information services 191
SusteIT 64, 67, 71, 127, 165, 214

text mining 96, 129, 152, 177, 186, 206, 207
The Future We Want 6, 7, 24, 88
total capital 17
Twitter 211

UCARE 64
UK Green Building Council 110
UNDSD 4, 16
UNEP 21, 23, 25, 60
UNESCO 5, 93
    open access policy 118, 142
UNFCCC 82, 83, 103
United Nations Division for Sustainable Development *see* UNDSD
United Nations Environment Programme *see* UNEP
United Nations Framework Convention on Climate Change *see* UNFCCC
United Nations Office for Sustainable Development *see* UNOSD
UNOSD 5, 6, 88

US Green Building Council 110
usability 11, 80, 81, 84, 87, 92, 96, 129,
    194, 204
  design issues 213-14
  metrics 167
  models 195
  research direction 205
  studies, digital libraries 82
usability and user-centred design 144-5
user-centred design 81, 95, 144-5, 167
user-centred services 51
user-generated data and content 200
user-generated information 103
user studies 2, 12, 80, 96

Web of Knowledge 80, 145, 149
Weka 96

Wellcome Trust 11, 48
  open access policy 91, 119, 130, 131,
    150
White House directive for open access 128
WikiMiner 96
wikis 212
WMO 23
World Bank 33
  open access policy 118-19
  repository 142
World Commission on Environment and
    Development 3, 21, 26
World Meteorological Organization *see*
    WMO
World Trade Organization *see* WTO
WorldCat 44, 162
WTO 25